When Dream Bear Sings

NATIVE LITERATURES OF THE AMERICAS AND
INDIGENOUS WORLD LITERATURES SERIES

When
Dream
Bear
Sings

Native Literatures of the Southern Plains

Edited by GUS PALMER JR.

Foreword by Alan R. Velie

University of Nebraska Press | Lincoln and London

Library of Congress Cataloging-in-Publication Data
Names: Palmer, Gus, 1943– editor. |
Velie, Alan R., 1937– writer of foreword.
Title: When Dream Bear sings: Native
literatures of the southern Plains / edited by
Gus Palmer Jr.; foreword by Alan R. Velie.
Description: Lincoln: University of Nebraska Press,
2018. | Series: Native literatures of the Americas and
Indigenous world literatures series | Includes index.
Identifiers: LCCN 2017058050
ISBN 9780803284005 (cloth: alk. paper)
ISBN 9781496208668 (pdf)
Subjects: LCSH: Indian literature—Great Plains—
Translations into English. | Folk literature,
Indian—Great Plains. | Indians of North
America—Great Plains—Folklore.
Classification: LCC E78.G73 W435 2018 | DDC
398.2089/97—dc23 LC record available at
https://lccn.loc.gov/2017058050

Designed and set in Charis by L. Auten.

For my wife, Carolyn,
my sons, Mark and Jeffrey,
and my daughter, Melissa

CONTENTS

1. Algonquian Language Family

CHEYENNE

6. Siouan Language Family

7. Uto-Aztecan Language Family

8. Language Isolate

ILLUSTRATIONS

FOREWORD

Alan R. Velie

Traduttore, traditore, "the translator is a traitor," a phrase originally used by Italians to complain that French translations of Dante were woefully unfaithful to their originals, is now universally applied to explain the difficulties of transporting a literary work from one language to another. However formidable the problems faced by the French when translating a poem from one Romance language to another, they were nothing like the obstacles faced by nineteenth- and twentieth-century explorers, missionaries, Indian agents, and scholars when they tried to render a tale from Kiowa or Cherokee into English.

The first translation of an Indian text into English was made by a Lieutenant Henry Timberlake in 1765. According to Brian Swann, Lieutenant Timberlake translated a song into heroic couplets; the result was more "version than translation" (1994, xxi). For the next two centuries English translations of tribal tales ranged from embarrassingly poor to interesting but not very accurate. This sample from a Kickapoo tale, translated by Truman Michelson for the American Ethnological Society in 1915, gives a good idea of what early translation was like:

> Soon that man came. As soon as his father came, he went to where the other was sitting. . . . He secretly gave him that little piece of meat. Suddenly that woman went out. Then the man asked his son again and again, "Where verily did you get this meat?"

This passage sounds a bit like the pidgin English Tonto speaks to the Lone Ranger, with the addition of the occasional archaism ("verily") that Hollywood likes to use when impersonating historical figures like Mark Antony or Cochise. Versions of tribal tales done by anthropologists who could actually write, like Alice Marriott, sound a good deal better, but are rough paraphrases of the originals.

The art of translation took a large step in the right direction in the mid-twentieth century when Jerome Rothenberg, Dennis Tedlock, Dell Hymes, Brian Swann, and others developed what Rothenberg termed "ethnopoetics." This new discipline involved using poetic forms—lines, verses, stanzas—to render the performative elements hitherto lacking in prose translation. Although one might argue that in dealing with oral tales, which are essentially a form of interactive drama, the ethnopoets substituted one distortion, writing them as verse, for another, transcribing them as prose, the results that Rothenberg et alia achieved were so superior to what had gone before that the objection would seem a quibble. What the ethnopoets achieved was very important: they transformed tribal tales from seeming to be a species of children's literature at best, revealing them to be powerful and moving works of literature. Ethnopoetics, which went hand in hand with renewed interest in language preservation, was part of the Native American Renaissance that brought new life to Indian arts, economic development, religion, and politics.

As impressive as the achievements of the ethnopoets were, they did not exhaust the possibilities of translating tribal tales into English. And, in order for the American reading public to appreciate tribal tales fully, a great deal more has to be done to educate them as to the nature of oral tribal literature. In *When Dream Bear Sings* Gus Palmer and his contributors have done a good deal to advance that understanding. The twenty-first century has given translators valuable new tools. As Palmer puts it:

> Nowadays the most significant improvement has been in the use of technology and modern equipment. Computers and other digital applications are readily available for users no matter where the work is undertaken. Digital processes have not only sped up the documentation of oral texts but have also helped to provide more complete scripts, including specially designed fonts and better recording devices that eliminate extra work and time. (xxxix)

But however gifted, knowledgeable, and well-equipped the translator of tribal tales, the problems he or she faces are enormous. Indian languages are so different in structure from English that a close translation that sounds anything at all like English is all but impossible to achieve. For example, take this excerpt from Durbin Feeling's word-for-word translation of the Cherokee story "Diary":

> I am just ill / if I say / no reason / I would be saying it / no / someone / truth/ He would not think / I am just alone. (171)

Each phrase between the slashes represents a Cherokee word. Cherokee is a poly-synthetic language, having a high morpheme-to-word ratio. In other words there are far fewer words in a phrase compared to English, each word being a compilation of several affixes. It is obvious from the passage from "Diary" that translating word by word from Cherokee to English simply doesn't work. Feeling's looser translation is far easier to understand: "There is no reason for me to say that I am ill because no one would believe me." This translation, however, conveys none of the rhythm or feeling of the original. Capturing that, to the extent they were able, was an important contribution of the ethnopoets.

As Palmer points out, Kiowa is even more difficult to translate into English than Cherokee:

> Kiowa vowels are contrasted through low, high, and high/low tones. The application of length and nasals also provides contrast in the production of lexical items, namely verbs and nouns. Without these vowel features even the elaborate pronominal system would not work. A typical Kiowa sentence will change in the arrangement of whether vowels are high, low, or high/low. (xxxii)

In other words, written English can only roughly approximate the meaning of Kiowa, with its tonal subtleties. That is the reason Palmer states that "Kiowa stories . . . [are] best translated in verse form." Poetry, with its greater ability to employ linguistic tools like rhythm and imagery, can more closely render the effects of a language like Kiowa.

Another difficulty is vocabulary. According to Palmer some of the most common words in English—for example, *love*, *hate*, and *goodbye*—have no Kiowa equivalents. Likewise there are many locutions in tribal languages that can only indirectly be rendered in English.

But structural difference between languages is only one of the difficulties faced by Euro–Americans in trying to understand tribal tales. Another major factor is that, although tribal tales bear some resemblance to Euro–American short fiction, the Indian conception of the nature and function of literature is fundamentally different, particularly in regard to what for lack of a better term we call "myth." Tribes make various distinctions among types of tales, but for the most part Indians divide stories between those of special importance, stories handed down from ancestors, usually dealing with culture heroes, which have to be told in accordance with special rules, and those of more recent vintage, dealing with contemporary events, which can be told at any time. For example, the Winnebago distinguish between *waikan* (what is sacred) tales, which take place in an age long past when animals talked, and *worak* (what is recounted) tales, which deal with more recent incidents (Radin 1956, 118).

The stories of special importance, which Western scholars call "myths," to quote Karl Kroeber, "arise out of and remain totally enmeshed in practical aspects of the life of myth tellers and myth listeners" (1998, 63). Western literature, by way of contrast, is what Kroeber describes as "'aesthetic' discourse," to be distinguished from "'practical' discourses" (63). In fact in the Western tradition the defining characteristic of literature, like that of any art form, is that it has no practical use. As long as a dummy is in a window displaying clothes, it isn't art. If you put it on a pedestal in your living room just because you like the way it looks, it becomes art, because you are using it purely for aesthetic purposes. With things composed of words we can make the same distinction: a manual is not literary art because we extract information from it and ignore the style of its language; a poem is literature because we pay close attention to its language while making no use of its information. By way of contrast, myths have traditionally played a very practical role in the lives of Indians: they are a guide to how to be a proper Kiowa, Cherokee, Sioux, or Arapaho. The importance of certain stories to tribal members can't be overstated, as a number of anthropologists have found to their chagrin. Swann tells of the misadventures of Barre Toelken among the Navajo. In his attempt to glean information about the Navajo trickster Coyote, Toelken transgressed Navajo taboos, resulting in severe misfortune, "deaths, injuries, accidents," among his informants (Swann 1994, xxx).

Another problem for the Western reader of tribal tales is genre, which shapes expectation. If we fail to recognize the genre of a work, we can't understand it even if we understand the language. For example, consider Americans' initial difficulties with playwrights like Samuel Beckett or Eugene Ionesco. When literate Americans went to the theater in the 1950s they expected a tragedy like *Death of a Salesman*, a comedy like *Blithe Spirit*, or a musical like *Guys and Dolls*. When presented with early examples of Theatre of the Absurd like *Waiting for Godot* or *The Bald Soprano*, they had no idea what was going on, even though they understood every word. I now tell my students to think of *Godot* or *Soprano* like volleyball in a church. Imagine that you stop by an unfamiliar church one Sunday to attend the service, but upon entering you see that the pews have been moved aside and people are playing volleyball. "What are they doing?" you ask the minister. "Playing volleyball," he says. "Haven't you ever seen volleyball?" Of course you have; the problem is you don't know what to make of people playing volleyball in a church on Sunday morning.

Western readers are likewise unsure what to make of tribal tales when they encounter them. Take for example the Wyandotte story "The Young Woman Fallen from Above." To an American who is educated but knows little of Indian culture, it would probably resemble what he or she would call a "fairy tale," a type of children's literature. When assured it was for adults he or she might be too polite to say anything, but might well think the story "primitive." This common misconception is based on a misapplication of Darwinism. Darwin's evolutionary paradigm is sound biology but, when applied to cultures, not only misleading but pernicious. To quote Karl Kroeber:

> The colonialist-imperialist mind-set that has dominated European ethnology for so long, especially in its tendency toward abstract theorizing and its dependence on the Eurocentric construct of "the primitive," could not . . . affirm the unique significance of small-scale preliterate cultural achievements. (1998, 12)

Tribal tales may seem cryptic to Western readers unfamiliar with the genre, but they are not primitive or simplistic. Indians are not evolving toward the ability to write novels: they are already there. Tribal tales may be old, but they are still being told in tribes whose members also read and write sophisticated works like *House Made of Dawn* and *Love Medicine*.

It is important to keep in mind that tribal tales are a form of drama, enactments in which the teller performs a tale to an audience that has heard the tale many times. The reason transcriptions can seem so cryptic and devoid of detail is that the audience knows the tale as well as the teller. Kroeber cites a typical Indian explanation of the brevity: "Our stories are short because we know a lot" (69). To complain of their brevity would be as obtuse as telling Ben Jonson his epigrams are too short.

As Kroeber points out, tribal tales omit "description, motive analysis, philosophizing, even figures of speech": "what seems a formal 'poverty' of many oral tales in fact testifies to the intensity of social transactiveness embodied in their exclusive attention to *events*" (70).

In their emphasis on events these tales share a trait with traditional tribal painting. If you look at the paintings of the Kiowa Five, or even later painters like Jerome Tiger or Otis Polelonema, you will notice that there is nothing in the background. The central figures appear against an empty monochrome field. Painter Edgar Heap of Birds explains:

> The image of Native art has historically been that of an abstracted image filled with intense conceptual narrative. . . . Native visual art is just part of a breathing system and networks with other components in the tribal culture. (Heap of Birds, email to author, May 20, 2003)

In other words, in visual art as well as literary, in order to put the focus on the essential meaning, much peripheral matter is omitted. Tribal members, having heard the story before, can supply the context. This technique allows for a certain amount of open-endedness and complexity to the tales. Kroeber states that in tribal tales

> representations of motivation . . . usually avoid both reductive simplification to a single dominating motive; . . . through a starkly "objective" narrative of specific actions they evoke in their listeners an imagining of the complex of considerations creating particular behavior. Such a rhetorical mode is especially appropriate in the retelling of familiar tales. Again, we must be alert to what we assume to be simplifications or omissions in myth tellings, recognizing them as in fact possible signals for audience imagining to which we are unaccustomed. (1998, 71)

With the rise of reader-response criticism in recent decades, Western literary critics have recently focused more attention on the role of the reader in providing meaning to a text. It is important to be aware of the role of the audience in providing meaning to a tribal tale. When considering what is left out of "The Young Woman Fallen from Above," we must be cognizant that less is actually more.

Finally it is important to note the effect tribal tales have had on recent Indian fiction. Since Scott Momaday kicked off what is now known as the Native American Literary Renaissance in 1968, Indian novelists have taken their place at the forefront of American writing. Momaday has won the Pulitzer and been nominated for the Nobel; Louise Erdrich's latest novel, *LaRose,* was reviewed on the cover of the *New York Times Book Review*. Indian novels have not only been bestsellers, they have become an important part of the American canon. In order to understand and appreciate these novels it is crucial to recognize their debt to tribal tales, particularly those about tricksters. Tricksters are represented in this volume by the Cheyenne, Osage, Caddo, and Plains Apache's Coyote; Kickapoo, Otoe, and Quapaw's Rabbit; and Miami and Comanche's Fox.

The Trickster is a universal archetype found in the folktales and fiction of every people—Odysseus, Reynard the Fox, Jacob in Genesis, Jack (of beanstalk fame), Br'er Rabbit, and Bugs Bunny are some of the most familiar. Although ubiquitous, he (the Trickster is usually, though not always, male) is accorded different importance or centrality by different peoples to their culture. No people take the Trickster more seriously than Indians. Virtually every tribe has one; he is almost always the central figure in their lore. Often he takes human shape: Manabozho of the Ojibwe, Saynday of the Kiowa, Napi of the Blackfeet. Often he is an animal: Coyote, Raven, Rabbit, Spider. Whatever his form he lives by his wits. Usually an underdog (David vis-à-vis Goliath), he survives in a dangerous world by playing tricks. He is also frequently the victim of tricks, berating himself as "Foolish One." Though totally amoral, particularly when it comes to sex, he is always viewed favorably by his people. And he is always peripatetic. Tribal trickster tales generally begin with some variation of the Kiowa formula *Saynday an he*, "Saynday was going along."

Students unacquainted with Indian culture might complain that the heroes of Indian novels are often shiftless layabouts: for example, Scott Momaday's Abel, Louise Erdrich's Gerry Nanapush, and James Welch's nameless narrator in *Winter in the Blood* spend most of their time chasing women and out of work. One might cite several reasons for this, but chief among them is the fact that they are essentially tricksters, modern avatars of Saynday, Manabozho, and Napi. Put tribal tricksters in a modern setting and they certainly wouldn't be bankers or any other sort of solid citizen.

In fact, to put tricksters in any written setting is to deprive them of much of their anarchic essence. Nanapush, Abel, and the narrator of *Winter in the Blood*, well drawn as they are, necessarily fall short of capturing the essence of the Trickster, principally because tribal tricksters are oral phenomena. Gerald Vizenor, the Chippewa novelist who has spent his career depicting tricksters in his fiction, concedes that "the trickster is a sign, a communal signification that cannot be separated or understood in isolation" (1989, 189). What he means is that the true Trickster exists only in oral enactment in which teller and audience imagine him together. As a people Americans have replaced orality with written discourse. Technology has only intensified this phenomenon—witness young people sitting together today, each reading his or her own electronic device in isolation. Whatever we have gained in becoming a culture that reads, we have also lost much. Gus Palmer and his associates have provided a window into the world of oral tribal literature. It is very much worth our while to look through it.

REFERENCES

Erdrich, Louise. 1984. *Love Medicine*. New York: Holt, Rinehart, and Winston.

Kroeber, Karl. 1998. *Artistry in Native American Myths*. Lincoln: University of Nebraska Press.

Marriott, Alice. 1963. *Saynday's People*. Lincoln: University of Nebraska Press.

Momaday, N. Scott. 1968. *House Made of Dawn*. New York: Harper and Row.

Radin, Paul. 1956. *The Trickster*. New York: Schocken.

Swann, Brian. 1994. *Coming to Light*. New York: Vintage Books.

Vizenor, Gerald. 1989. *Narrative Chance*. Albuquerque: University of New Mexico Press.

Welch, James. 1974. *Winter in the Blood*. New York: Harper and Row.

ACKNOWLEDGMENTS

Without the support, collaboration, faith, and trust of the many persons involved in Native languages and literatures, this volume would not have been possible. Each contributor, colleague, acquaintance, and friend is recognized, thanked, and appreciated in this unique undertaking. I am especially grateful to Brian Swann, whose tireless efforts have made the volumes in the Native Literatures of the Americas and Indigenous World Literatures Series a success in so many ways. I have never met Brian but know of his work in poetry and translations. Special thanks for support, encouragement, and friendship go to Daryl Baldwin, David Costa, Lawrence Hart, Connie Yellowman, Barbara Goodin, Alice Anderton, Doris McLemore, Gary McAdams, Todd Fuller, Shelly Wahpepah, Donna Longhorn, Jared Roubedeaux, Mark Awakuni-Swetland, Garrick Bailey, Lori G. Ware, Craig Kopris, Sherry Clemons, Tanya George, Wayne Pushitaniqua, Lisa Norman, Karen Hildreth, Wayne Lehman, Keli Mitchell, Misty Wilson, Elizabeth Kickham, Josh Aaron Richards, and a host of others without whose help this book would not have become a reality. An extended appreciation to Matthew Bokovoy, Heather Stauffer, Elizabeth Zaleski, Vicki Low, Lindsey Auten, Andrea Shahan, Rosemary Sekora, Tish Fobben, and all others I may have inadvertently overlooked or forgotten.

Now, a special thanks to the Department of Anthropology at the University of Oklahoma for support, encouragement, the use of technology, materials, and the time needed to write. My grateful thanks to Jacqueline Reese and the staff at the Western History Collection and the Doris Duke Collection at the University of Oklahoma, who provided transcribed texts and background information about tribal people and speakers where such material was unavailable elsewhere. Appreciation and gratitude must also be extended to the following Indian tribal nations and organizations whose generous help made the volume possible: Comanche,

Plains Apache, Kiowa, Fort Sill Apache, Caddo, Wichita, Delaware (Lenape), Ponca, Omaha-Ponca, Otoe Missouria, Osage, Kaw, Tonkawa, Pawnee, Quapaw, Miami, Ioway (Northern), Cheyenne, Absentee Shawnee, Potawatomi, Wyandotte, Seneca-Cayuga, and Meskwaki. Finally I wish to acknowledge my life partner, Carolyn, without whose helpful presence, encouragement, and love I would have not been able to carry out this work. *Àhô!*

INTRODUCTION

This book comprises Native literatures from storytellers of the Great Southern Plains. Many of the Indian tribes that dwell in these lands share the shifts of great changes of season and weather. Their stories tell of many of the striking and wonderful things that have taken place upon that particular landscape. Here the weather is among the harshest known in the world. In summer the sun plays a central role in the sky, parching the land until it becomes dry and hotter than molten glass. In winter some of the coldest weather in the world is known here when winds come out of the Arctic North, bringing sleet and snow.

Many nomadic tribes moved up and down the corridor between the Rocky Mountains in the west and the great Mississippi River to the east. They camped here and there, ranged far and into the depths of the land following the great buffalo herds. Their stories tell of the wonderful adventures they had, of hunting and camping near the rivers, always keeping within close range and in sight of the mountains where they felt most at home. This was where their gods lived.

Many stories tell of the magical places and things the people saw and heard long ago. It was a time when the land was dark and there was no sun. Dangerous giants and beasts roamed about, and the people were fearful for their lives and hid in the forests and canyons. Some of the stories recount the time when the Trickster called together the people to tell them about the land to the east, where there were strange beings who possessed a fiery ball of light they played with. It was a dangerously hot light, but it lit up the land and everything round about so you could see and move about freely and happily. And so the Trickster organized a detail of animals that went there and took away the light and brought it to their land where it lit up all the world.

This is one version of how the sun came to be. There are many more.

While many of these tribes call the Plains landscape their home, others arrived later, driven forcibly westward by the federal government to provide more space for advancing white settlements in the East. Lest they forget who they were, these recent arrivals brought with them their tribal stories and myths, accounts about their tribal heroes and their emergence into the world. Their stories, now transcribed from the ancient language of their people, are translated into English. Many of these accounts were committed to memory and but one generation from being forgotten and disappearing forever. They make up the oral tradition of the people and are the best examples of the human experiences of these unique people. Some of the narratives are but remnants of former times when the people thrived in their homeland far away, while others recount the time they were dispersed to unknown places to settle, to a landscape that was strange but that in time they became familiar with and made their own.

While some of the narratives in this volume appear as tribal narratives and stories, myths and folktales, others are personal sketches and poems. These Native literatures appear in their original tribal form and translation or in English only. It should be pointed out that the translation of Native American stories, myths, legends, and other personal narratives into English is difficult and not without controversy. There are, however, also useful things that come out of translation. A translator of an original text will often bring something unexpected to a translation, something different and new; something that will vibrate with an energy; something that will fill the mind of the reader with wonder and awe; something that the reader will want to experience again with the same amount of enthusiasm and will search diligently for in similar sources of pleasure. It is the devoted and responsible translator who will work very hard to assure human experience comes bubbling to the surface of our consciousness when we read his or her work. In this way, we may unexpectedly realize the capacity and potential of language for the first time—not that we haven't experienced it before, but this time it has perhaps been of a rare quality and rich in feeling, so that we are moved in a profound way. This is of course but one dimension of our literary experience. We are discussing oral literature and not written literature here. We are exploring areas of literature recently discovered and appreciated.

Much oral literature has come down to us in printed form and is often quite technical. Some of the work in this volume has been transcribed by a system of writing that reflects as closely as possible the sound of Native words as they were originally spoken. This is important for many reasons but, for now, if we consider how rapidly these original Native languages are disappearing, it is profound and even heroic that individuals would attempt to present writing forms and narratives as we find here.

Indeed many of the transcriptions in this volume are products of much devoted labor and facilitated by orthographies created by tribal speakers or linguists. These heroes are both Indians and non-Indians. Some are professionally trained; some are devoted practitioners, with boundless energy and determination, of the tribal language. Of these two, I am most impressed with the latter, because these are the ones for whom language survival and continuance is most urgent, for whom heritage languages are the very hallmark of who they are and what is most pressing during these difficult times. But that is something we can discuss later. Let it suffice for now that language survival is at the heart of much of this work and can be seen in the narratives presented in this book.

Before going on, let us explore a few concerns regarding the transcriptions and translations that may be found in this book.

Consider the following textual analysis of the Wichita narrative, "Turtle, Buffalo, and Coyote."

| 1 | a. ka:?a: ?a:kó:kha:r?a | | |
| | b. Once upon a time | | |

| 2 | a. kik?i:s | khi?as | kiyakihite?ecaki |
| | b. turtle | poor thing | he was sitting at the edge, they say. |

This text contains tense, person, number, and adverbial forms, including some impressively long polysynthetic constructions. Aesthetic or poetic concerns are of necessity lacking and will be illustrated later. I have done similar work with Kiowa. It is useful to do interlinearized translations but their use satisfies other, non-literary interests and pursuits. Recently more in-depth work has revealed stylistic applications regarding Native oral narratives. Because Native oral literatures are spoken and heard in the vernacular, persons unfamiliar with these languages can miss essential features of storytelling. When ordered in printed form, these texts often follow forms familiar to non-Natives. Such forms may be rendered in English, with rhyme schemes, line metrics, and other useful poetic devices clear only to English readers. They satisfy readers who are familiar with English versifying and have almost nothing to do with the original language. In this way, much is lacking in terms of Indian poetics, if there is such an animal. Dell Hymes and others have attempted to produce texts close to indigenous Native voices, but admit that this is exceedingly difficult. Even so, there is much good work that has helped us pay more attention to Native American oral literature. Brian Swann, Jerome Rothenberg, and William Clement, to name a few, have contributed and continue to contribute a great deal to the appreciation of Native oral literature.

This concern with translations has raised other important issues that need explication. One of these is the translators' familiarity with the language they are working with. Kenneth Hale (1969) complained that many linguists often lacked sufficient understanding of tribal languages and were therefore unable to produce useful translations. In the same article he proposed providing speakers of Native languages with an opportunity to train in linguistic programs and then return to their speech communities, where they might produce better works in their heritage language, including translations of oral works. In this way, a new generation of language workers could work from within their own communities to produce better and more useful work than former ones. At present, almost all the contributors in this book have done or are still doing language work with an Indian tribe. Some are tribal members and speakers while others are not. Some have had professional language training while others have not. In cases where workers are trained there are often more opportunities for them to learn the most up-to-date methodologies for doing fieldwork. What is more, these workers often have access to the latest modern technologies and software programs. With a little assistance much work may be accomplished on tribal properties or in the tribal community. In addition to this, there are often opportunities to work collaboratively in the speech communities as well as in academic settings where other research and library resources are available. At the university there are funding sources for research and study; graduate students often collaborate with faculty as well as assist in fieldwork. At the university where I work I have often had as many as three students assisting me. They interview and record speakers; transcribe and translate long lines of discourse; document topic forms and usages for dialects, if any; and perform other language-related work. In all of these settings tribal workers are afforded many kinds of opportunities to study and improve how they do language work. In our department we offer a master's degree in applied linguistic anthropology and have had much success recruiting and training students, many of whom are members of tribes in the state and elsewhere. Research and theses have been completed for Choctaw, Chickasaw, Kiowa, Alabama-Coushata, and Pawnee, to name several. Although most of the work focuses on the linguistic aspects of these languages, several have examined original texts, interpretation, and discourse analyses. Many of these students have worked and are still working closely with tribal language programs. The best success I have had is in training students in the recording, transcription, and translation of Kiowa stories. Teaching students to transcribe and translate a Native language has been the most challenging, yet the most rewarding, work of all.

Ezra Pound, T.S. Eliot, Stanley Kunitz, and others have written about the enormous weight of translating Chinese or European poems, knowing that they must allow the poem not only the freedom to illuminate and grow in the minds and imaginations of readers but also to evoke the deepest natural feeling on its own terms—something Native speakers seem more conscious of, as suggested by Hale and others. To translate a piece with any precision and sensibility requires a translator to incorporate and apply the most special kind of sensitivity and skill. Many, if not most, translations done by non-speakers of a language tend to produce a more *literal* kind of work, missing crucial emotional aspects that usually only native speakers are conscious of. This is largely due to the fact that translators just want the piece to be understood, more or less. This strategy may allow one to understand what the work is trying to say or to gain knowledge, but it often does little to help the reader experience any depth of feeling or thought that may be at the heart of the matter. What Hale proposed was serious and revolutionary, but it made sense. Native speakers were, and often are, absent from language work. The question arose as to who was better qualified to explain, explicate, or interpret what was, according to Hale, natural to Native speakers themselves. At the time, around 1960, there was little known language work in Indian communities and precious few tribal people doing language work. It was not until the 1990s, when the Native Language Act was passed by Congress, that any serious attempts were made to lessen language shift or loss. Some activities were going on in Indian Country, but they focused more or less on tribal traditions and customs, social practices, and lifeways. Occasionally, there were individuals and groups meeting sporadically in isolation, mostly to socialize and tell tribal stories. These small, impromptu get-togethers were enjoyable to participants and at least kept alive the desire to converse in their native tongue as best they could.

The desire to converse in my native Kiowa was always at the heart of my work. In that work I sought to translate mostly prose pieces, what we might call *stories*. I knew many of my readers were going to be literary scholars, anthropologists, and perhaps even linguists. For that reason I employed word-for-word translation. I am glad I did because the work was received fairly favorably. Even at that time I thought about doing a more literary translation but didn't, for lack of time. Since then I have translated some Kiowa stories and other short pieces I thought were best translated in verse form. This seems to work fairly well for Kiowa because of the obligatory system of vowel tones. Kiowa vowels are contrasted through low, high, and high/low tones. The application of length and nasals also provides contrast in the production of lexical items, namely verbs and nouns. Without these vowel features even the elaborate Kiowa pronominal system would not work. A typical Kiowa sentence will change in the arrangement of whether vowels are high, low, or high/low. Phonotactic constraints, rules that specify the structure of syllables permitted in a particular language, determine how Kiowa words are pronounced (Finegan 2004, 543). Because Kiowa is an unwritten language, speakers must be aware of how a word or a string of words may shift from low to high, or vice versa.

Consider the following example:

Ka̱hi̱:gau, gàt âijàu haya.	Tomorrow, I'm going somewhere.
Ka̱hi̱:gau, **háun** gàt ái:jáu haya.	Tomorrow, I'm **not** going anywhere.

Notice the presence of negative *háun*, which causes the verb *âijàu* to change to *ái:jáu*. There are many other examples that show the importance of the shifting elements of sound in strings of words that in some instances can change the entire sense or meaning in Kiowa. In my Kiowa work I have tried to pay attention to features of sound and their enormous usefulness in communication, whether in simple, everyday conversation or in storytelling.

I still do much of my work this way because I feel most at home working with my native Kiowa. It is easier for me to treat translation in a number of ways, depending on the purpose of the pieces I'm working on. I have also worked with *peyote* songs, ritual oratory, and personal narratives. What I have been aiming at are sound elements, echoes, or reverberations as they occur in words or strings of words. In traditional Kiowa storytelling, verbs are routinely suffixed with a hearsay marker.[1] When telling stories or recalling past experiences, Kiowas will often add this suffix onto verbs, in order to recall a past speech or event. I've determined that this is an indicator that sets a distance between ordinary conversation and storytelling; in this way it "sets apart" experiences or events in a story from ordinary ones, things carried out on a normal day, as it were. Unlike English, where one can recount what was said or experienced simply by supplying adverbs such as "reportedly" or other phrases to indicate something occurring in the past, indigenous languages often apply simple verb markers. It is a complex feature in indigenous Native languages, only recently appreciated as a special feature in the verb complex. Readers will find examples of this extraordinary storytelling device in many Native literatures.

To give an example of its usefulness in storytelling, consider the Kiowa formulaic opening *Cáuigú á cí:dê hábé* (The Kiowas were *reportedly* camping). *Once upon a time* is a fairly equivalent storytelling formulaic opening well known among English speakers that more or less prepares listeners for an account that will be given or "storied." It is a convenient device and may be applied to many stories. A Kiowa storyteller might simply say "Cáuigú á cí:dê hábé," and that is all it would take to set the stage for the telling of a story. When Kiowas hear the formulaic opening they know that a story is going to be recounted and they prepare themselves to listen and respond. Listeners will often participate actively in recitations by nodding their heads or uttering some manner of agreement. In the case of a live performance of traditional Kiowa storytelling, much emphasis is demonstrated by means of bodily gestures and movement. I want to point out that these features and usages can be illustrated among the literatures in this volume. Although this book is not meant to treat complex linguistic forms, it is always interesting to see how these things work and how they often occur in oral native literatures and nowhere else.

A good many texts and translations in this volume have been previously recorded and/or published. Others are more recent works published for the first time. In the case of earlier work, translations are reprinted as new translations by individuals. This is perhaps the best way to present these literatures at this time. It is difficult to locate and present much original native literature because there are fewer and fewer original recordings or transcriptions. This does not come as a surprise, as many, if not all, native languages and literatures in their original forms are unavailable. Tribal people are attempting to revitalize, renew, or maintain whatever there is left of their heritage languages. In almost every case we are aware of how hard it is to locate speakers who are able to help build or rebuild speech communities as they once existed. Conferences and meetings are held annually in various parts of the country to try to discuss ways to keep native languages alive. This has created an acute sense of responsibility in Indians working diligently to save what is left of their tribal lifeways. It is as if the ground beneath the people has opened up like a great sea wave to swallow them up whole along with whatever else is left of their tribal life.

The best example of success in matters of language preservation seems to be taking place only in the large native communities—namely where Indian families reside with many who still speak the language of their forebears. For example the Navajo or Diné reservation is an ideal place that is not only huge but also governed by the people themselves—on their own terms. Here, it is still possible to find tribal people carrying on daily conversation in their native tongue in the towns, at public gatherings and ceremonies, and in the home. Studies reveal that speaking one's heritage language in the home with family members seems the most desirable way in which tribal languages can thrive.[2] Other, smaller, non-reservation tribal nations face more obstacles, because English is still the overwhelming choice of language in the schools, businesses, and other public institutions that dominate the people—Native languages cannot compete under these conditions. This is something that can't be helped. Try as they might to keep their languages alive, many Native peoples give in to the English language because it obliterates smaller, weaker speech communities like a giant wave engulfs tiny islands.

Tribal groups living off reservations and in urban settings face more difficulties in maintaining their heritage language. Indian tribal people who reside outside of the historical tribal area are often fragmented into smaller family units. Support is often lacking to keep tribal traditions and practices alive. The chance to meet occasionally to accomplish any reasonably meaningful results is often rare. In settings such as social centers, churches, and other public facilities, Indians sometimes conduct language classes when possible, as well as participate in feasts, singing, dancing, and other social or tribal ceremonies.[3] Urban meeting places in the large metropolitan areas seem to provide ideal opportunities for rebuilding social and cultural activities, many with language-learning components. Some of these are supported and staffed by people from tribal communities back home. In many cases, a common meeting place and time is called, perhaps the only one of its kind created to help displaced families and individuals come together, with the ultimate goal of restoring what is Indian and good in the Indian way of life. Indian people who live away from their ancestral homeland will often harken back to memories of the time when their families lived closer together and the fabric of tribal life seemed accessible all the time. They remember their close friends and relatives and wish to restore themselves somehow to their tribal identity and lifeway. Most people who come from a strong tribal heritage and background will maintain close connection to these things because it is a good thing. This sense of belonging and balance is especially keen among American Indians even today. Modern times and technological progress have done little to change Indians and their way of life. It was perhaps the one important feature that the U.S. government wished to destroy as it set about ways to obliterate Indian tribes in this country. The going wisdom at the time was that the essential way to change Indians was to resettle them and take away the vast land holdings that were always theirs.

In 1887, the federal government enacted the General Allotment Act to settle Indian tribes on 160 acres of land where many Indian families still reside today.[4] These tracts of land, known as "Indian Country," still provide a place where Indians live, work, and raise their families. Further this is a place where they can practice their tribal customs and tribal traditions. For example the Kiowas revived their gourd dance tradition in the late 1950s because the people wanted to evoke some sense of their tribal lifeways and they knew that by reviving the old songs and dances this would restore them to something in a meaningful way. This ceremony spread out over the years and has now become a popular, pan-Indian festival of song and singing, dancing and social interaction, taking place in almost every sector of this country. An inter-tribal gathering, gourd dancing has brought Indian people together not only to sing and dance but also to form friendships and strong bonds. Remarkably gourd dancing has unified Indians almost effortlessly in spirit and an attendant sense of well-being. The Blackleggings Warrior and Native American Church traditions, two other traditions of the late 1950s, have enjoyed a revival and also helped to form strong tribal and inter-tribal relations between Indians.

One of the main outcomes of these revivals and practices is that Indians have become more aware of their tribal heritage. Moreover they are more conscious of their heritage languages, including oral traditions. Once Indian people begin to rebuild, renew, or revive the language of their forebears, they also remember their origin stories, oratories, tribal traditions, and tribal history. The result is that storytelling takes on new meaning for the people. Something in oral literary forms evokes a sense of the historical past and restores Indian heritage without taking away anything of modernity or the sense of forward motion in modern living and lifestyle. Some translations in this volume were recorded by tribal elders out of this renaissance and were transcribed and translated through the efforts of individuals working in cultural heritage and language programs. Some of these tribal historical accounts can now be read for both enjoyment and learning, two of the goals of this anthology.

If the advancement of cultural heritage and languages are possible outcomes in this book, the variety of native literatures also contribute to the understanding of readers. *Under Green Corn Moon: Native American Lullabies* is a collection of lullabies from Indian Nations all over America recorded by Silver Wave Records, Boulder, Colorado. Collections like this not only provide a source of enjoyable reading but excellent material for learning. An advertisement for *Under Green Corn Moon* informs readers that performers on this recording represent sixteen different Indian tribes, indicating the diversity of tribal participation. Other books such as *Kiowa Voices I & II* include songs, singing, and other tribal lore and legends. These works round out a list of resources for teaching and learning, as well as sources for good general reading. With a simple internet search it is possible to locate similar sources that can be downloaded. With modern technology all kinds of learning materials are available for almost any interest, including information about storytelling and oral traditions, native literature genres, special treatments of literatures, themes, and special features such as magical realism, to name a few.

Other aspects of native literatures focus on intangible matters that often only tribes find cogent and useful. It should not come as a surprise that readers are often unable to fully understand some works in translation because they contain metaphysical concepts and ideas that appear to be strange. One need not be overly concerned when confronted by material that translators themselves are unable to make clear. Still, it is helpful to be aware of what is there and how it works. To even adequately produce a work that can stand on its own is wholly admirable; translators attempt to do this as often as they can. In any translation it is almost always impossible to go from one text to another without losing something in transition, so diametrically different are languages, one from another. There is often precious little one can do in a work but hope for the best results or outcome. When I was working with Kiowa texts I often struggled to explain in translation what was going on at the heart of some stories. I had a Kiowa idea of what it was but then to transmit it into English was next to impossible. Take for example words such as *love, hate,* or *goodbye,* commonly used English terms that are completely absent in Kiowa. This is not because the people didn't experience these human emotions. They just weren't put into words. And so I had to summon up words and sometimes combinations of words or concepts I thought would best express these sentiments. I realized many Native languages also lacked words that expressed these otherwise common things and ideas in English. In my Kiowa classes I have taught students who were forever wanting word-for-word translations of Kiowa into English when there was none to be had. In a story where no such words exist, one has often to rely on other means to express such things or simply use the closest thing in English. Readers usually get the point. They more or less make sense of what is going on in the context: things going in and out, out, in, and around. It is context then that becomes important in terms of objects and things, place, landscape, and other physical presences. In this volume many of these problems were no doubt encountered and had to be resolved, not to mention allegory, irony, humor, and other intricate and hard-to-explain concepts that are, as I pointed out, intangible, metaphysical. Translators often attempt to incorporate "the living center" or spirit of a narrative to engage the most participation from their readers. Now we all know translators vary in how they think about or employ words. Understandably, if translators working with Native texts are going to encounter some difficult central matters that may be charged with high emotion and deep meanings, they may have to forgo completing the work. It suits them to represent only what they understand in the most essential way in the completed work. It may result in not reaching the level of depth and meaning called for in the original piece but draws as close as it can to that existential place and should be appreciated for only that. Translators have been confronted with these concerns over millennia. The point is many would-be translators try to get at the heart of the matter; they want to evoke by means of writing the original human essences or meaning; they wish to enter into a world or domain they may have never experienced themselves; they want to do this but do not always succeed. In translation work, we try to do all we can to come to grips with the whole language. When we come upon the inexplicable, we falter, wishing we could do more to get at the heart of things. The great German translator Walter Benjamin (1968) put it best when he observed that the task of the translator consists in reproducing in the language into which he is translating the intended effect of the original. He was of course focusing on European novels and poetry, translated from one language to another or to several. Still, his explanations about translation are relevant here. They are useful to those of us who want to learn more about working with languages in a way that helps to highlight literature.

While many translations in this book were accomplished by people who are speakers of their Native language, others were contributed by non-speakers, as I mentioned elsewhere. Some contributors are not professionally trained translators. Their contributions are of personal interest, and the work they do is more or less afforded by their natural abilities. In many cases revitalization of their tribal language is at the heart of their work. That is why volumes such as this one can help as a resource to examine grammar, word formation, sentence structure, and other related linguistic features. As a reading resource, the literatures present aspects of tribal culture, oral tradition, and verbal arts. Whether oral literature is transcribed in the original native language and then translated into English or translated directly into English matters not in the least, because we realize how surprisingly quickly these things can disappear or be forgotten during these times of rapid indigenous language and culture loss worldwide. The loss of oral literatures in even one language and speech community is a loss for all of us. To read and share the human experiences contained in these pages is to realize the great gift and power of language and words that come down to us. It is the hope that the oral literatures published in this book, old and recent, translated for the first time or retranslated from older sources, will benefit and extend the enjoyment of literature for many readers. In some cases translations were in need of reworking. This does not mean their original condition was inferior. Studies indicate more recent technology has afforded newer or at least improved methods to accomplish translation work. The translation of indigenous verbal arts has improved as a whole. In this book, those retranslating older works were encouraged to explain how they came to translate their selections so that readers might understand what has changed in the methodologies undertaken in this kind of work. In other words we wanted to create a discourse regarding the new translations, how these selections were made and why, among other things. I recommended a possible formatting scheme for contributors to follow but soon realized they wanted to format their contributions according to their own tastes and wishes. Contributors were therefore allowed to present their work in whatever style most suited them. Following this thread of reasoning we saw how differently these works compare with those produced in other similar volumes, if only to see how things have changed or perhaps how they have improved over time.

There is a long history of American Indian oral literatures in this country. As noted elsewhere, missionaries, soldiers, government agents, railroad surveyors, anthropologists, and other non-Indians undertook collecting and recording early literary works. There were no particular methods through which this work came to be. Most translators undertook the work fairly single-handedly, interviewing, taking dictation, making recordings, and writing. Even now, much of this kind of work follows no authoritative plan and is still largely achieved by means of collaboration in a spirit of reciprocity and respect. Nowadays the most significant improvement has been in the use of technology and modern equipment. Computers and other digital applications are readily available for users no matter where the work is undertaken. Digital processes have not only sped up the documentation of oral texts but have also helped to provide more complete scripts, including specially designed fonts and better recording devices that eliminate extra work and time. In addition to this there is an even greater conscientious effort among language professionals to work in the best interests of tribal speakers and tribal communities, an awareness that helps not only in the recovery of earlier recordings, translations, and texts but also in the actual writing of new translations and interpretations. With the imminent danger of indigenous language loss, contributors are more aware of how their contributions may help speech communities retain, maintain, and even invigorate Native languages. All of this has created a new bond among all language workers, with a new spirit of collaboration, trust, and zest, without which little would be accomplished. We are given new ways to do translations all the time because there is a growing concern not only to work collaboratively in these important matters but also to be conscious of the race against time that is rapidly eroding human languages and cultures everywhere.

In Indian Country, language revitalization is at the heart of many tribal initiatives and efforts. Heritage languages stand a better chance of remaining spoken languages than they did, say, fifty or so years ago. This is of course due to the commitment of students, individuals, and the scholarly community. In this regard I like to think of the ongoing work in documentation and dictionaries conducted by Douglas Parks and linguistics students at the University of Indiana, working closely with the Pawnee people; the language work conducted by Sky Campbell and Jade Roubedeaux with the Otoe-Missouria community at Red Rock, Oklahoma; and that of the Lenape linguist Jim Rementer, another dedicated worker in the Delaware language program in the Bartlesville community in Oklahoma. There are many others, including Barbara Goodin, working with the Comanche Tribal Language program and always promoting and urging tribal participation despite there being few if any Comanche speakers alive. Professionals in Indian studies programs, linguists, poets, anthropologists, and others are rallying with tribal communities to retrieve, revive, renew, or otherwise preserve what remains of heritage languages. The desire of most Indian people is almost always to find or create better ways for their languages to be learned and spoken by future generations of the tribe and, perhaps to a lesser extent, to document or analyze their language. Many young people from individual tribes are studying and training in new and useful ways to help their heritage languages revive and stay alive. It is not surprising to find other similar language revitalization projects in communities around the world, such as those in China, New Zealand, and Hawaii, which in some instances are networking with many Native efforts in this country. Nowadays almost every area of language and culture appears to be of concern to the world community. This is an important and healthy sign that language and cultural groups are aware of impending language endangerment and loss; many are attempting to work in wider, stronger circles to bring about positive change. These changes even affect how other people feel about these things. Not only are communities striving to maintain their languages, they are also incorporating ways to revive their tribal traditions and lifeways—no cultural stones are being left unturned.

Interestingly there is a kind of bonding that occurs among many dedicated and hardworking groups. Unknown until recently, Indian tribes themselves are networking in unique and unexpected ways. For example groups discuss how some of the things they set out to accomplish failed or succeeded, things they were unable to do before because they didn't know anybody else who was doing them. This creates a desire to bond with other groups. It produces collaborations where new ideas and applications, strategies, and work can develop and flourish. When people begin to work closer together there is growth in awareness of the good things in life. They realize they can do more and better things than when they worked in isolation. An unexpectedly strong and wholesome atmosphere and spirit develops within new associations like the growth of a great tree, full of new vigor and hope with branches full of leaves reaching out.

Finally I want to extend my personal appreciation and gratitude to my own Kiowa people for their support and faith in me to complete this work. My own work in Kiowa storytelling apprised me of recordings and led to some translated texts I was able to achieve with speakers like Parker McKenzie, Cornelius Spotted Horse, Dorothy Kodaseet, Florene Taylor, John Tofpi, Gus and Alice Palmer, and Oscar Tsoodle, to name a few. There were a host of other Kiowa speakers who assisted in one way or another in the Kiowa community where I undertook this work. The experience was truly gratifying, and I hope together we were able to bring Kiowa storytelling to better levels of appreciation and understanding. Nineteenth-century translator-documenters of the Kiowa language and texts include James Mooney and Albert Gatschet, while early twentieth-century translators include John P. Harrington, Elsie Clews Parsons, and Alice Marriott, all of whom are well-known figures in anthropology and early fieldwork and whose works are still sought out by researchers. To this day these important and resourceful figures from long ago are still contributing to languages and cultures, as well as language description and documentation, all materials essential to further study by researchers and scholars alike. These contributions have deepened interest and made a huge impact in indigenous languages and literatures worldwide. This volume will be another resource to add to the existing stock of work that benefits the social sciences and humanities. When the entire assembled volumes of the Native Literatures of the Americas and Indigenous World Literatures Series are complete, the work will represent a truly great moment in American letters and literature and assure the place of indigenous verbal arts in the canon of literatures of the Americas and the world. Àhô!

NOTES

1. *Evidential* or *evidentiality* is the term linguists employ to indicate this sort of verb ending.
2. For more information, see Leanne Hinton and Kenneth Hale, *The Green Book of Language Revitalization in Practice* (San Diego: Academic Press, 2001).
3. Recently, Native American Church religious ceremonies have come to be practiced in many urban Indian communities. There is a growing community, for example, in Norman, Oklahoma, where young families conduct peyote meetings and carry on activities just like those held in Indian Country around the state. The ceremony is carried out in a tipi, following all the protocols of the peyote ritual down to the songs, prayers, cedar, and fire.
4. The Allotment Act of 1887, also known as the Dawes Act, provided for the distribution of Indian reservation land among Indian tribes. Its goal was to make successful farmers or ranchers out of Indians. The remaining "surplus" land was opened to white settlement. The general outlook of the act reflected a genuine interest in the welfare of Indians overall, but in many cases it was a failure because community life came to be characterized by poor living conditions, diseases, and abuse by neighboring whites.

REFERENCES

Benjamin, Walter. 1968. *Illuminations*. New York: Schocken Books.
Finegan, Edward. 2004. *Language: Its Structure and Use*. Boston: Thomson Wadsworth.
Hale, Kenneth. 1969. "American Indians in Linguistics." *The Indian Historian* 2: 15–18, 28.

PART ONE
Algonquian Language Family

CHEYENNE

Cheyenne Stories and Storytelling Oral Traditions

Gordon Yellowman

Wah-dum is the Cheyenne word for "welcome," meaning welcome to my place, home, residence, tipi, and dwelling. *Huh-dawh* ("long ago") is a Cheyenne word that begins a story or recounting of an origin story in a geographical historical place, sacred place, or cultural landscape.

My grandma Nish-kit, the late Mary Alice Yellowhawk, once told me that there is a time and place to do storytelling; she said to never tell certain stories in the night or at nighttime. I asked her why and she said because if you tell certain stories in the nighttime, you will grow a humpback or become humpbacked.

Now, I don't know whether to believe her or not, because it could have just been a disciplinary way of keeping us from staying up late or it could have been mythical, meaning superstitiousness. Regardless, these were the traditional Cheyenne customs and rules and we, as Cheyenne children, all had to abide or follow the rules; if we chose not to there would be physical and spiritual consequences. To this day I have not told stories in the night; I dare not to because I do not want to go humpbacked. Storytelling is an art and a responsibility, for it reflects the identity of who we are as Cheyenne people. History, culture, and lifeways are reflected in our oral histories, language, and culture arts.

Cheyenne storytelling is an art tradition that's passed on to the next generation; it's a dying art and responsibility. There are four seasons that exist in the Cheyenne universe: spring, when renewal-of-life stories are told; summer; fall, when stories of changes in colors are told; and winter, when stories of old men and old women are told. Each season reflects the livelihood of the Cheyenne.

Storytelling of astronomy, the stars, was the responsibility of the Cheyenne Star Clan, a clan that consisted of Cheyenne ceremonial ladies. Many of these women received their knowledge while taking part in the seasonal summer animal dances, ceremonial dances for healing and renewal. My grandmother Mary Alice Antelope was a member of the Star Clan and also held a prominent role in the animal dances.

There are many reasons why we tell stories. The four primary reasons for storytelling for the Cheyenne are 1) the prehistoric times of the mammoth, the origin stories; 2) the prehistory of the cultural landscapes, adaptations, geographical areas, and sacred sites of the Cheyenne; 3) historic times, transitions, atrocities, movements, and relocations; 4) our past and the future, using our past to move into the future.

The Bear and the Coyote

Translated by Joyce Twins

na hetóhta'haov ne-hetóhta'haov
I'll tell you a story.
Nahkohe estaameneheohtse'tanoho meo'o
A bear was following along a path.
hapo'e nahaohe o'kohome moneheneheohtse'to hehe
Likewise there a coyote was following it.
nehe'se e stoo'e'ovahtsehoono
Then they met [up together].
Nahkohe e statsehetohoono o'komomeho
The bear [he] said to the coyote,
no'hehnestse he'tohe nameo'o e xhetohoono
"Move aside. This [is] my path," he told him.
hova'ahane, hapo'o no'hehnestse he'tohe nameo'o e xhetaehoono
"No, likewise [you] move aside. This [is] my path," he told him.
tsexhe'seoo e seoo'evo vo'tahtsevose exhe'ke me'ehnehoo'o xao'o
While they were arguing a skunk slowly appeared.
Hahtome he'tohe nameo'o exhetohonoo
"Scram! This [is] my path," he told them.
Exhe'ke nema'evonehnehoo'o
He slowly turned around.
exhe'ke hesehosohnehoo'o
He slowly went backwards.
tseh voomovose estanesehe' nevo'aheotsehoono
When they saw him, they took off in two directions.
esaa naha'oomehesesto tosa'e tsehesease ta'xevose
They were not caught sight of where they took off [to].

7

Cheyenne Story—Dogs Used to
Carry Burdens in Days before Horses

Birdie Burns, Cheyenne
Recorded and transcribed by Julia A. Jordan

Clear up to that time they didn't have horses. That's when they first came across that sea, when they walked. And they had dogs—big dogs—like I told you, they must have been these big Siberian huskies. They had some dogs like that. I know what they look like. They're kind of cross-bred with wolves. They're just like wolves. Some of them got real big and some weren't as big. Maybe those dogs were that big at that time. They're the ones that they used to pull their poles and their camping outfit. The dogs would just be in bunches to themselves, but they knew where the people were going. People were walking on foot and these dogs would be somewhere in a big group following. They didn't follow right behind them. They were to themselves. But they knew where the people were going. The dogs carried the tipi poles on their sides. As far back as they can remember they had tipi poles.

They were trained to follow the crowd. And then when they came to a place where they were going to camp, maybe for the night, these women did all the work putting up the tipis. And they were the ones to say where they were going to camp. And they stood there where they were going to camp, waiting for the dogs. Maybe they were still coming somewhere. And then when the dogs caught up with them, the dogs kind of waited around and looked around where their master was. Then these women began to holler. They began to holler for their dogs. And each dog knew his master's voice. This dog just went right to where his master was. They didn't have names like we name our dogs [today]. They just had the same call. The women had the same call.

Cheyenne name for dog is *'oiskiso.*

8

Cheyenne Story—Man Who Prophesied Coming of Horses and White Men Long Ago

Birdie Burns, Cheyenne

Recorded and transcribed by Julia A. Jordan

A long time ago, when they were all—I guess you know the Indians always had a big camp—they never scattered. And someone appeared to them. They didn't know who he was. Just like at the beginning when the buffalo used to eat the humans—the Cheyennes—and someone appeared there showing them how to make bows and arrows. And the buffalo were so surprised when these people that they had been eating turned around and killed them and ate them. And this must have been the second time when this—whoever he was—appeared to the Cheyennes. And he was the one that prophesied. He must have been an Indian prophet—a Cheyenne prophet. He prophesied to the Cheyenne tribe that if they didn't behave or if they didn't do right that these things were to come upon them. First he taught them never to commit murder and never to steal. And never to repossess anything that they already gave to someone. I think that's that. I never did hear his name. I don't know whether it happened at the same time after that or whether he said it the same time when he was giving the Indians—the Cheyennes—these laws.

But there's another place where he told the Cheyennes, "If you don't live right—if you keep getting away from your ways—you're going to get married young. You're going to get married young and you're going to marry your own relatives—your own kinfolk. And you're going to begin to get gray at a young age if you don't live up to the teachings that were given to the Cheyennes. And there's a person that's going to come among you people. Beware!"

He was cautioning them. He said, "That person is the one that's going to bring you something that's going to make you keep wandering—keep wandering, keep

9

wanting to go. You'll never be settled anymore. He's going to bring something that his mane will touch the ground."

He didn't say "horse" but that's what he meant. They didn't know the word for horse because they had never seen it. He said, "Something's going to have a mane, and that touches the ground, and his tail's going to touch the ground. And this creature"—he didn't say "horse"—"he'll move his head just like this."

You know how horses look when they're wild and want to go, like the way racehorses do when they're going to run. He described that it was going to be like that. So I guess he meant horse. He meant the horse. And sure enough when the Cheyennes got hold of these horses, they just kept going and kept going and roaming and moving. And their mind began to—they weren't settled anymore like they were when they were on foot. They just took their time moving, and took their time camping, and they just took their own time. But when the horse came in, see how far they moved? From this side of South Dakota clear on to where we are right now.

How Stories Were Told at Night by an Old Lady

Birdie Burns, Cheyenne
Recorded and transcribed by Julia A. Jordan

Birdie Burns was in her mid-sixties during the time of these interviews. She was born and raised in the Clinton area by traditionally oriented parents and knows a great many old-time stories and much information about the former Cheyenne way of life. Her father was Kias, a sub-chief or band chief, and her mother was Sage Woman. Her father's father was Middle Wolf ("Wolf-Going-Through-A-Crowd") and her mother's father was High Backed Wolf, who, among other things, participated in the Battle of Adobe Walls. Birdie was raised in the Mennonite Church but in recent years has joined the Baptist Church. Her father was a peyote man for a time, but he gave up the religion when his son, Birdie's brother, died. He then became active in the Mennonite movement. Birdie has been married to Ed Burns for many years, and they have one son, Edmond Burns, and a daughter. She also has a son by a previous marriage.

Birdie's husband, Ed Burns, was present at this interview and participated for a few minutes at the beginning of each side of the tape. The transcriptions of the Cheyenne terms given here are only approximate. —J. Jordan.

Well, at the beginning they crossed that big sea. And they kept roaming south. And then they got to those big pine trees, and they found shelter under the roots of those trees. Well, I guess they thought they could live outside. I heard this story when I was a little girl. Like I said, it's from my great-grandmother . . . You know when we sit around at night one would start telling something and then he or she would remind that next person that was visiting, and then they'd start out like that again. And one person just didn't sit and tell it. See, they kind of remind each other, and this one, whatever he left out, then this one would add to it. And that's the way they keep their stories. You know they didn't write. And if any young person is in there, well, he gets to learn what was way back there.

11

It was over here after they had houses where I started hearing them. But way back then they must have had tipis. They say that before they tell these stories they gather in one home first. And whose home they're meeting in—this old lady would what we say now, she had to serve refreshments. And that time she cooked berries, kind of an Indian pudding. And coffee and maybe fry bread or something like that, and then they'd start telling these stories. That's the way they kept up these old stories. Friends and neighbors, too. Yeah. Here it was just relatives what this old great-grandmother talked about. We were just all cousins sitting around listening to her. We'd ask her to tell stories. Well, her daughter was there. She was maybe just about sixteen or seventeen years old—younger than her mother. And my father and uncle and their wives and my mother. Just the family. They'd ask her something about a certain thing—why it happened. Because she was old and she knew, well, she'd start telling that way. And she'd say, "It happened at that time—." And that's where I listened. Many times I'd go to sleep listening to her. And maybe I'd have sense to hear it [somewhere else]. But I didn't have sense enough to know that I should learn all I could back there. It was just like hearing about "The Three Bears" way back there. You're not interested in what you learn when you're young. [She was telling you these stories in the Cheyenne language.] Yeah, that was the only language they had. She would be sitting on the floor. On the beds. This grandmother that would often visit that told these stories, she was a real old lady. You couldn't get her to lay on the bed. She'd rather sit on the ground. And then they had an open fireplace. They had beds on the floor. And then an open fireplace. Being an aunt to my father and uncle, she'd have fresh meat hanging above this fire. And while she was telling stories, her daughter would get down some of that meat. She'd say, "Cook some meat for my nephew." Well, her daughter would get that meat down and a piece of fat, you know, all smoked, and she'd cook it over the fire. And at the same time, she'd be cooking coffee. And she used to serve refreshments instead of my aunt and mother and uncle and father serving the refreshment. The old lady did. See, that was her love for her people. She'd get that meat down, and, oh, we just enjoyed eating even if it was midnight. And she was that kind of a good old lady.

Birdie's Grandmother's Story of How Corn and Buffalo Were Given to the Cheyennes

Birdie Burns, Cheyenne

Recorded and transcribed by Julia A. Jordan

Well, the way she started telling it, she said it was at the foot of a big mountain somewhere in South Dakota. And she said the camp there. Their traditions were always [face your camp] to the east. They had a big camp—kind of moon-shaped, only a little bit closer—towards the east [opening to the east]. And that's the way they camped toward that mountain. And every morning they would have some kind of a game. The games they used to play, maybe. Certain groups played against some that came from another group. And then they had several different groups, I guess, these Cheyennes at that time—young people. And the older ones took part. Like in foot races and all kinds of games that they had at that time. And while that was going on—they'd moved that wheel, too. I guess you've heard about that wheel. They used to make a round wheel and the bull's-eye was in the middle. They used buffalo rope [thongs]—lariat—it was just long string of buffalo hide. And they braided it somehow in this wheel [a gaming wheel] and inside there was a bull's-eye, and they'd throw an arrow, and the lucky one would win if he hit that bull's-eye. And that was one of their games at that time. And I think that was what they were doing. And this boy kept having a dream—one of the boys. Of course, I don't know how you would translate it—but you've heard this corn in the wind, how those leaves blow—the sound that they make—that was this other boy's name. And this one was named Tassel. But those were unknown yet. They had their own names that were given to them when they were born. They still went by that. And this boy was afraid to do what he was asked in his dream. He had that dream several times, over and over. And at the same time another boy must have had the same dream, way from another group. Because when they

13

first saw each other, one was coming from that side and this other one was coming this way. And, well, he made up his mind he was going to try it. And I guess at the same time that other boy thought he was going to try it, too. They didn't know that they had both made up their minds the same day. This was the early part of the morning. When the other boy looked toward this way—this direction where this boy was coming—he was dressed just—. In their dream their grandmother told them to dream a certain way and wear paint a certain way. And she must have told this one in his dream how to dress—just like the way she told this other one.

When that boy looked that way he saw this boy coming dressed just the way he was dressed and it kind of made him mad. "Who is this trying to imitate me, and how did he know I was asked to dress like this?"

Well, when this boy saw the other boy coming he thought the same way. So instead of going toward the east like they were asked to do, they stood there looking at each other.

And so one of them spoke and said, "Are you trying to imitate me?" This one asked. And this one said, "Well, I was thinking that too myself, that you were trying to imitate me."

He said, "No."

Well, this boy asked, "Who told you to dress like that—and why?"

And that boy answered and said, "My grandmother that lives in that mountain. Now where did you get yours?"

And this boy said, "My grandmother that lives in that mountain, too."

Well, they were kind of both surprised. So they said, "Well, let's go." They didn't argue anymore or didn't get madder. They just made up right there that they were going to be partners. So one of them took the lead. And all these, they just stopped their game. They were just watching them—these boys coming from different directions dressed alike and wearing paint alike. They just looked at them going toward this mountain. Everybody just dropped what they were doing and just stood there. These boys were going. It must have been quite a ways off to that mountain. They finally got to the foot of the mountain and right above there was water coming out from the side of the mountain. And these people just wondered what they were going to do when they entered this—going toward the mountain. Maybe some thought, "What's getting into them? Are they getting crazy or what?"

So the one that was in the lead got his buffalo robe and covered his head. And he went right to this water—I guess you would call it a fall—he just went right in there. And this second one, he done the same thing. Cover himself and went in there. And they wondered if they were coming back out alive, these people that were watching.

They watched all day long. They never saw a sign of them anywhere. Well, some of them just gave them up for good. They knew that they went in the mountain and they didn't expect to see them again. Well, some thought, "They'll be coming back. They have a reason for doing that."

Toward the evening, when the sun was going pretty low, there they came. And, oh, out here, they didn't see buffalo for so many years. They were just half-starved. No buffalo all them years. And they were having a hard time. And maybe these two were prayerful boys. And that's why they were blessed like that—why they were both called like that.

So at a certain time of the evening, there they appeared. They came out the way they went in—in that water. Through that water that was running. One of them appeared first, and then the second one. This first one, he was carrying a bowl, a big wooden bowl. They were wondering what he was bringing out and where did he get it. Everybody was just wondering.

So they kept coming closer and closer from these people that they left. And when they got there—oh—when they got to that mountain, the one that must have been in the lead, he kept going and kept going until they came to a place that looked like it was daylight in there. Looked like it was as light as the sun—these days when it's real bright sunshine. It looked just like that. It was that bright. And it was in the mountain.

When they got closer to this grandmother, she already saw them. She said, "You're welcome, my grandsons. I've been singing for you. Come and sit down over here," she said. "Come and sit down over here, Tassel."

And they just looked all around, these boys.

"Come on." She called this other boy whose name means some kind of a sound that these corn leaves make. You've been in a cornfield when the wind blows—you can hear all those. I don't know if you call them leaves or what. And she set them down. So she gave them this meat that was already cut in little pieces. It was meat cooked over the fire. It had a lot of fat in it. And they both sat down. And in another dish she gave them corn. So they both started eating, because there was hardly anything to eat where they came from and they were very hungry.

And after they filled up and ate all they wanted, she told them, "Look over there." She pointed out that way. As far as they could see there was a big field of corn—a green cornfield. And beyond that somewhere, "Look," she said. "I'm going to turn this buffalo loose in the morning." She said there was a large herd of buffalo up that way. So she said, "I want you to take this food back to your people."

Because she must have known that they were hungry and at the point of starvation. So she said, "These names I called you, I give to you from today on. Your name is going to be 'Tassel' and your name is going to be—" I can't call the name. I just have to describe it. *Ma aki.na* is "Tassel." That's my son's name—Edmond Burns— Edmond H. Burns. And this other one is *nisθ ɛ na' hof* [Cheyenne transcriptions only approximate]. So they started back out. That was when they appeared all of a sudden, coming through this water again—this waterfall. And they saw them coming, just the way they followed each other going in, so they were following each other coming back.

When they came close to the people they saw these men—these boys—carrying wooden bowls. And, "Get back, everybody! See what they brought!"

So everybody kind of sat back. And those boys came right in the middle. They must have been standing in a circle. So they put down a big bowl of meat that was already cut up, just ready to put in your mouth. She had cut it into little pieces.

He set it down. Fat in it, and meat, cooked over the fire. And another wooden bowl with just nothing but roasting ears. And then these boys got up and stood back and they said, "This is for you. Our grandmother gave it to us for you to eat. Now you men—." They used to put men in those days first, because the ladies come last because the boys get killed. They fought for the women. It's not like white people—ladies and gentlemen at that time.

So the boys sat down first and they filled up. Whenever they got enough they got up. They said, "Come on. Some more come and sit down."

That thing didn't run out until those last little orphans—they were forgotten— they were playing around and someone said, "Say, we're forgetting those little orphans over there."

So one of the boys went over there and brought these little orphan boys and sat them down. The little boys went after it. And they were the ones that ate up the meat and corn.

And that's how they got this corn. *Hma:m nhots* [last syllable is voiceless].

ABSENTEE SHAWNEE

Shawnee Poems

Narrated by Pauline Wahpepah
Introduced by Gus Palmer Jr.

Like many Native languages, both Kickapoo and Absentee Shawnee are endangered. The Shawnee pronunciation guide, and the greeting and poems in Shawnee that follow and are translated into English, are by Pauline Wahpepah. Shawnee is Pauline's first language. She is also a speaker of English and Kickapoo. Pauline Wahpepah is among the last few speakers of both Kickapoo and Shawnee. She especially enjoys speaking, teaching, and talking about the Shawnee language. The poems she writes in Shawnee reflect her interest in the natural world. She thinks about the living things around her in Shawnee and then writes about them in Shawnee. The English translation is a rendering of the same object of interest she thought about in her native Shawnee memory first and then wrote in English.

The Absentee Shawnee community is located in central Oklahoma, where many of the things she writes about can be found. The Absentee Shawnee Indian tribal office is located in Shawnee Oklahoma. The Shawnees arrived in Indian Territory around the 1830s, removed to Oklahoma by the Indian Removal Act of 1833. The Shawnees were settled first in Kansas prior to coming to Oklahoma.

Pauline's family is descended from Tecumseh, the famous Shawnee war chief who assembled neighboring tribes along the Eastern Seaboard in resistance to the advancing white settlements. Today there are approximately three thousand tribal members of the Absentee Shawnee tribe.

Shawnee Pronunciation Guide by Pauline Wahpepah

Consonants:
b, h, k, l, m, n, s, t, w, y
k sounds like soft 'q'
t sounds like soft 'd'

Vowels:

a = 'ah'

a = 'a' in 'cat'

i = 'e'

o = 'oh'

e = 'e' in 'get'

u = 'u' in '**h**uh,' not used very much

Blended sounds: *by, bw, ch (j), kw, mw, nw, sh, shw, sk, sw, th, thw, tw*

I came up with this pronunciation guide from English sounds, so learners will be more familiar with the sounds instead of learning new symbols for sounds.

Ho!

Hello!

Haki wasi iasamamo?

Are you feeling well?

MIKITHIYA

tasi onthewa

spammiki tasiwayenthe

imsilotaki tasi

nomeko ina

mikithiya

EAGLE

Is flying.

Up high, floating

In a circle.

Riding the wind

That eagle.

IMKWA

imkwa ni newa

in tasi nibawi

ki newa

tanawa ina imkwa

weh, kitothami petathi

webtrhe ina imkwa

BEAR

I see a bear.
Do you see him?
Where is the bear?
You're too slow.
He is gone.
The bear.

KIISATHAW

spammaki habiwa
biyatabaka kinawa
nekani kisakwa sibemtha
pakshimoke
wi ahkwabi

SUN

Up high he stays.
At dawn you'll see him.
All day long he will travel.
At dusk
He will rest

BABAKI

Ni nama babaki.
Nisa ba mikina.
Bataki nisaha.
Lani babaki.
Ki wabataba babaki.

FLOWER

I see a flower.
I shall pick it.
I shall return.
There is the flower.
We shall look at the flower.

KICKAPOO

The Motorcyclists

Mosiah Bluecloud

"The Motorcyclists" is one of many Central Algonquin stories that I have collected. "The Motorcyclists" was found in a stack of tattered papers in a dusty box in the basement of the Kickapoo Secondary Administration building in McCloud, Oklahoma. Five stories and a syllabary were recovered. On the syllabary was a note in the language from the possible author of the stories. The author asked that non-speakers learn their heritage language. The author also joked that no one ever believes his stories and so he writes them down in the hopes that they will not be forgotten but retold again and again through the breath of generations to come.

Ehpapakethumehaki

Nekutenu'i niisui manithaki, epepakethuemehaki nihaachimaki esaiyaachi eesikii-weneskahiichi meethihi. Kapuutue pieutamuuki witheniikaani iinahi ehteeki aatheni mieki enanakethiaachi nenesi awachikanaki awatathuaachiki. Iini maa-haki niisui ehpapakethuemehaki keaweaki papakethuhahi. Iini ehpitikeaachi iini witheniikaani, chihi iinahi tasitheniewa nekuti metuthenenia tasimiichia bisteiki.

Iini sehe iiniki ehpapakethuemehaki ehmaikunepachihaachi iini'ni metuthene-nia'ni. Iinahitai nahekuepiaki ehapiniichi. Iini sehe iina nekuti manitha utapena-maewa iini bisteiki iini ehpakietaki iini pehteki ehatuuchi iinahi unakaniki. Iini iina kutakeha ehmenuuchi iini kaapihi menuniichi ehkiisi aaneta menuuchi iina manitha, chihi chapukinekewa iinahi kaapiheki, iini sehe ehnanatuhkuihaachi.

Iini aakui chahi iina metuthenenia aachi auwiyehi inueechi. Seeski pathekuia iini ehtepahaki eesiwitheniichi. Iini ehweputheechi nuiya iinahi uuchi itheniikaniiki.

Iini tenaami eniketaachi iiniki ehpapakethumehaki ehpiichi menuitaachi ethek-iahaachi iini'ni metuthenenia'ni. Iini iina nekuti ehpapakethumeha ehkanaiichi kanuunewa iini'ni iskuethahi'ni mikecheiniichi'ni iinahi ithenikaaneki. Manahi ehnueechi, "aakui yetuke iina metuthenenia itheniniichi'ni, aakui aachi auwi-yehi inueechi'ni ehpenanakeechi," yaaha ine'we iini'ni iskuetheha'ni iina ehpa-pakethumeha.

Iini iina ehkanaiichi iskuetheha, 'uwe', ine'wa iini'ni ehpapakethumeha'ni, "aakui eiki yeetuke nahekuenikeechi," yaaha iina iskuethea. "iinuki ewepipaukekuuchi apiskamuheewa niisui papakethuhahi," yaaha iina iskuetheha.

The Motorcyclists

Once two of those motorcyclists, I'll tell you about them, went around every-where doing bad things. Once they went to an eating-place where the very big carrying stuff [semitrailer] stop to eat along the road. Those two travelers were using motorcycles. They entered the eating-place where, there, an Indian man was eating a beefsteak.

Then those motorcyclists went over and bothered that Indian man. They went over there and sat on either side of him. Then one of them grabbed the beefsteak and bit into it and returned it back to the plate. The other one drank the coffee he [the Indian] was drinking and after drinking some that guy put his fingers there into the coffee and tried to get the Indian mad.

The Indian didn't even say anything. He just got up and paid for what he had eaten and he left from there, that eating-place.

They were really laughing at him those motorcyclists. They were delighted that they'd made the Indian mad. Then one of the motorcyclists spoke saying to the girl working there in the eating-place. This is what he said. "That Indian who was eating here isn't much of a man, he didn't say anything after what'd been done to him," he said to that girl.

And then the girl spoke. "Well," she said to the motorcyclist, "and also it looks like he doesn't know how to drive," the girl said. "Just now driving off he ran over two motorcycles," said the girl.

LENAPE

The Lenape Story of the Origin of the Woman Dance

Lillie Hoag Whitehorn
Transcribed by Bruce Pearson and Jim Rementer
Translated by Nora Thompson Dean
Introduced by Jim Rementer

Told by Lillie on August 22, 1977, at her home in Anadarko.

Introduction

The Lenape or Delaware Indians are members of the widespread Algonquian language family. At one time Lenape was spoken over an area of almost 22,000 square miles and the original homeland was all of New Jersey, eastern Pennsylvania, southeastern New York State, and the northern part of the State of Delaware.

Europeans first encountered the Lenape in 1524. The Delaware Tribe was the first tribe to sign a treaty in September 1778 with the newly formed United States government. Nevertheless, the tribe was forced to retreat westward in the face of expansion. The Delawares were relocated time after time by the United States government; to Ohio, Indiana, Missouri, Kansas, and finally, in 1867, to Indian Territory (now Oklahoma). The language was widely spoken into the mid-twentieth century and was preserved in the latter half of the century by elders who did much to encourage documentation of the language.

"My late mother told us that a great while ago this was the origin of the singing for the women when they dance." Thus Lillie begins the story that was told to her. It is impossible to know how long ago this might have taken place. We do know that a very similar story was told by a Delaware named Willie Longbone from northeastern Oklahoma in 1939 and the two groups have been apart for over two hundred years.

In an effort to keep the language and the stories of the Lenape people alive, this story and many others are now found as told in Lenape on the Lenape Talking

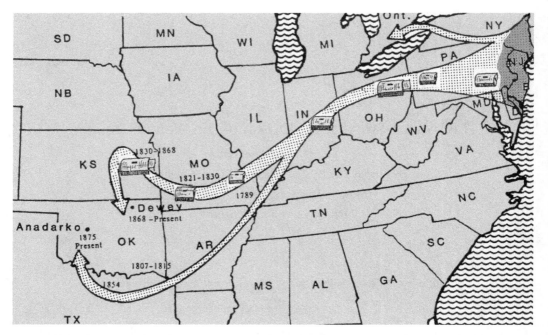

FIG. 1. Delaware Tribe relocations. Map created by Jim Rementer.

Dictionary (www.talk-lenape.org). The dictionary contains words and sound files from both groups of Delawares located in Oklahoma and is being used as a learning tool by tribal members who want to know more about the language and stories of their ancestors and by other interested people.

The Lenape Story of the Origin of the Woman Dance

This version includes the Lenape story of the origin of the woman dance by Lillie Whitehorn found at the Lenape Talking Dictionary (http://talk-lenape.org/stories ?id=44 and http://talk-lenape.org/stories?id=48).

Kènu hùnt yukshe ntëlkuk ntëlachimwin nèk xkweyok
This is a story that was told to me about

ènta naxku'hëmënt ènta xkweyok mëkùchi shëk këntkahtit.
when they sing exclusively for the women when they dance.

Lò'mëwe waka nkahèsa ntihëlëkunèn lò'mëwe, kìtlòmwe,
My late mother told us this a great while ago

hùnt yukwe nën wënchixën yu xkweyok ènta naxku'hëmënt ènta këntkahtit.
about the origin of the singing for the women when they dance.

Kènu hùnt lòmëwe Lënapeyok hùnt mah lòmëwe naxènawki
Long ago the Delawares lived in three parts,

nèk wikha'tuwàk Lënapeyok, Pëleyok òk Tùkwsitàk na làpi
the Turkey clan, the Wolf clan, and then this Turtle clan.

Pukuànkuwàk. Pè wàni Pukuànkuwàk na në ntëlhakein. Na wèmi Turtle-Clan. [?].
The Turtle Clanspeople are my clan. Then

hùnt nihëlàchi wèmi wikha'tuwàk.
they lived together, but by themselves [apart from other clans?].

Na hùnt na kwëti lìnu òk xkwe nihëlàchi pali' wi'kuwàk
There was a man and a woman who lived by themselves

pali'ichi, òk kwitëtëwoo hùnt tànktitu na
a short distance away, and they had a little son who was just then

pilaechëch, kënchawèna a'lëmi ahpamske.
beginning to crawl. [A little later she uses the word for crawl.]

Na wixkawchi kta hùnt të'luwèn na lìnu tëlao hùnt nèl wicheòchi
Then one day the man told his wife,

witaèmachi tëlao hunt, "Nkata may alai, nkata may alai,
"I want to go hunting, I want to go hunting,

nkata may ntu'nao chikënëm." Na hunt tëlan na xkwe,
I am going to look for a turkey." The woman said,

   "Na ta nëni!"
   "That's good."

Na hùnt alëmske na lìnu. Na na xkwe nutikeyok na
The man left, and the woman stayed home with

kwitëta hùnt. Na na pilaechëch hùnt kënchawèna a'lëmi kàski ahpamxsu.
her little son. The boy was just now beginning to crawl,

Lenape Story of the Woman Dance   31

òk nihënipu, ku xane kwiakwi kàski pëmëske.
and he could stand occasionally, but he couldn't walk yet.

Na hùnt kahta sukëlan, alàshi alëmi kahta kùmhòkòt. Na
Then it began to look like rain and was getting cloudy. Then

hùnt na xkwe kwëchin hùnt, shëmu'ch, kchi hùnt.
outdoors, or rather, she went out.

Na wètë'nëmën èt ma [supp] kwipëlënay, na ìka è hakiha'kànink.
Then she got her hoe and went to the garden.

Lòmëwe èt kwipëlënay ènta hnakatèmën ènta kwipëlënay nèkao Lënapei'
It was the old type of hoe like the Delawares used before they

hùnt kènu aku' sëkahsëni' nihëlàchi manitaonu na ahtuhwi' taompikàn.
had iron as it was made out of a deer's jaw.

Na hùnt na tìli hnakaktàmëneyo ènta hakihèhtit. Na hùnt ìka
That was what they used to use when they made a garden. She went to

tòn hakihakënink èt ma na xàskwim alëmi mèchi kahta mata kwëni
the garden to hoe her corn, which hadn't yet started

kahta xu suwalu èt. Na hùnt na titehan nà xkwe,
to tassel. Then the woman thought,

"Ntèpi a na alënta në skiko tëmitehëmën òk munënëmën." Na
"I could cut down or pull up some of the grass [weeds?]." Then

hùnt ìka tòn na xkwe. Na kèxiti hùnt òhëlëmìchi
the woman went there. It was just a short distance

na ènta tòkihakanëmëwoo, na hùnt tòlëmënakwsin.
to where their garden was, and she began to work.

Na èt mah mèchi na yu mahtèxën ènta kahta sukëlan,
Then it was just about to rain,

na hùnt ìka wënchi pèthakhòn. Na naka xkweyo hùnt kènu
and all at once it thundered. Then that woman

ìka talhukwën nèl pèthakhùweyo hùnt. Na alëmi tkaiti alëmi
was struck by the thunders. It then began slowly

sukëlan. Nakè kta hùnt kshilan hùnt, na
to rain. Before long it rained hard, and

pèpèthakhòn.
it thundered repeatedly.

Na èt ma na mimëns kawi' wëlè wikihtit
That child must have been asleep over there in the house.

tali. Na èt ma tukihële na nòtunaon nèl
Then he awoke and began to look for

kòhèsa. Na kwilai, na ktùkxwsu hùnt na
his mother. When he couldn't find her, he crawled

mimëns kòchëmink tali. Na mëlimu.
outside. Then he began to cry.

Na èt ma na mayayxkwi na lìnu pèchi ktëki. Na
About that time the man returned home.

kèku yu wëneyòn në kwitëta pèxwsit,
Suddenly he saw his little son crawling toward him,

na hùnt wètënan. Na litehe hùnt, "Kèku èt ta
so he picked him up. He thought, "Whatever

èlsit." Kèku èt ta wënchi ku na
is wrong with him?" Something was because

ninkalaio në kwisa na xkwe.
the woman never left her son.

Na wètënan, hùnt na pwëntu'xòlan, wëli
So he picked him up and carried him inside; he was really

skàpsu hùnt. Na tkaiti alëmi òk pàkëlan. Na hùnt
wet. Then it slowly began to stop raining.

kwëchin hùnt na lìnu, na kwënan na kwisa, na
He went outside, carrying his son, and

tòlëmi ntunaon nèl xkweyo në wiatemachi. Na hùnt
and he began to hunt for his wife. Then

mweshatàmën winki hakiha'kànink e. Na hùnt nëni
he remembered that she liked to go to the garden. Then

tòneyo ènta ìka pahtit na mòxkawoo nèl xkweyo.
they went there, and when they got there they found the woman.

Kèku hùnt waka shenkixin, èt ma ìka
She was lying there dead, as it was there

tòlhukwën èt ma pèthakhuweyo hùnt. Na wëli
that the thunders struck her. She was really

lusu hùnt wëli sëkinakwsu. Na ktëki hùnt
burned and she looked very black. Then the man went

na lìnu hùnt na tòlëmu'xòlan na kwitëta. Na
and got his little son and carried him.

alëmskeyok nèkao eyok èlànkumachi wikhatihtit, na
They left to go to where his relatives lived, and

mòy luwèn. Na wèmi yu tali wehumawtin hùnt.
he went to tell them. They then all notified each other at that place.

Na na sakima wèhumao òk wèmi awè'n lan. Na hùnt kènu
The chief was notified and all the people. Then

na achimulsahtuwàk hùnt. Na nalan naka xkweyo
they held a council. They went after the deceased woman

na pè'shëwan. Kèku èt ma waka wëli
and brought her. The deceased one was really

lu'suwa ènda ìka alahukuk nèl pèthakhuweyo. Na hùnt
burned when she was struck by the thunders. Then

kènu na achimulsuwàk hunt.
they had a council.

Na hùnt kanshelì'ntàmuk èli alahukuk nèl
They were surprised because she was struck by those

pèthakhuweyo. Na hùnt na kwèti lìnu luwe' hùnt, "Ntèpi a ni
thunders. One man said, "I could

ktëki' pèshëwa," luwe hùnt. Kwèti na lìnu hùnt, "Nuwatun ni
bring her back." The man said, "I know

a ènëmën wënchi a ktëki' pèshëwan." Na hùnt luwe, "Na
what I could do to bring her back." Then he said, "That's

ta nëni!" Na luwe hùnt, "Shëk neyukwëni xu neyukwëni xu
it!" Then he said, "But for four days

nsakhakèn," luwe hùnt, "neyukwëni xu nsakhakèn. Xu wënchi
I will be gone," he said, "I will be gone for four days. I will

opànk nta. Xu nkënëm kènu shuhòhòktët. Nal xu na
go to the east. I will hold this little gourd rattle. This is what

nkënëmën," luwe hùnt. "Na pèshëwàke na xkwe ktëki
I will hold," he said. "Then if that woman is to be

pèshëwàte nèch këmanituhëmo li mawhwin, mawhwinch," luwe
brought back you will hold a dance, you will have a dance," he said.

hùnt. "Wèmìch," luwe hùnt, "nihënisha nek xkweyok
He said, "All the women will be two at a time

tèkawtuwàk. Na na kìkuwi na xkwe, kìkuwi nek xkweyok nàlch nèk nisha
behind each other. The old women will

nikàniyok," luwe hùnt. "Na yushe'," luwe hùnt, "alàshi
lead," he said. "Then it will seem like

a èluwèt newëna na xkwe ènta newihtit nàlch
when the women are in fours we will see that woman

na newa na yukwe naka nàni," luwe hùnt, "ènta ktëki
on the fourth [day?]," he said, when he

pèshëwat. Nàlch mahuwàk mawhwin," luwe hùnt,
brings her back. "Then they will have a dance," he said,

"asuwàk nèk lì'nuwàk, na nèk xkweyok òkakeyok,"
"The men will sing, and the women will dance in a circle,"

luwe hùnt. "Na ènta mawhwihtit, na yushe ènta newën
he said. "Then when they have this dance for four times

ènta piskèk," luwe hùnt, "xu ìka wìchi, ìka wìchi
at night," he said, "she will be there, she will be there,

xu, nal xu nàn. Nàch na lìnu kwënao nèl
that will be her. The man will carry

kwitëta," luwe hùnt. "Na hùnt na
his little son," he said. "Then when

pàxke na xkwe na xu tëlao nèl witaemachi,
the woman steps aside she will tell her husband,

'Mili na kwitëtëna.' Kàchi kahta ku milièkhèch, kàchi milahich,"
'Give me our little son.' Don't give him to her,"

luwe hùnt, "èli ìka lënamawtèch na ta chich
he said, "because if he hands him to her she will never again

kwëtkënaio xu chimi tòlëmuxòlao wë'ntahkwi awè'n
return, and she will take him to where a person goes forever,"

eyat," luwe hùnt. "Na kàchi kahta awè'n melimwihich,"
he said. "Don't anyone cry,"

luwe hùnt. "Awè'n mëlimwite pòlitun nëni, na ta chich
he said. "If anyone cries he will ruin it and I can never

nkàski ktëki'. Mpalitakwën, na xu ènta ktëki
bring her back. He will ruin it for me, and in the future I cannot

awè'n kàski pèshëwàk." Na luwe hùnt, "Këmawhwihëmòch ta."
bring anyone back." Then he said, "You all have a dance!"

Na hùnt kìchi hùnt na në le. Na yu
It really happened [the dance]. Then

ènta neyukwënàkàt hùnt mawhwin hùnt. Na yu newën
they had held a dance for four days. On the fourth day

ènta piskèk nèka wìchi na xkwe ktëki pè èt ma ìka wìchi
when it was night, the woman returned and there with the people

witke, ìka wìchi këntke nèk xkweyok ènta këntkahtit.
she danced, she danced with those women.

Na wëneyòn hùnt na witaemachi, na pòxkèn
Then she saw her husband, and she stepped to one side.

hùnt. Na tëlan hùnt, "Mili na kwitëtëna. Ntahola na
She told him, "Give me our little son. I love him,

nkwitët, nkata neyo." Na hùnt na lìnu chitani
my little son, I want to see him." The man tightly

kwënao na kwisa. Nèli na lënamihtit luwe hùnt
held onto his son. While they were doing that [dancing]

kèku èt ma na hilusës wëntahkwi hùnt pali' wiku
an old man who lived separately came toward them.

na hilusës hùnt. Ku tëmiiki ìka wìchi awènike', nkëme'
He was not often there among the people, he was always

pali'. Na hùnt ìka pòn, na hùnt të'luwèn, "Nuxwitët,"
separate. He came there and he said, "Grandchild,"

hùnt tòlëmi mëlimwin. Luwe hùnt, "Nuxwitët, kehëla èt
and he began to cry. He said, "Grandchild, you have truly

ma ki ktëki kpa. Nulelìntàn newëlàn," hùnt.
come back. I am glad to see you."

Na ènta na lënink, ènta na lat nèl uxwisa,
When he did that, when he told his granddaughter that

na naka xkweyo ta èt ta hùnt. Ku chich nèhkwësi',
then that deceased woman disappeared. She was not seen again,

ku chich ìka wìchi.
never was there again.

Na hënt yukwe nëshè ènta mahwin nëni wënchixën në Lënapei'
Now this is where it comes from when they have the Delaware

xkweyok ènta naxkuhëmënt hùnt. Na nëshè shëk nkàski sakawchimwin.
Woman Dance. This then is the length of the story.

Na na ntihëlë'stàmën waka nkahèsa òk nuhëma
This is what I heard from my late mother and grandmother

ènta achimwihtit. Shë yu ntëluwènsin ènta Lënapeyàn,
when they told stories. My Delaware name

ntëluwènsi Wèntataèxkwe. Naka nuhëma
is Wèntataèxkwe [Where the Flowers Come From Woman]. My grandmother

ntìli wìlkwën. Pahsi ni Anadahkuxkwe. Waka nuxa sakima
named me that. I am half Caddo. My late father, a chief, was named

luwènsu Enoch Hoag, mèkënihëlak tìli sakimain Hasinai'.
Enoch Hoag, and he was the last chief of the Caddo.

Nàni ntëlhakein Anadahkuxkwe. Pahsi ni Anadahkuxkwe òk pahsi
That is my tribe of the Caddo. I am half Caddo and half

Lënapèxkwe. Nkahèsa naka Lënapèxkweyo luwènsu
Delaware woman. My mother was a Delaware woman and her name was

Kweihtitti ènta Lënapeyëwènsit.
Kweihtitti in Delaware.

Na ènta shëwanàhkowènsit luwènsu Nellie Thomas Hoag.
In English her name was Nellie Thomas Hoag.

MIAMI

Myaamia "Story of Fox and Wolf"

Narrated by Kiišikohkwa (Elizabeth Valley) to Albert Gatschet
Introduced by David J. Costa

Background on the Myaamia and Their Language

The Myaamia, also known as the Miami, are a tribe of the southern Great Lakes area. Their original homeland was in what is now Indiana, western Ohio, and the southern edge of Michigan. The Myaamia spoke an Algonquian language often called "Miami-Illinois." The groups speaking Miami included the Myaamia proper (*myaamiaki* 'downstream people'); the Wea (*waayaahtanooki* 'whirlpool people'), along the middle reaches of the Wabash River; and the Piankashaw (*peeyankihšiaki* 'torn ears people'), in the southwest of Indiana around present-day Vincennes.

The groups known as the "Illinois" in that state spoke dialects extremely similar to those of the Myaamia and other Indiana groups; the two best-known groups speaking Illinois were the Kaskaskia (*kaahkaahkiaki* 'katydids'), in the southwest of the state near the Mississippi River, and the Peoria (*peewaaliaki*; etymology unknown) to the north, along the Illinois River. The closest neighbors and linguistic relatives of the Miami-Illinois–speaking groups were the Kickapoo, Meskwaki, Potawatomi, Sauk, and Shawnee.

By 1832 all Miami-Illinois–speaking groups were forced to leave the Illinois area. They first emigrated to eastern Kansas, in and around present-day Miami County, where they stayed for over thirty years. In 1867 they were forced to move again, relocating south to Indian Territory, where they settled in the Quapaw Agency, in what is now Ottawa County in the northeast corner of Oklahoma. The Wea and Piankashaw were likewise forced out of Indiana in the first few decades of the nineteenth century, temporarily settling on lands adjacent to the Peoria in eastern Kansas. In 1867 they accompanied the Peoria and Kaskaskia on their relocation to the Quapaw Agency and, soon after arrival, merged with the Peoria. These groups coalesced to form the modern Peoria Tribe of Indians of Oklahoma, an amalgam of the Kaskaskia, Peoria, Wea, and Piankashaw.

In 1846 the Miami Tribe, as a sovereign entity, were forcibly removed west to their reservation lands, leaving behind approximately three hundred individuals in Indiana, and settling for about a quarter-century in eastern Kansas, next to the Wea and Piankashaw. In the 1870s they, too, were relocated to the Quapaw Agency in Indian Territory, where their descendants live to this day as the modern Miami Tribe of Oklahoma. Of the Myaamia who stayed behind in Indiana, to this day their descendants mainly live in the northern portion of that state, around or near the Wabash Valley.

There are no longer native speakers of Miami-Illinois in either Oklahoma or Indiana, though there are vigorous efforts in both states to revitalize the language. In Oklahoma the last fully fluent speakers passed away in the first half of the twentieth century, though a few semi-fluent speakers lived a few decades past that. In Indiana, the last people with some native knowledge of the Myaamia language survived until at least the early 1960s, or possibly as late as the early 1980s.

The Miami-Illinois language was very extensively documented over a time span of more than two hundred years. Early eighteenth-century Illinois is recorded in three dictionaries and a prayer book from the French Jesuit missionary period. The Miami-Illinois language was recorded sporadically throughout the nineteenth century, but extensive documentation of the modern language did not begin until the late nineteenth and early twentieth centuries. From the 1890s through 1916 the speech of the last generation of fluent speakers was documented by Bureau of American Ethnology (BAE) linguists Albert Gatschet and Truman Michelson, and by Jacob Dunn, a lawyer and avocational linguist from Indiana.

Background on Elizabeth Valley

Elizabeth Valley, sometimes known as "Vallier," was a Myaamia woman born in western Ohio, probably in 1813. Her Myaamia name was Kiišikohkwa, literally 'Sky Woman,' and she did not acquire an English name until considerably later in life. Though born in Ohio, she moved to Indiana at a young age, where she was raised among the Eel River band of the Myaamia. She probably left Indiana in 1846, during the main removal of the Myaamia to Kansas. Once in Kansas she married Frank Valley of the Peoria tribe, with whom she had a son, Lovely Valley, born around

1848–50. From this point on she spent the rest of her life living among the Peoria, though she continued to be counted on the Miami annuity rolls for several years afterward and was thought of as Myaamia by many in the Peoria community. Frank Valley and his family moved from Miami County, Kansas, to Indian Territory in April 1869, after which Kiišikohkwa first starts to appear in written records as "Elizabeth." She died in Oklahoma on February 1, 1899, at about eighty-five years of age.

Kiišikohkwa worked with Albert Gatschet in 1895, in the course of his extensive work on Miami-Illinois for the Bureau of American Ethnology. From her Gatschet obtained six traditional narratives, most of them animal stories.[1] In his work with Kiišikohkwa, Gatschet had to employ the services of the Wea speaker Sarah Wadsworth as an interpreter, since Kiišikohkwa apparently did not speak English. Gatschet did not record much personal information about Kiišikohkwa, simply stating:

> Vallier's father was a Miami who lived in Ohio—and she was born there also. Then they moved to Indiana—then to Kansas, then [Oklahoma]. [She] is good looking for her 80–85 years; hair only partly white, skin very dark, not much burnt; smoking tobacco. (Gatschet, n.d.)

Kiišikohkwa was in fact the oldest individual from whom Miami-Illinois texts were ever obtained, as well as the only Miami-Illinois speaker any linguist ever worked with who did not speak English. Consequently the stories and language obtained from Kiišikohkwa are especially valuable for their exceptionally conservative, older style, and are probably the truest to the precontact speech styles and story traditions of any Myaamia speaker recorded in the nineteenth century.

About the Text

Kiišikohkwa's *Story of Fox and Wolf* was collected by Albert Gatschet sometime in 1895. It is found in Gatschet's original field notebooks preserved at the National Anthropological Archives in Suitland, Maryland (Gatschet, n.d.). The original text consists of four handwritten pages, in Myaamia with a loose word-for-word English translation. Gatschet later wrote out a slightly reanalyzed and cleaned up version of the story, probably for the purpose of eventual publication, though Gatschet never actually published any of his Miami-Illinois materials. Nevertheless, Gatschet's first version of this story is used here, as it is clearly truer to the story as Kiišikohkwa told it.

On the Presentation

Gatschet transcribed Kiišikohkwa's speech in his own rough version of the orthography in common use among BAE workers of the time, which suffers from being both inconsistent and phonetically imprecise. This has been retranscribed here into the modern standard Miami-Illinois spelling system, which has the advantage of representing all the distinctive sounds of the language as well as being used in present-day instructional materials among the Myaamia tribe. In his original elicitation, Gatschet does not really translate whole sentences, but merely provides very loose glosses of individual words. Since Gatschet's glosses of individual words are rather rough, the translation provided here is my own, based on my study of the Miami-Illinois language. Further complicating the interpretation of Gatschet's materials is the fact that he does not reliably indicate where sentences begin or end, nor does he always mark quotations. Thus quotation marks are supplied here to indicate quoted speech, periods are used to mark the ends of sentences, question marks are filled in to mark questions, and commas are used to mark clause boundaries.

Transcription and Pronunciation

The Myaamia story presented here is given in the standard writing system in use among the Myaamia tribe. In this system, the consonants *p, t, k, h, l, m, n, s,* and *w* have basically their expected English values.[2] The letter *y* represents the sound in English 'yarn.' The letter *c* is always pronounced like English 'ch' as in 'church.' The only special letter used is *š*, which is for the 'sh' sound as in English 'show.' The sounds *p, t, k, c,* and *s* are all voiced when they come immediately after nasal consonants; this means that *mp* is pronounced like 'mb,' *nt* is pronounced like 'nd,' *nk* is pronounced like 'ng' (as in English 'hunger'), *nc* is pronounced like 'nj' (as in English 'injure'), and *ns* is pronounced like 'nz.' When the consonants *p, t, k, c, s,* or *š* are preceded by the letter *h*, they are pronounced with a small 'h' sound immediately preceding them, what is sometimes called preaspiration, an extremely common feature of Miami-Illinois pronunciation.

In addition, there are four vowel letters in Miami-Illinois, *a, e, i,* and *o*. The vowel sound *a* is pronounced roughly like the vowel 'o' in 'pot'; *e* can be pronounced either like the 'a' sound in 'bad' or the 'e' sound in 'bed'; *i* is pronounced like the 'i' sound in 'bid'; and the vowel sound *o* is usually pronounced something like the vowel 'o' in 'note,' but can sometimes be pronounced like the vowel 'oo' in 'look.' In addition all four Miami-Illinois vowels can occur long, in which case they are written doubled: *aa*, *ee*, *ii*, and *oo*. These vowels are pronounced longer and more drawn out than their short equivalents, and can also sound slightly different: *aa* is like the 'a' in English 'father' or 'fall'; *ee* is something like the 'a' in English 'made'; *ii* is like the 'ee' in English 'feed'; and *oo* is usually pronounced like the 'oo' in English 'food,' but can also be pronounced like the 'o' sound in 'rode.'

About Fox and Wolf

At the top of the first page of the original manuscript of the story is a title *paapankamwa aalhsoohkaakani*, literally "fox story."[3] *Aalhsoohkaakani* is a Miami-Illinois word often rendered in English as 'winter story,' those traditional narratives that can only be told in wintertime.[4] As such, they contrast with more ordinary stories, such as historical accounts, personal anecdotes, or autobiographical narratives (Miami-Illinois *aacimooni*), which could be told at any time of year. In his work with various Myaamia and Peoria speakers, Albert Gatschet was told that winter stories "were not to be told in summer time, lest these monsters would come out at night, get into the beds of those recounting [them], going directly for the relator. There were many of these stories, and when they were related on right cold days, the weather would become still colder." In yet another place Gatschet said that "the Peoria and Miami story tellers say that when these legends and animal stories are told in summer, snails, snakes, and frogs of all kinds, toads will gather and suck the story tellers in their butts at the anus. Shawnees believe the same thing."

Fox is a very important trickster in the folklore of the Miami-Illinois–speaking peoples; several stories about Fox and his interactions with Wolf were collected from various Myaamia and Peoria tribe members. In addition to the "Story of Fox and Wolf" presented here, there are two short Fox and Wolf stories obtained by Jacob Dunn from Indiana Myaamia speaker Gabriel Godfroy, a version of the story in Peoria elicited by Truman Michelson from George Finley, and three versions in English also obtained by Truman Michelson (two of them from Peoria Nancy Stand and the third from an unidentified individual).[5] All of these stories are thematically similar, being humorous accounts of attempts by Fox (*paapankamwa*), always ultimately successful, to trick and steal from from Wolf (*mahweewa*). While Wolf is much bigger, stronger, and fiercer than Fox, he is also considerably less intelligent and more impulsive. After continually getting tricked by Fox, Wolf usually angrily tries to retaliate against Fox, though his attempts at revenge inevitably fail and result in Wolf's own humiliation and, often, death, while Fox always escapes unscathed and well fed. While the prominence of Fox as a trickster is apparently unique to Miami-Illinois–speaking groups, similar stories are found among neighboring tribes, most notably an extremely similar Shawnee-language "Story of the Fox and the Wolf" (haathθohkaaka waakočehθi čhiine mhweewa) collected by Gatschet from the Loyal Shawnee Charles Bluejacket around 1878.[6]

Paapankamwa Aalhsoohkaakani (Fox Story)
Narrator: Kiišikohkwa (Elizabeth Valley), Myaamia, to Albert Gatschet, 1895

Paapankamwa peempaalici. Paapankamwa kiimoteta pimi. Meehci kiimoteta, meehkaayonaaci amiihsitonaakanahi.

Fox was walking around. Then Fox stole some grease. After he stole it, he greased his whiskers.

Neehi-'hsa mahweewali aašitehkawaaci. "Keetwi, iihši, meeciyani? Meehkaawitonani."

Then he met up with Wolf. "What have you been eating, little brother? Your mouth is all greasy."

Neehi-'hsa: "Alikonci eekotenki. Kiila iihpisiyani, teepihsaayani."

Then Fox [said]: "It's hanging over there. You're tall, you can reach it."

"Pimi niiyaašilo, iihši."

"Take me there to the grease, little brother."

"Ooniini eekotenki pimi," iilaaci ahseensali mahweewali. Neehi mahweewa eempihsaaci. Neehi-'hsa poohkantanki ašihsayi waawaapiihkiciaki. Neehi šeehšahakoci misaahaki antepikaninki. Neehi paapankamwa keeweešinawaaci ahseensali. Neehi maacaamwita ciilahkionkiši.

"The grease is hung up here," [Fox] said to his older brother, Wolf. Then Wolf jumped up. And then he bit a hole in the hornets' nest. And they stung [Wolf] all over his head. And Fox laughed at his older brother. Then he ran away into the underbrush.

Aapooši meehkohkawaata ahseensali. Neelapaalayohseeci paapankamwa. Kiimoteci kiihkoneehsahi. Eenswaholaaci. Soonkacilici, neelapihsaaci, ansooyinki kiihpilaaci.

And once again, [Fox] met up with his older brother. Fox was walking along with his tail rattling. He had stolen some fish. He tied them together. They had frozen solid, and they rattled where he had tied them on his tail.

Aašitehkawaaci ahseensali. Neehi-'hsa "Taaniši iišileniyani, iihši, seekiinaci kiihkoneehsinsaki?" iilikoci ahseensali mahweewali.

Then [Fox] met up with his older brother. Then his older brother, Wolf, asked him, "What did you do, little brother, to catch all these little fish?"

"Aašoohkooni poohkahamaani, ceemonkaalaweepiaani waapanwi," iilaaci. Noonki ahseensali weenimaaci.

"I cut a hole in the ice and sat down and stuck my tail in it all night," he said to him. He fooled his older brother then.

Neehi-'hsa mahweewa aašoohkooninki poohkahanka. Ceemonkaalaweepici waapanwi, kati kiihkoneehsinsahi sakiinaaci. Naahpa-'hsa aašitatinki ansooyi. Aalweelici, kati saakaciweeci. Neehi-'hsa šaahšaakahakoci mihšimaalhsali.

And so Wolf made a hole in the ice. He sat down and stuck his tail in it until the morning, so as to catch some of the little fish. And then his tail froze in the ice. He couldn't get out. And then he was clubbed to death by a white man.

Neehi-'hsa aayaahkami maacaamwici paapankamwa. Eehkwa piici niiyaaha wiiyaahkita.

Then Fox ran away for good. He's probably there still.

Eehinki eehkwaapiikaasita.

That's as far as it goes.

NOTES

1. An English translation of Kiišikohkwa's *Story of Wiihsakacaakwa* is presented in Costa (2005, 308–13).
2. For a full explanation of the sound system and grammar of Miami-Illinois, see Costa (2003).
3. This is written ‹papangámwa halthukákani› in Gatschet's original.
4. This word is also commonly seen as *aalhsoohkaani*. The two words often seem to be interchangeable, though in one place Jacob Dunn claimed *aalhsoohkaani* meant 'story' while *aalhsoohkaakani* meant 'collection of stories.'
5. Versions of all these stories are given in Costa (2010).
6. This text is preserved in Albert Gatschet's manuscript #68 at the National Anthropological Archives (Gatschet 1878–79).

REFERENCES

Costa, David J. 2003. *The Miami-Illinois Language.* Lincoln: University of Nebraska Press.

——. 2005. *Culture Hero and Trickster Stories.* In *Algonquian Spirit: Contemporary Translations of the Algonquian Literatures of North America,* edited by Brian Swann, 292–319. Lincoln: University of Nebraska Press.

——. 2010. *Myaamia neehi peewaalia aacimoona neehi aalhsoohkaana. Myaamia and Peoria Narratives and Winter Stories.* Oxford OH: Myaamia Project.

Gatschet, Albert. 1878–79. Notebook with Vocabularies, Texts, Notes (Shawnee and Potawatomi). Manuscript #68, National Anthropological Archives, Smithsonian Museum Support Center, Suitland, Maryland.

——. n.d. Vocabulary and Texts. (Three original Miami and Peoria field notebooks). Manuscript #236, National Anthropological Archives, Smithsonian Museum Support Center, Suitland, Maryland.

POTAWATOMI

Pondese: Old Man Winter and Why We Have Spring Today

Translated and introduced by Justin Neely

This story is a traditional Potawatomi story about the origin of spring. The story was translated by myself, Justin Neely. Our language is an Algonquian language and is related to other languages like Sac & Fox, Shawnee, Kickapoo, Ojibwe, and Odawa, to name a few. There are Algonquian languages from the East Coast to California. Our tribe originally came from the Great Lakes and before that we have oral stories that we came from the East Coast. In the reading I mention the trailing arbutus. This flower is considered by some the tribal flower. It is one of the first flowers that come up in spring and is an indicator that spring has arrived. There are seven groups of Potawatomi in the United States and two in Canada. There is a northern and southern dialect of Potawatomi but both are mutually understandable although there are a few different vocabulary terms for certain objects and verbs. Some other good resources for learning about the Potawatomi Tribe are Alanson Skinner, who wrote a series of anthropological pieces in the 1930s that include a number of traditional tales. James Clifton, Ruth Landes, and David Edmunds also wrote some good books on our tribe. Traditionally we had a number of stories that we would only tell in the wintertime, particularly stories that involved Wiske or Nanabozho. These stories included the trickster figure Wiske, who would often play jokes on the people but who was also the one who taught us how to do different ceremonies and made the various animals the way they are. The Citizen Potawatomi Nation is located in Shawnee, Oklahoma. We have over 25,000 tribal members. We have over 9,000 that live in Oklahoma and a number in California and Kansas, as well as all the fifty states. We are one of the most, if not the most, treatied tribe in U.S. history. We signed over forty treaties with the United States, a few with France, and a couple with Great Britain.

Each treaty pushed us further out of the Great Lakes. We were removed forcibly a number of times, including in 1838 on our Trail of Death, first into Missouri and then into Kansas. Finally we sold our interest in land in Kansas and bought land in Oklahoma, where we are now located.

Pondese: Old Man Winter and Why We Have Spring Today

1. Kiwezi jiptebe bidek wde wigwamem mkomi zibik. Gechwa kekya nagwzet mine yekwzenagwzet. Gaga she bon bbomgek mine gechwa gaga ate mgek wde-shkode. Wabankwet mine kikichkanet. Wigwamek nshikewbet mine mteno ga nodaget shke bonimgek zagech.

   An old man was sitting inside his house by an icy stream. His appearance was old and tired. Soon winter would be over and his fire would be extinguished. His hair was white and he ached in his joints. He was sitting all alone in his wigwam with only the sound of fresh snow falling outside.

2. Ngot gishget, epich atemgek nkweshkwan ni sesksiyen. Kyetnan wenzet o kwe. Mnowabmenagwzet wde-shkiwzhgem mine mno shomigwet. Kwe ga byedot bgoch waskonedoyen mine ga biskonyet gechwa wiwkwan wishkpemishkos.

   One day as his fire was going out he met a young woman. She was very beautiful. She had pretty eyes and a great smile. This woman brought wild flowers, which she wore on her head.

3. "Noseme" ga kedot o Kiwezi nchiwenmo ewabmenan. "Bidgen widmoshen Ni pi je epabmadzeyen? Wishkezwnen gwidmowen mine da zhechkeyan. Nesap gda widmo mine ejiptebygo nomek."

   "Grandchild," said the old man, "I am happy to see you. Come in and tell me where you have traveled. I will tell you my strengths and things that I can do. You should do the same and we will sit for a while."

4. Kiwezi edapnan ni pwagenen bidek wde-shkemot mine ga gish wdemawat wdo-pwagenem ewebkiktowat.

   The old man picked up his pipe from within his bag and after they had smoked they began talking.

5. "Nesewen nbodajge" ga kedot o kiwezi "Zibek dokmejewen mine gechwa sen wishkezemgek."

"I blow my breath," said the old man, "and streams slow and become still as if they are hard like rock."

6. Sesksi nnese "Waskonedoyen zagkiwat nekmek shena mshkodek."
"I breathe," [the young woman said,] "Flowers spring up here and there on the prairie."

7. "Nweweb ninseske," ga kedot o kiwezi, "mine bonimget gechwa waboyan kwech igwan kik. Bnakwi gi datbekwen epich kiktoyan mine nnese pne-shiyek nemashiwat wase kiwen. Wesiyek kkezowat nde-nesewen mine zigdekiwen mine bikwa sen."
"I shake my hair," said the old man, "and snow falls and covers the earth like a blanket. Leaves fall while I talk, birds fly to a distant land, and the ground freezes hard like a stone."

8. "Nwewebninseske," ga kedot o sesksi, "mine gezhobisamget kik. Gtegadek bzegwiwat gechwa gachiyewat penojeyek. Pneshiyek giwewat ga gish notakewat ekiktoyan mine ge nin nde-nese ngezomget gi zibik. Mno notak-chegemget wegwendek ebmoseyan mine jayek wesiyek nchiwenmowat."
"I shake my hair," said the young woman, "and warm showers fall on the earth. Plants rise up like small children. Birds return home after they hear my voice and also when I breeze the rivers melt. Beautiful music plays wherever I walk and all the animals rejoice."

9. Jeshek mokze o gises ga gshatemget megwa shena ode kik. Kiwezi bon kiktot.
Just as the sun was rising it began to get warmer and warmer on the earth. The old man stopped talking.

10. Ojindis mine jijikekwea Ngemwat beshoch shkwademek. Mine gda mno magwe ni waskonedoyen kwech igwan ode dokanmek.
The bluebird and robin were singing close to the door and you could smell flowers on top of the gentle breeze.

11. Waben o sesksi egi wabman ni kiweziyen mine sesksi ga kkenman ni pondeseyen. Mbish bmejewen wde shkizhgwen epich bzegwi o gises shpem-segok. Megwa tkozet o kiwezi ga yawet.

In the light of the morning the young woman saw the old man and she knew that he was Pondese.[1] Water flowed from his eyes. The sun rose up above as the old man got shorter and shorter.

12. Gekpi gezo o nene. Cho gego demget wde-wigwamem nesh je trailing arbutus[2] zhenkasot. Gechwa wabmeskwam mine wabshkezo waskonedo. Finally the man melted. There was nothing in his wigwam but the trailing arbutus. It was a pink and white flower.

Iw
The end

---

1 Pondese is the spirit of the north. Also known as old man winter or the winter-maker.

2 Trailing arbutus, sometimes called a Mayflower, is a pink and white flower said to be the first flower to appear with the arrival of spring. It is considered by some to be the Potawatomi flower.

PART TWO

Athabaskan Language Family

PLAINS APACHE

Coyote and Rock Monster

A PLAINS APACHE TALE

Narrated by Alonzo Chalepah Sr.
Transcribed by Harry Hoijer
Reanalyzed and introduced by Sean O'Neill

Introduction

This story was related to the linguist Harry Hoijer in 1935—at the height of the American Depression—as he passed through from Chicago, where he was teaching linguistics, to the American Southwest, where he was carrying out long-term linguistic fieldwork among the Athabaskan communities there, including the Jicarilla and Chiricahua tribes. Along the way he often stopped in Oklahoma, mostly to work with the Tonkawa Tribe, in the northern part of the state near the Kansas border. Occasionally he stopped in Anadarko, about an hour south of the capital, Oklahoma City, where he was fortunate to meet with a small band of Athabaskans, then known as the Kiowa-Apaches.

Today this group is officially known as the Plains Apache Tribe of Oklahoma, though the old expression "Kiowa-Apache" is still familiar to many members of the community, as the now-outdated term once defined them in government documents and an earlier wave of academic writing. Though no longer in vogue this old designation was current during Hoijer's stay and captured at least a part of the tribe's ethnohistory. On the one hand it reflects their intimate relationship with the Kiowa Tribe, with whom they have been politically aligned for centuries, while also highlighting their even closer ties to the Apaches (and Navajos) of the American Southwest, in terms of common linguistic descent—as members of the larger Athabaskan stock.

Soon after arriving in Anadarko, Oklahoma, for a short visit, Hoijer was fortunate to encounter Alonzo Chalepah Sr., who was both a fluent speaker of the language and an expert in folklore and traditional culture. So much was condensed in that brief historical encounter between Chalepah, a respected elder in the Plains Apache Tribe, and Hoijer, a budding linguist who was then teaching at the University of Chicago, where he finished his degree under the direction of Edward Sapir, a pioneer in the field of linguistics and a major figure in the study of Athabaskan languages, including Hupa in northwest California and Navajo in the Southwest. Hoijer himself went on to develop the fields of anthropology and linguistics, as a future professor at the University of California at Los Angeles.

Alonzo Chalepah Sr., for his part, belonged to a family with a long and distinguished role in leadership in the tribe and that was instrumental in passing these traditions, including religion, onto the next generation. O'Neill, the author of this piece, himself came to know many of Alonzo Chalepah Sr.'s descendants, including Alonzo Chalepah Jr., the grandson of the teller of this tale and bearer of the family's distinguished name—as well as a keeper of these traditions in present times. Over a period of perhaps a week or so, the two men—Hoijer and Chalepah—documented the structure of the language for future generations, leaving this text behind as an artifact, alongside a handful of other stories and notes on the structure of the language. In the next generation Hoijer's student William Bittle went on write a dissertation on the grammatical structure of the language (Bittle 1956), while leaving behind an extensive archive for posterity (see Webster 2007).

The moment of Hoijer's visit was epic in still other ways. The Dust Bowl was unfolding in the region, with its epicenter near the Oklahoma panhandle. Many people in the Plains Apache community, perhaps a hundred miles away, still recall massive clouds that swept up in the distance. Even closer to home, for many in the community, were the days of "Indian Territory" in the nineteenth century, when the area was established as a supposedly permanent home for many tribes, including the Plains Apaches, that had been removed from their ancestral homelands. Despite their long persecution, going back several centuries, at the hands of the U.S. government, the Plains Apaches had once been nomadic, before being relocated to what was then known as Indian Country to settle with their Kiowa neighbors. It wasn't long, of course, before this land was taken away from its original inhabitants and annexed as the frontier state of Oklahoma in the early twentieth century, much to the chagrin of many of the Native peoples who had hoped to live here in peace, after being driven away from their own homelands throughout the larger continent.

What is clear from the Plains Apache oral tradition is that their ancestors traversed a vast territory, as recounted in their folklore about place-names, which span from today's Mount Rushmore, at the northern extreme, to the Gulf of Mexico—as far south as Mexico City—toward the southern limit of their regular travels. Many members of this community today still tell the lurid tales of the conquistadors they once encountered in Mexico and on the Plains, while recounting stories about monkeys, as the telltale signs of their ancestral travels in the heart of Meso-America. For many members of the Native American Church, which has deep roots among the Plains Apache, peyote is still an important religious sacrament, giving many in this community a regular reason to return to Mexico in the spring, to collect the plant where it still grows in abundance.

The ethnonyms of the Plains Apaches—their names for themselves—are many and instructive in this setting, providing further evidence of their complex past. For many, *Ghad-dindé* says it best, an expression that translates as "Cedar People," referring to their long-standing cultural practice of making incense out of the dried and crushed needles of cedar trees, for use at religious ceremonies. More common, though, is the now-familiar word *Na'isha*, which appears on flyers and billboards in the area, announcing ceremonies and meetings of the Plains Apache Tribe. The word literally translates as "thieves," which reflects on their reputation as tricksters, in the sense of those who have the power to outsmart their opponents, something that is still a matter of stealthy pride for many in the community. The corresponding word in Kiowa is *Samet*, which tells much the same story, translating as "Stealers," perhaps in part referring to their status as an adopted ethnic enclave among the Kiowa, during the time when the Plains Apache took refuge among their more numerous neighbors on the Plains. This name Na'isha is itself based on a transliteration of the slightly longer Plains Apache expression *Nadíí'įįsháá*, which is harder to capture in the orthography (or writing system) of English and much harder for non-fluent speakers to hear in rapid succession. Another common variation on this theme is *Na'ishan Dene*, which is another way of referring to the Plains Apaches, as the "People Who Are Thieves (or Tricksters)."

Like many stories that circulate in among the Plains Apaches, Coyote plays a starring role in this tale, as he does in general throughout the Plains, the Southwest, and even the Pacific Coast, where this beloved character was a daily visitor around the camps and trails (see Bright 1993). When telling stories in the evening, the signature howling of the coyote nearby was also a poignant reminder of the ever-present status of this popular figure. Throughout the Native societies of the American West, Coyote often teeters in suggested status between a starring role as religious figure, shaping the world as we know it with his beneficent acts, and that of secular mischief-maker, whose actions are comical and worthy of disdain, with perhaps a tinge of ironic respect. With this liminal role, on the edge of both the sacred and the profane, Coyote stories are easily revamped from group to group, with minor changes to the plot (see Bahr 2001; O'Neill 2015). Even at the outset, as Rock Monster plots against him, it is clear that Coyote is the protagonist of the tale, the one whom the audience roots for, hoping that he will outwit the enemy—in this episode, the innumerable and ever-antagonistic Rock Monsters.

Given that the story was volunteered during a chance encounter between an expert speaker and a short-term visitor, the cultural and historical sources of the tale remain unclear to this day. The most likely scenario is that the story belongs to the genre of the folktale, as a familiar episode that was recounted before friends and family in the course of everyday life—in part for entertainment, but also in part for spiritual enlightenment. In this way, the folktale engages with the sacred realm of oral literature, bringing it to bear on everyday situations (see Basso 1996). Coyote, for instance, is a visible figure, not just in myth but throughout the day, giving one reason to dwell on these stories and think about their meanings in everyday life. Often Coyote is a hero, outsmarting those who plot against him, as he does here; just as often Coyote is a clown, giving the audience a reason to laugh, even as they admire his gift of silliness. So comparing someone to Coyote in conversation could be taken as a compliment, but it could just as well be said to impart a criticism—suggesting, perhaps, that one is being silly or even dangerous.

Traditionally in the Plains Apache community, these stories are told in the evening, going late into the night—at one time in a tipi and around a fire, burning within to keep the company warm. For some families, the older tradition of telling stories in a tipi has been replaced in current times with any suitable shelter at a distance from the usual living space, such as an underground storm shelter. As the ethnographer Gilbert McAllister explains (as reported in Boatright 1949, 17), based on his experiences among the Plains Apaches in the early 1930s:

> It was in the evening around the fire that the old men, the grandfathers, told stories ostensibly to their grandchildren, but everyone sat around listening.

These stories embodied the lore of the tribe, the customs, the traditions, the hopes, the ambitions, even the failures. They were a form of escape, of relaxation, as well as an unconscious means of cultural indoctrination. Though the stories had been told innumerable times, the narrator had utmost attention. All listened eagerly, impatiently, and roared with laughter at the same old climax. A stranger would have thought the story had never before been told. One by one the children fell asleep, but the storytelling went on and on. Old men listened to other old men, seemingly absorbed in a story they had heard a thousand times.

The story opens in a typical way for a southern Athabaskan speech community, with a straightforward announcement, on the part of the narrator, of the identities of the main characters. Giving the spoken equivalent of a title line, Chalepah rattles off the names of Coyote and Rock Monster, who would have been familiar to most Plains Apaches at the time, pairing them with a conjunction but without any associated action, just as a Navajo narrator would in an Arizona context (see Kozak 2012). Among the Athabaskan communities of the Northwest Coast, on the other hand, the central characters are rarely introduced or even mentioned at the outset; instead, the audience has to infer their identities according to their familiar deeds (see O'Neill 2012; Scollon and Scollon 1981). So in terms of this contrast between the oral styles of the Northwestern and Southwestern Athabaskans, the Apaches of the Plains clearly adhere to the more familiar Southwestern style of narrative delivery.

Orthography and Pronunciation Guide

The sounds of Plains Apache are a challenge to write in standard letters of the Roman alphabet, as some are similar to those of English while others have no parallel, such as the special barred-l sound (ł) or the tones (á) and nasalization (ǫ) on the vowels The orthography given here is similar to those in use among the Navajos and Apaches of the Southwest, making the languages *look* as similar at first glance as they in fact *sound*, in terms of signature aural textures. Not surprisingly many of these sounds are shared by other languages of the Plains, including the neighboring Kiowas as well as the larger Siouan family, which includes Ponca, Osage, and Quapaw (in Oklahoma) as well as Lakota, Omaha, and Dakota in the Northern Plains. These sonic similarities echo the long-term social contact among the peoples of the Plains, which probably gave rise to these loose similarities in raw sound over many centuries, even while each language ultimately sounds quite distinctive.

The vowels of Plains Apache, for instance, pose several immediate challenges to the Roman alphabet, by incorporating features of tone, length, and nasalization into the palate of habitual sound-production. Following the current system in vogue among the Navajos and Apaches of the Southwest, tone is marked here with an acute accent (*á*) when high, while left unmarked (*a*) when in the contrastive low position. Hoijer himself wrote the low tones with a contrastive grave accent, to match the acute accent on the high tones, which is in some ways redundant given that the two-way distinction between high and low can be more succinctly summed up with an acute accent in contrast with no accent—or an unmarked low tone. Nasalization, which occurs alongside tone, is marked with a simple hook, meaning that a nasal vowel with a low tone bears nothing more than the hook (*ą*) while a high nasal vowel bears two modifications (*ą́*), with accent above and a hook below. Length is simply marked with single (*a*) versus double vowels (*aa*), marking sonic duration in an iconic or visually suggestive way, in terms of writing convention. Long vowels can, furthermore, move between the two positions—high and low—giving rise to rising and falling tonal contours, marked with a high tone on the first (*aá*) or second (*áa*) vowel, respectively. Beyond these characters for tone and nasalization, the basic vowel positions of Plains Apache loosely correspond to the standard values of Spanish; the basic positions of the Plains Apache vowels, in terms of the International Phonetic Alphabet (IPA) are given as follows in brackets: *a* [ʌ], *aa* [aː], *e* [ɛ], *ee* [ɛː], *i* [ɪ], *ii* [iː], *o* [ʊ], *oo* [oː].

The consonants, on the other hand, seem to pose less of a challenge at first glance, despite their subtle departures from the familiar sounds of European tongues. One of the most striking sounds, for the English speaker, is the so-called barred-l [ɬ], which is like the whispery 'l' of English 'clean' or 'slurp,' though with more friction still. On the other hand many Plains Apache sounds hold values roughly parallel to those of English, including *s* [s], *z* [z], *t* [tʰ], *k* [kʰ], and *y* [j] (as in English 'yes'). Others hold only slightly different values, such as *d* and *g*, which are not as resonant as in English, where the voicing is full; in terms of the International Phonetic Alphabet, these can be represented as follows: *d* [t] and *g* [k]. In this way the contrast between *t* [tʰ] versus *d* [t] in the Plains Apache writing system is based on the presence or absence of aspiration [ʰ] rather than *voicing*, as it is in English voiceless [t] versus voiced [d]. Another series of sounds, represented as digraphs in the orthography presented here, ultimately signal a single sound unit with a pair of two associated characters, including *sh* [ʃ], *zh* [ʒ], *tł* [tł], *kh* [kx], and *gh* [ɣ]; the first two sounds correspond to the *s* [ʃ] of 'sugar' and the *z* [ʒ] in 'azure,' though the others are without parallel in spoken English, sounding like a *g* or *k* released with noticeable friction. Another sound in Plains Apache consists of a 't' sound followed by a barred-l, which corresponds to IPA [tł]. Still other letters are followed by an apostrophe (such as *t'* or *ts'*), which represents a subtle sonic effect, consisting of a slight popping sound with the release of the consonant or consonant cluster in question. Among linguists these sounds are known as ejectives, since the vocal chords briefly close and push upwards like a plunger, creating pressure in the mouth, which is then suddenly released, creating a short (and subtle) "popping" sound, which strikes some as sounding almost metallic. These sounds, in terms of their values in the International Phonetic Alphabet, are as follows: *t'* [t'], *ts'* [ts'], *ch'* [tʃ'], *tł'* [tł'], *k'* [k'].

The keen observer who pays close attention to the representation of sounds in this performance will also notice some striking onomatopoeia towards the end of the tale, with the elongated hissing (or fricative) sounds that emulate the sound of the small bird; see Webster 2009 for parallel examples of onomatopoeia in the speech play and poetry of contemporary Navajo writers. One could only have been so lucky to have been with Hoijer that day, hearing the actual telling of this tale as it unfolded on the plane of actual sound! For now this is the best we can do, capturing that encounter on the printed page, with some suggestion of the sounds!

ZÁZAGHą́ą́ DÁ' NÍ'SGYEE   COYOTE AND ROCK MONSTER

I.

Ní'sgyee'	Rock Monster
náníìchį̇'dą́'	on the road
gakxash	they were coming [as a group].
Zázaghą́ą́ gǫǫłtsą́ą́	Coyote saw them [Rock Monster and party].
Daado'ádighíshnííł	What shall I do?

II.

Zázaghą́ą́ sháąhát'ee'	Coyote—he jumped in
'iją́ą́dééghwosh bijig	cockle burrs—in them
daadǫ́ǫ́s'iją́ą́dééghwosh	he crawled around.

Bikxáágaa	On him
'áłééchighwee	all over
be'aagaa	they stuck to him.
Goshtł'ish yijig	Much—in it
dá'ádé'íłxał	he rolled around.
Nániíchi'éé	In the road
deeshchį́į́	he lay down.

III.

Ní'sgyee'	Rock Monster
waniíjáá	he came there.
Biną́ą́ał'į́į́	He looked at him.
Bich'ą́deejáá	He went from him.
Łe'híídó'	Another one
wanáánáágáá	he came there also.
Bich'ą́'náádeesgá	He went from him, too.
Náánááłe'	Another
Bich'ą́'náádeeshgáá	he went from him, too.

IV.

'Eetł'aahíí	The last one
biną́ą́ł'į́í	he looked at him.
Bihą́ądídáá	"His fur
dígǫ́ǫ́déé	it's good.
k'aaqééł	Quiver
'ádighíshghį́į́	I'll make it,"
nish	he said.

V.

Dáábidįįłchį́į́	He picked him up.
Miighíí	He carried him.
bideesghį́į́	Carrying him, he started
níiza'yáá	to a distance
silį́į́	it became.

VI.

Shichitł'ą́ą́	"My brother
'ijááná'	what
léédiłgyih	you fear it?"
Doo-'ijááabeede'shgih	"I don't fear anything,"
nish	he said.
Ní'sgyee'	"Rock Monster
łe'ijáá heeshį́'	something—maybe
béendí'gyih	you fear it."

VII.

Haa	Yes,
daahiłgį́į́dee	small bird,
hijaayé	little me,
héédééshgih	I fear it!
Dááná' ´áaníí	What noise does it make!
Tssssst	"*Tssssst*,"
nish	he said.
'Ą́ą́xandéé	Close
gódeegee	his ear,
yideesní	he made a noise:
tssssst	*tssssst*
tsssst	*tssssst*.

VIII.

Bi'shį́į́dees'is	He ran away with him.
'igaabighį́į́'t'e'	He threw him (obj).
Zázaghą́ą́	Coyote
gołdeesdaa	chased him.
Got'į́'	To him
yidí(x)łní(x)'	made a noise.
Zázaghą́ą́	Coyote
náá(x)hą́ą́ghígah	he turned back.

Free Translation and Structure of the Tale

COYOTE AND ROCK MONSTER(S)

I. Coyote Witnesses the Rock Monsters' Appearance
Rock Monster was coming down the road [with a party]. Coyote saw them [coming].

II. Coyote's Reaction
"What shall I do?" Coyote thought. Coyote then jumped in cockle burrs, crawling around in them. They stuck all over him. He rolled around in the mud, and then lay down on the road.

III. The Rock Monsters Come to See Coyote, Scope Him Out
Rock Monster then came there to look at him. As he went from him, another one [in the group] came there as well, and also went away. Another one came up and ran off as well.

IV. The Last Rock Monster Tries to Make Coyote into a Quiver
When the last one came to look at him, he said, "His fur is good; I'll make it into a quiver!"

V. Coyote is Trapped, and Taken Away
Then, [the last Rock Monster] picked up [Coyote]. He started carrying him, eventually going a good distance.

VI. Stirring Fear as Way Out of the Predicament
"My brother, what do you fear?" he [Rock Monster] asked. "I don't fear anything," [Coyote] answered. "Rock Monster, maybe you fear something," Coyote responded.

VII. Little Bird Makes Fearsome Noise, Causing Distraction
"Yes, little me, I fear the sound of a small bird." "What noise does it make?" he said. When [Rock Monster] put his ear close up, it made a noise: *tssssst, tsssst!*

VIII. Coyote Flees, Perseveres
[Coyote] ran away with [the little bird], then threw him off. Coyote he chased him, making a noise toward him. Coyote then turned back.

Bahr, Donald M. 2001. "Bad News: The Predicament of Native American Mythology." *Ethnohistory* 48 (4): 587–612.

Basso, Keith. 1996. *Wisdom Sits in Places: Landscape and Language among the Western Apache.* Albuquerque: University of New Mexico Press.

Bittle, William. 1956. "The Position of Kiowa-Apache in the Apachean Group." PhD dissertation, University of California at Los Angeles.

———. 1963. "Kiowa-Apache." *University of California Publications in Linguistics* 29: 76–101.

Boatright, Mody C., ed. 1949. *The Sky is My Tipi.* The Texas Folklore Society. Austin: University Press in Dallas and the Von Beckmann-Jones Company.

Bright, William. 1993. *A Coyote Reader.* Berkeley: University of California Press.

Kozak, David L., ed. 2012. *Inside Dazzling Mountains: Southwest Native Verbal Arts.* Lincoln: University of Nebraska Press.

O'Neill, Sean. 2012. "The Politics of Storytelling in Northwestern California: Ideology, Identity, and Maintaining Narrative Distinction in the Face of Cultural Convergence." In *Telling Stories in the Face of Danger*, edited by Paul Kroskrity. Norman: University of Oklahoma Press.

———. 2015. "Translating Oral Literature in Indigenous Societies: Ethnic Aesthetic Performances in Multicultural and Multilingual Settings." In *The Legacy of Dell Hymes: Ethnopoetics, Narrative Inequality, and Voice*, edited by Paul V. Kroskrity and Anthony K. Webster. Bloomington: Indiana University Press.

Opler, Morris, and William E. Bittle. 1961. "The Death Practices and Eschatology of the Kiowa Apache." *Southwestern Journal of Anthropology* 17 (4): 383–94.

Sapir, Edward, and Harry Hoijer. 1942. *Navaho Texts.* William Dwight Whitney series, Linguistic Society of America.

Scollon, Ron, and Suzanne Scollon. 1981. *Narrative, Literacy, and Face in Interethnic Communication.* Norwood NJ: Ablex Publishing Corporation.

Webster, Anthony K. 2007. "Reading William Bittle and Charles Brant: On Ethnographic Representations of 'Contemporary' Plains Apache." *Plains Anthropologist* 52 (203): 301–15.

———. 2009. *Explorations in Navajo Poetry and Poetics.* Albuquerque: University of New Mexico Press.

PART THREE
Caddoan Language Family

CADDO

The Wolf and the Wren

Narrated by Sadie Bedoka Weller
Transcribed by Wallace Chafe

The following story was told in the Caddo language by Sadie Bedoka Weller on August 10, 1961, in Anadarko, Oklahoma, and was transcribed by Wallace Chafe. Mrs. Weller was born in 1901 and died in 1970. She spent much of her childhood with an aunt and uncle who passed on to her many Caddo traditions. George A. Dorsey's *Traditions of the Caddo* (1997) contains seventy Caddo stories that were collected during Mrs. Weller's childhood, but only in English. Further stories told by Mrs. Weller and transcribed by Chafe can be found in *Caddoan Texts*, edited by Douglas R. Parks (1977, 27–43), where this story appears on pages 33–35. Another of Mrs. Weller's stories, "Coyote Becomes a Mortar," was published with a detailed linguistic analysis by Chafe in *Native Languages of the Southeastern United States*, edited by Heather K. Hardy and Janine Scancarelli (2005). The story presented here obviously incorporates parts of the European story "Little Red Riding Hood" combined with Native American elements. Borrowings of this kind from European sources were common, as was the inclusion of a song like the crow's song here.

1 Ahya'   tiki: bah'nah   háh'í:'a'   tsínda:kístsi'.
   in the past far   it is said   she was present   little wren
   It is said that long ago there was a little wren.

2 Bah'nah   ná: sá:sin'   tut'iyas'nihah   dawat.
   it is said   that one   her mother   she prepared for her   basket
   It is said that her mother prepared a basket for her.

3 Túmbah'nah   ná: t'i'   chiyuhtsi'   kahni:dih'a'   ná: dawat.
  she told her   that one   little one   wren   to take it   that one   basket
  She told that little wren to take that basket,

4 Ku'á:na'   kánímbaka'   nassah'áwdih   ná: ínniyah   háh'ihsa'   tá:shah.
  over there   she told her   when you arrive there   that one   somewhere   he's there   wolf
  "When you arrive over there," she told her, "somewhere there is a wolf."

5 Bah'nah   tushdáwá:'ah   wa'nah   ha'ahat   tut'iyas'nihah.
  it is said   she laid it down for her   everything   nicely   she prepared for her
  It is said she laid it down for her, preparing everything nicely.

6 Nátti'   há:yuh   bah'nah   tushdímbíhnidah   kakkanduts'ah.
  there   on top   it is said   she laid it on top   mud
  There on top it is said she laid some mud.

7 Kánnúmbaka'   ná: dúhya'   nassáybáw'a'   sínáh   dah'úmbah'nah.
  she said to her   that one   now   if you see him   this   tell him
  She said to her, "Now if you see him tell him this.

8 Dí: 'ibat   tsi'nadihah.
  this   grandfather   I'm taking it
  'I'm taking this to my grandfather.

9 Tsichandu'nadihah   t'án:k'uh   kah'a'nih'a'.
  I'm taking mud to him   pipe   to make
  I'm taking mud to him to make a pipe.'"

10 Bah'nah   háhiyah   háhiyah.
   it is said   she went   she went
   It is said she kept going.

11 Ku'á:na'   bah'nah   hákah'í'asuh.
over there   it is said   he came
Over there it is said he came.

12 Kánímbaka'   "Kúydà:dihah?"
he said to her   where are you going
He said to her, "Where are you going?"

13 Kánnúmbaka'   "'Ibat   tsichandu'nadihah   t'án:k'uh   nah'a'na'."
she said to him   grandfather   I'm taking mud to him   pipe   to make with it
She said to him, "I'm taking mud to my grandfather to make a pipe with."

14 Ná: tá:shah   kámbaka' "Kúy'a'   hít'usbah.
that one   wolf   he said   here   let me see
That wolf said, "Here let me see.

15 Sínáh   kut'ihah   'wín't'a'.
like that   I'm that way   also
I'm like that too.

16 Kú:'nutah   nast'án'a'na'   t'án:k'uh."
I like it   if I make it   pipe
I like to make pipes."

17 Bah'nah   'isikáwní:yah.
it is said   he put his hand in
It is said he put his hand in.

18 'Wáy'shah!
Oh dear

19 'Wán't'i'   dika'hay   dínt'áhnah.
    whole   thing   he ate hers
    He ate all her things.

20 Bah'nah   sínátti'   hákíyánniyah.
    it is said   then   he chased her
    It is said then he chased her.

21 Ku'á:na'   bah'nah   hákakkidáwsa'   ká:k'ay'.
    over there   it is said   he was sitting on something   crow
    Over there it is said a crow was sitting on a branch.

22 'Ahashshah   bah'nah   háhnáy'áwsa'.
    really   it is said   he's singing
    It is said he was really singing!

23 Kúsidí: ná: t'i'   kámbaka'   "Hákkutáyní'asuh   ná: tá:shah."
    pretty soon   that   little one   she said   he's following me   that   wolf
    Pretty soon that little one said, "That wolf is following me."

24 Sínátti'   bah'nah   kánímbaka'   "Dà:yahyuh   kúkku:sú:'a'."
    then   it is said   he told her   get in it   in my nose
    Then it is said he told her, "Get in my nose!"

25 Bah'nah   sínátti'   dí: á:yhah   kúh'isú:'a',
    it is said   then   this   she got in   in his nose
    Then it is said she got in his nose,

26 bah'nah   'ukkih   bah'nahway'   ná: tsah   tá:shah   hússaháyní'asuh.
    it is said   really   in fact   that   Mr.   Wolf   he was following
    it is said in fact that Mr. Wolf really was following.

27 Kámbaka'   "Sidí: hít'ínámmah."
    he said   this way   she flew
    He said, "She flew this way."

28 Bah'nah   ná: ká:k'ay'   'ahashshah   dáhnáy'áw:sa'.
    it is said that   crow   really   he's singing there
    It is said that crow really was singing there!

29 Kín'a'nihah   kán:day.
    he's making it   [wooden]) bowl
    He was making a bowl.

30 Bah'nah   háhbak'ihsa':
    it is said   he's saying it
    It is said he was singing:

Wolf and Wren

tu wa ka ka tu pa ni na   tu wa ka ka tu pa ni na

ku na wi ta ka   ku na wi ta ka   tu wa ka ka

31 'Ahashshah   bah'nah   táh'áwwishshiyah,
    really   it is said   when he arrived there
    Really it is said when he arrived there,

32 ná: tá:shah   bah'nah   háhúmbak'ihsa',
    that   wolf   it is said   he is saying to him
    it is said that that wolf was saying to him

33 "Ná: sídat'ihah,   'ahashshah   ha'imay   háka:sú:dí:t'a'."
    that   what's wrong with you   rally   big   your nose is swollen
    "What's wrong with you, you have a really swollen nose."

34 Kánnúmbaka'   "Si'ídàn:t'a'?
    he said to him   what happened to you
    He said to him, "What happened to you?

35 Wít   híssa'bin'   kúkà:nihsa'   ná: kán:day'?"
    self   you hit it   while making it   that   bowl
    Did you hit yourself making that bowl?"

36 "Hun'nah.   Híkku'bin'   na   nidun   kúyhtsitáy:wan."
    no   it hit me   by   ball   while I played
    "No. I got hit by a ball while I was playing."

37 Baka'   "Nuka'   sah'atáyánnáhdu'wa'   kúkà:suhí'usa'?"
    he said   maybe   you are able   where you blow your nose
    He said, "Are you maybe able to blow your nose?"

38 Bah'nah.   "Kakúdah'náwkáy:bah?"
    it is said   without your feeling pain
    It is said. "Without feeling pain?"

39 Kánímbaka'   "Hawwih.   Tsitáyántáybáw:'a'."
    he said to him   all right   I'll try
    He said to him, "All right. I'll try."

40 Bah'nah 'ukkih kudí: náh'ínánniyah.
  it is said really over there she flew

It is said she flew away.

41 Chiyuhtsi' bah'nah di:yúníh'nah.
  wren it is said she escaped

It is said that the wren escaped.

REFERENCES

Chafe, Wallace L. 1977. "Caddo Texts." In *Caddoan Texts*, edited by Parks, Douglas R., 27–43. Native American Texts Series 2 (1). Chicago: University of Chicago Press.

———. 2005. "Caddo." In *Native Languages of the Southeastern United States*, edited by Heather K. Hardy and Janine Scancarelli, 323–50. Lincoln: University of Nebraska Press in cooperation with American Indian Studies Research Institute, Indiana University, Bloomington.

Dorsey, George A. 1997. *Traditions of the Caddo*. Lincoln: University of Nebraska Press.

PAWNEE

The Old Woman and Her Grandson Blessed by a Voice

Narrated by Dollie Moore, Pitahawirata Pawnee
Translated and introduced by Douglas R. Parks
Interlinear files by Joshua A. Richards

Introduction

A major genre in the folklore of the Pawnee, and all northern Caddoan tribes, is that of a pitiful old woman who has lost her husband and children in an enemy attack on their village. The old woman, who then has no male relatives to provide for her, builds her lodge on the outskirts of the village where she is among the most vulnerable to enemy attacks. In this story, she typically has a grandson who is powerless and unable to provide for the two of them. Inevitably the grandson is blessed by a supernatural power. Subsequently, after he performs mysterious feats in the doctors' lodge, people in the village give the boy and his grandmother presents of food and robes so that they are no longer poor. There is also an important lesson in this story: after one is given mysterious power, one should never share that power with another person.

A member of the Pitahawirata band, Mrs. Moore recorded this story and various other ones in the late 1960s when she was in her seventies. She was a fluent speaker of South Band Pawnee and was exceptionally knowledgeable about Pawnee culture and oral traditions.

The Old Woman and Her Grandson Blessed by a Voice

1	taturaa²iiwaatista	pakuraaruhuuru²	si²ahriitacikskaapaakisu	cuustit
	I'm going to tell about	a voice	that pitied them	old lady

Now I'm going to tell about a voice that pitied an old woman

a   piiraski.
and   boy.
and a boy.

2   taku   witiituhku   piitahaawiraata.
     Someone   there's a camp   Pitahawirata.
     There was a Pitahawirata village there.

3   reesaaru²   witiituriku   rawa   heruu   ahrukstaatawe²
     Chief   has this camp now   and   it was the custom
     The chief had this village, and now it was the custom at that time

     heruu   reesaaru²   uúkatat   witaarítat   he
     then   chief   [on the] west   [would be] camped and
     for chiefs to have their lodges on the west side, and

     suuhuri   heruu   cihtahaahriri²   heruu
     along   There   on the edge,end [of the camp]   there
     along the edge of the village

     si²ahraarakariku   cuustit   a   piiraski.
     Camped   old lady   and   boy.
     an old woman and her grandson were camped.

4   siwitikaapaakis   taku   wesikareehraaruhku   sirakuuticisu   teekskurit.
     They were poor   someone   they didn't have   relatives   close.
     They were poor and did not have any close relatives.

5   iriikuuhraaruuraakita   tiirukstahwaawari   raawiirakuuru²
     For the reason that   when they camped from place to place   [some enemy] scouts
     For that reason, when they camped in different places, some enemy scouts

taku[?]   sikurihkuutit   i[?]aasti[?]   a   isaasti[?].
there   they might have killed   his father   and   his mother.
might have killed the boy's father and mother.

6   rawa   iriraaruuraakita   ckara   iisiraaku.
    Now   that's the reason   alone   they were.
    Now that is the reason they were alone.

7   eeweekuuhriihi[?]   tiiraturaa[?]iiwaati   reeckuuhki
    It must have been   this story I'm telling   [in the] fall
    This story I'm telling must have occurred in the fall

weekuuhrikstaaraahkaruuku.
when they were through planting.
after they had already planted their crops.

8   he   cuustit   weekuuhratakawa   iriikuuhrukstaaraahkaruuku.
    And   old lady   they were plentiful   what she had planted.
    And the crops that the old lady had planted must have been plentiful.

9   rawa   e   iriikuuhrasaku[?]u   piiraski   witaahteehuru[?]
    Now   and   there was a day   boy   he used to be around
    Now one day the boy was hanging around

iriirakica   iriruusikuruhriiku.
where there was water [that is, a creek]   where they camped.
the creek near where they were living.

10   he   raawiitakaaraa[?]isu[?]   caahriks   ahriitpakaraaru[?]at   piiraski :
     And   all at once   person   called him   boy
     And all at once a human called out to him.

11 "ruusikeeskuuhra   aka²   iriiraruhruurahku   pitku   pahuks
   Go get me   your grandmother   from her garden   two   pumpkins
   "Go get me two of the best crooked-neck squash

   sirakuuhreera   reekaacu²."
   two of the best   crook neck squash.
   from your grandmother's garden!"

12 heruu   ahri²at   piiraski   ruuwituciihuuru².
   Then   he went   boy   he obeyed.
   So the boy obeyed.

13 pitku   si²ahratarikut   reekaacu²   ruusi²ahriritawiraa²at   irii²ahrakica.
   Two   he picked   squash   he took them down   where the water was.
   He picked two squash and then took them down to the water.

14 heruu   ahriwaaku²   caáhriks :   "siisuksawiha²i   he
   Then   he said   person   Throw them in the water   and
   Then the person told him, "Throw them in the water and

   witi²isutkiriktaaruurukut."
   you must hold your eyes.
   you must shut your eyes."

15 e   iri²ahruuta   piiraski.
   And   he did that   boy.
   And the boy did that.

16 iiwee²ahrareewaataara   hiruu   si²ahrihaawari²   kíwaaks.
   And when he looked   there   [two] were swimming   swans.
   And when he looked there were two swans swimming there.

17 rarahkiickeeciki   ruuhriiwaara.
    Long-necked ones   pretty ones.
    Long necked ones, pretty ones.

18 heruu   ahriwaaku²   piita :   "rawa   weetatuhraa²iitawu.
    Then   he said   man   Now   I've shown you.
    Then the man said, "Now I have shown you.

19 rawa   ruusiisukstikata²at."
    Now   pick them up.
    Now then pick them up!"

20 weewitisakuriisat.
    It was getting evening.
    It was becoming evening.

21 ruusi²ahririkata²at   pahuks.
    He took up   pumpkins.
    Then he took up the pumpkin.

22 rawa   kskiiti²iks   sakuuru²   iriwituutaari².
    Now   Fourth   days   he did that.
    Now he did that for four days.

23 heruu   ahriwaaku²   ikaari² :   "kirikee ruu²ut   pahuks
    Then   she said   his grandmother   Why are you   pumpkin
    Then his grandmother asked: "Why are you taking these squash

    tiisirastitawiraawu?"
    take these down?
    down [to the stream]?"

24   heruu   ahriwaaku⁷   piiraski :   "atíka⁷   kaasucireecis."
     Then   he said   boy   Grandmother   you'll find out.
     Then the boy said, "Grandmother, you will find out."

25   rawa   kskiiti⁷iks   iiweerasákuhku   heruu   ahriwaaku⁷
     Now   fourth   when it was day   then   he said
     Now when it was the fourth day,

     caahriks   ii⁷ahriitpaawaktiku :   "ruu   pitku   sikeesiritawira⁷a⁷
     person   who was talking to him   There   two   fetch, go get two
     the person who was talking to him said: "Go there, fetch two more

     hawaa   pahuks   hawaa   sirakuuhreera."
     also   pumpkin   also   two of the best.
     squash—two of the best."

26   he   kituu⁷u⁷   iisiraritawiraa⁷.
     And   all of them   he brought them down.
     And so he brought all of them down to the stream.

27   heruu   ahruci⁷a   piiraski :   ruuwituciihuuru⁷   kskiiti⁷iks
     Then   he did it   boy   he obeyed   four [swans]
     Then the boy obeyed and there were four—

     weewitúhraaru⁷   askuraa⁷u⁷   witirakutkiriktaaruurukut   he
     there were [that many]   the same thing   he grabbed his eyes   and
     the same way—he shut his eyes and

     wee⁷ahrareewaata   he   kskiiti⁷iks   ahriraraawaari⁷   kíwaaks.
     [when] he looked   and   four   were swimming around   swans.
     when he looked there were four swans swimming around.

28 rawa   heruu   ahriwaaku²   caáhriks :   "rawa
    Now   then   he said   person   Now
    And then the person said, "Now

    ruusukstarikata²at   páhuks!"
    take up   pumpkin.
    pick up the squash!"

29 iiweerararikataata   pahuks   heruu   ahriwaaku²   ikaari² :
    And when he took up   pumpkin   then   she said   his grandmother
    And when he took the squash up to their dwelling, his grandmother asked,

    "kirikee rasuutaari²?"
    What are you doing?
    "What are you doing?"

30 heruu   ahriwaaku²   piiraski :   "tahraarakuusku²   kickat.
    Then   he said   boy   I'm putting them   in the water.
    Then the boy said, "I'm putting them in the water.

31 ruukeecihtawiraawa   he   isuhraa²eerit."
    Let us go down   and   you will see the way [of it, he did it].
    Let's go down to the stream and you will see what happens when I do it."

32 heruu   si²ahritawiraawa   si²ahrararaa   pahuks.
    Then   they went down   they had   pumpkin.
    Then they went down with the squash.

33 heruu   ahriwaaku²   pakuraaruhuuru² :   "iriweetúraahe   aka²
    Then   he said   voice   That's good   your grandmother
    Then the voice said, "It's good that

ahrasicirastawiraa'a.

you brought down.

you have brought your grandmother down.

34 weetatutpaawaktiksta.

I'm going to talk [that is, teach] to her.

I'm going to talk to her [that is, reveal a mystery to her].

35 weesitatuutacikskaapaakisuksta.

I'm going to take pity on you two.

I'm going to take pity on the two of you.

36 rawa   sukstaara'i   pahuks."

Now   put in   pumpkin.

Now put the squash in the water!"

37 heruu   ahriraara'i   pahuks   hiruu   ahriraaraawari'

Then   he threw in   pumpkin   there   were swimming

Then he threw the squash into the water, and thereupon there were

kiwaaks   ruuhríwaara.

swans   pretty ones.

swans, pretty ones, swimming around.

38 heruu   ahriwaaku'   cuustit :   "aaka'a   iriwesitaskuutacikskaapaakis

Then   she said   old lady   Oh   you're sure taking pity on us

Then the old lady said, "Oh, my, you are certainly taking pity on us

tii'iriweerasuutaara."

what you're doing."

by what you are doing."

39   heruu   ahriwaaku⁷   pakuraaruhuuru⁷ :   "tiiweesiratuutacikskaapaakisu
     Then   he said   voice   Since I'm taking pity on you
     Then the voice said, "Since I am taking pity on you,

     he   reeticka⁷   raskutawaruukaaara.
     and   I want   you to perform.
     I want you to perform.

40   kuraa⁷u⁷   weerihtawaruukaara   ruukaasi⁷at   he   ispaaku⁷
     Doctors   when they perform   you must go   and   tell them
     You must go there when the doctors perform their feats and tell them,

     'taticka⁷   ratkutawaruukaara.'"
     I want   me to perform.
     'I want to perform.'"

41   heruu   ruu⁷ahrikata⁷at   cuustit   heruu   ahriwaaku⁷
     Then   went up   old lady   and   said
     Then the old woman went up to the village and said

     kuraakitáwi⁷u⁷ :   "taticka⁷   ratkutawaruukaara."
     [to] the head doctor   I want   me to perform.
     to the leading doctor, "I want to perform."

42   heruu   ahriwaaku⁷   kúraa⁷u⁷ :   "aaka⁷a iriweetúraahe.
     Then   he said   doctor   Oh   that's good.
     Then the doctor said, "Why, that's good.

43   kaasirikáta⁷   tahraaktawaruukaarista   iriikuuhrasaku⁷."
     Come up   we're going to perform   some day.
     You must come up when we are going to perform on a certain day."

44   rawa   iriwee²ahraasakuura   heruu   ahrirarat   páhuks   heruu
      Now   when the day came   then   she took up   pumpkin   and
      Now when the day came she took up the squash and

      ahriwaaku²   ahruhreehku   kuraakitawi²u :   "keeci   sikaaskuucikickawarit
      said   she meant   head doctor   only   you must put water in
      said, talking to the head doctor, "You must put water into

      aspaaksu²."
      hide.
      a hide [to form a pool]."

45   witikskaruukúsuuku²   reehkukíraraahu   a raahkukiraaru.
      They used to make them   when they hauled something   to contain water.
      They are what we used to make for hauling water.

46   karikstara   kucki   tii²iriiweeruuta   tiítiiri.
      They didn't have   buckets   like it is   now.
      We didn't have buckets like we do today.

47   tiiweeruraaheera.
      It's good.
      Now it is a good thing [that we have buckets].

48   rawa   heruu   ahri²at   cuustit   ruu²ahrucicirasat   piiraski.
      Now   then   went   old lady   and took   boy.
      Now then the old woman went and took the boy with her.

49   ruusi²ahrirarat   pahuks.
      The two took   pumpkin.
      The two took the squash.

50 rawa   heruu   ahriwaaku?   kúraa?u?:   "awit   tastawaruukaarista."
   Now   then   he said   doctor   First   you'll perform.
   Well, then the doctor said, "You are going to perform first."

51 heruu   ahrí?at   cústit   iriikuuhruutuhuuru?   he
   Then   she went   old lady   she did what she had to do   and
   So then the old woman did what she had to do, and

   ahraraara?i   piiraski   pahuks.
   put in   boy   pumpkin.
   the boy put the squash in the water.

52 hiruu   ahraraaraawari?   kiwaaks   ruuhríwaara.
   There   were swimming around   swans   pretty ones.
   Then there were swans—pretty ones—swimming around.

53 rawa   iiweesiraraareehac   kukarawituci?a   haawa?.
   Now   when they got through   she did nothing   more.
   Now after they finished their performance she did nothing more.

54 heruu   si?ahrirariikatahat   ruusi?ahruceekcírasat   kíwaaks   he
   Then   they took out   then they brought   swans   and
   Then they took the swans out and brought them home

   piiraski   ahruutaktakiictacareepu   witikiictaaraasta.
   boy   tied their necks   strung them together.
   after the boy tied their necks and strung them together.

55 ariisit   ahratawiraawu?   iriisi?ahraakariku   cuustit   a   piiraski.
   Themselves   they went down   where they camped   old lady   and   boy.
   The old woman and the boy went down to where they were living.

56 kíwaaks   rawa   iiwee²ahrawa²uureerit   he   ístu   hiruu
    Swans   now   when they stopped   and   again   there
    Now when they stopped there, the swans

    ahri²it   pahuks.
    they were   pumpkin.
    were squash again.

57 heruu   ahrirarahiikat   piiraski   karacaape.
    Then   took them in   boy   tipi.
    Then the boy took them into their tipi.

58 ckara   siwiteekariku.
    Alone   they were camped.
    Their camp was not near anyone else [they were off by themselves].

59 heruu   ahriwaaku²   iiweesiratawiraawaara   iriirakica
    Then   he said   when they went down   where the water is
    Then, after they went back down to the stream,

    heruu   ahriwaaku²   pakuraaruhuuru² :   "rawa   haawaa
    then   he said   voice   Now   again
    the voice said, "Now

    sitatuutacikskaapaakisuksta.
    I'm going to take pity on you two.
    I am going to take pity on you two again.

60 taticka²   tiítiiri   ruuraskuuta   he   iriiraakaawi   karaarataa²u²
    I want   today   you to go   and   where it is   earth lodge
    I want you to go to the earth lodge,

he   reewataaraarista   ruuraaruuteewatahtakaahaksta   iriireecusaakaratawi.
and   ray of light   the light will drop through   where the smokehole is.
and a ray of light will drop down through the smokehole.

61 heruu   isucirasat   piiraski   heruu   isiwaaku⁷: 'taticka⁷
    Then   you must take   boy   and   you must say   I want
    Then you must take the boy, and you must say, 'I want

    raskukuutacikskaapaakisu.
    you to take pity on me.
    you to take pity on me.

62 taticka⁷   piiraski   tiiraariki   rakukataata   tiiraawataaru'
    I want   boy   this   to go up   this ray of light
    And I want this boy to climb up the ray of light,'

    he   kuwitucicakta⁷uhkaawe."
    and   it was like a ladder.
    which was like a ladder."

63 heruu   ahriwaaku⁷: "he   iiweerakata⁷uhtarit   heruu
    Then   he said   and   when he goes up   then
    Then he said, "And when he goes up,

    rireewatpaa   he   kuruhraa⁷iituskuus.
    he'll look around   and   he say a good word for you.
    he will look around and say a good word for you.

64 he   isiwaaku⁷   'cikstit   raaruureetawiraa⁷a⁷   istu.'"
    And   you must say   in a good way   let him come down   again.
    You must say 'In a good way, let him come back down again.'"

65 he   iri²ahruuta   piiraski.
   And   he did that   boy.
   And the boy did that.

66 iiweesi²ahratawaruukaara   ckara   siwitikaku   karaarataa²u².
   And when they performed   alone   they were in there   earth lodge.
   They performed when they were alone in the earth lodge.

67 irii²ahruksakahwaarukstii²u   ahrikstawaruupaahri.
   It was The Wise House   where they used to perform.
   It was the holy dwelling where the doctors used to perform [their magic].

68 heruu   ahrikatá²at   piiraski.
   Then   went up   boy.
   Then the boy went up [the ray of light].

69 cuustit   witiwaawaaku²   iri²kuuhrawaawaaku²   pakuraaruhuuru²
   Old lady   said everything   what was said to her   [by] the voice
   The old woman said everything that was said to her by the voice—

   iriirakuutuhuuruu²a.
   the way of it.
   the way that it should happen.

70 heruu   ahrikatá²at   iiweerawiitit   ku²ahrawaaku²
   Then   he went up   and when he sat down   he said a prayer
   Then he went up [the ray] and when he sat down he said a prayer

   tiiraawaahat   sirihkuutacikskaapaakisu   a   ákitaaru²
   [to] the Heavens   to take pity on them   and   tribe
   to the Heavens, asking that He take pity on them and

rihkuutacikskaapaakisu.

to take pity on.

take pity on the tribe.

71   istu   ruu²ahreetawiraa²a²   cikstit.

       Again   then he came down   in a good way.

       Then he came back down in a good way.

72   raaruuwiteetawiraa²a².

       He just came down.

       He merely came down.

73   rawa   heruu   si²ahriwa   ruusi²ahrikaa²iispa.

       Now   then   they [du.] went   they went home.

       Now the two went back to their lodge.

74   rawa   tiiheeweeraheesa   iriweekuuhrasakuuruksta   heruu   ahrí²at

       Now   the next day   when that day is going to be   then   she went

       Now the next day, when it was going to be day, she then went

       he   kuraakitawi²u²   ahruhraarikaa² :   "haawaa   istu

       and   head doctor   told   Also   Again

       and told the head doctor,

       taticka²   ratkutawaruukaara."

       I want   me to perform.

       "I want to perform again."

75   heruu   ahriwaaku²   kuraakitawi²u² :   "iriweetúraahe.

       Then   he said   head doctor   That's good.

       Then the head doctor said, "That's good.

76   raheesa   haawaa   áwiit   irikaasihírasa   istawaruukaara."
     Tomorrow   Now   first   you will be first   if you perform.
     Tomorrow you will again be the first to perform."

77   haawaa   tiiheeweeraheesa   haawaa   ruusi²ahrawa   piiraski.
     Again   the next day   also   they came   boy.
     Again the next day she and the boy came.

78   iiwee²ahrarahkaawi   heru   ahriwaaku²   cuustit   piiraski
     When they were all in   then   she said   old lady   boy
     After they were all inside [the lodge], the old woman said to the boy,

     ahruhrehku :   "rawa   sukskata²at   tiiraawataara."
     she meant   Now   go up   this ray of light.
     "Now go up this ray of light!"

79   heruu   ahriwaaku²   piiraski :   "taticka²   ratkukataata   tiiraawataara
     Then   he said   boy   I want   to go up   this ray of light
     Then the boy said, "I want to go up this ray of light,

     he   iiwee²itkita²uukut   he   ihreewatpa   he
     and   when I get to the top   and   I'll look around   and
     and when I get to the top I'll look around and

     ku²ihraa²iituskus   heruu   cikstit   ruu²itiriitawiraa²."
     I'll offer a word of prayer   then   in a good way   so I can come down.
     offer a word of prayer, so that I can come down in a good way."

80   rawa   irisi²ahruuta   cuustit   iriweerawaaka.
     Now   they did it   old lady   what she said.
     Now the two of them did what the old woman had said.

81 heruu   ahrikata²at   piiraski.
   Then   went up   boy.
   Then the boy went up.

82 ahrawiitit   iriireecusaakarátawi   karaarátaau²u².
   He sat down   where the smokehole is   earth lodge.
   Then he sat down by the edge of the smokehole of the earth lodge.

83 he   istu   ruu²ahreetawiraa².
   And   again   he came down.
   Then he came back down.

84 cikstit   raaruuwiteetawiraa².
   All right   he just came down.
   He came down safely.

85 iiweeratawiraa²a   he   tiirawíhat   kúraa²u²   raawitiitasku
   And when he came down   and   these [sit.]   doctors   were dismayed
   And when he came down these doctors were dismayed and

   ahrihwicka²a   'kirikee tasuu²ut   takee weetasiitacikskaapaakis.'
   they wondered   what he did   who has taken pity on them.
   wondered what he had done and who had taken pity on him [and his grandmother].

86 heruu   si²ahrikaa²iispa   iiweesirakaa²iispara   ruuwiteeraara²
   Then   they went home   and when they went home   came [behind]
   Then they returned home, and while they were going home people were coming

   caahriks   he   si²ahreeruhraruuwa   aakawaahcisu²   a   raa²iksu².
   people   and   they brought the two   Food   and   presents.
   behind them, and they were bringing food and presents for the two.

87 raahiirit   weesikarawitikaapaakis   cuustit   a   piiraski.
   Finally   they were poor no longer   old lady   and   boy.
   Finally the boy and the old woman were no longer poor.

88 iriikuuhrasaku²   piiraski   raaruu²ahrikata²at   irii²ahrahuriiwaawi
   And one day   boy   went out   where they lived
   One day the boy just went up to where the

   piira²u²   kara²ahririikaapaakisu   heruu   ahraarahkusisaari².
   children   who were well-off [that is, not poor]   and   they were playing.
   children of wealthy families lived and were playing.

89 kuraa²u²   ahráracawe   ahríhwaki²: "sikeeciiturukut
   Doctors   who belonged to it [the organization]   they said   Let's catch
   Some doctors who belonged to a society in the doctors' lodge said, "Let's catch

   piiraski   he   rikata²at   heruu   iriiruutaara
   boy   and   he could go up   then   what she did
   the boy so that he can go up the way he did

   iirukstawaruukaari   ikaari²."
   when she was performing   his grandmother.
   when his grandmother was performing."

90 si²ahriicicirasuukat   karaarataa²u²   heruu   ahririíwaki²:
   Then they took him in   earth lodge   and   they said
   So they took him into the earth lodge, and then they said,

   "kee²isuuta   irirasuutaara"   iriikuuhruciksuhuuru²   tiirukcaákariki.
   Do   what you did   what he did   yesterday.
   "Do what you did!" when he performed yesterday.

91 iiwee?ahrakataata   he   ahruraahurahac   iriirákuwaaka   raakutawiraa?a.
   and when he went up   and   he forgot   what to say   to come down.
   And when he went up he forgot what to say in order to come down.

92 heruu   ahriwaaku?   kúraa?u? :   "rawa   sikstawiraa?."
   Then   he said   doctor   Now   come down.
   Then the doctors said, "Now come down!"

93 heruu   ahriwaaku? :   "ruusisucikskaksa?   atíka?.
   Then   he said   Go call   my grandmother.
   Then he said, "Go call my grandmother.

94 weetikuraahurahac."
   I have forgotten.
   I have forgotten what to say."

95 ruusi?ahriicihurat   ikaari?   heruu   ahree?a?   ikaari?
   Then they went after   his grandmother   and   came   his grandmother
   Then they went after his grandmother, and then she came

   heruu   ahriwaaku?   irisikuuhruutuhuuru?   raaruuwiteetawiraa?
   then   she said   what they had to say   they came down
   and told him what he had to say to come down

   piiraski   cikstit.
   boy   good.
   in a good way.

96 rawa   heruu   ahriwaaku?   cuustit   raktiiki   ahruhreehku :
   Now   then   said   old lady   grandson   she meant
   Now, then the old lady told her grandson,

"haawaa   istu   irikareesuci²a.
Also   again   don't do it.
"Don't do that again.

97 tacakuutacikskaapaakis   caahriks   eekareeri²   haawaa   heetaku
    He took pity on us   Person   and we can't   also   someone else
    A person took pity on us, and we cannot just give his power to anyone else—

    haawaa   raaruu²aaciriiraa²u   tiiráraaku.
    also   just give it   this gift away.
    we can't just give this gift away.

98 kutara²   caahriks   he   weereecakuutacikskaapaakis.
    It belongs to   person   and   he took pity on us.
    It belongs to a person and he took pity on us.

99 weetaciiraara   he   raaruuraakita   tiirácihku   cikstit
    We have his way   and   why we're here   that's the reason   good
    We now have his power, and that is the reason that we are having good

    tiiweeracaku   tuuréspaahu   cikstit   tiiweeracihraakawaawaahcu."
    the days   come   good   when we're eating.
    days coming to us and we are eating well."

100 ee   ahrawaaku²   cuustit :   "haawaa   istu   irikareesuci²a.
    And   said   old lady   Also   again   don't do that.
    And the old woman said, "Don't do that again.

101 haawaa   istu   kuuseetákusi"   hreuu   ahriwaaku².
    Also   again   you'll get stuck   then   she said.
    You'll get stuck up there again!" she said.

102 rawa haawaa cuustit a piiraski weesikareehrikaapaakis.
   Now   also   old lady and boy   they were well-off.
   And from then on the old woman and the boy were well off.

103 iseerit piiraski weeraaruuwitiiku.
   Famous boy   he was.
   The boy was indeed famous.

104 si²ahreeruutakcirasaahu   aruusa² a kuusiraahkurahwitat.
   They kept bringing to him horses and something for them to have as bedcovers.
   People just kept bringing him horses and robes to have as bed covers.

105 rawa taku iriweeruutiraa²iitusteehat.
   Now here is the end of the story.
   Now here is the end of the story.

He Goes Over and the Burning Log: A Wolf Story

Narrated by Harry Mad Bear, Skiri Pawnee
Introduced and translated by Douglas R. Parks
Interlinear files by Joshua A. Richards

Presented here is a typical Coyote or Wolf story of the Skiri Pawnee. Although most tribes name their trickster Coyote in English, the Skiri vacillate between Wolf and Coyote. The narrator uses Wolf's name, He Goes Over, most of the time, but refers to him in English as Wolf, so that term is used where appropriate in the English translation. The narrator is Harry Mad Bear (Ti²aakaciksuuku², 'He Has Good Thoughts for People'), whose first language was Skiri and who was in his mid-seventies when the story was recorded in 1967. He was an excellent speaker of his language and a great raconteur. In the presentation of the story the initials HGO are used when references are simply "he" in English so that the reader is able to follow the story line more easily. Otherwise the translation closely follows the Skiri wording of the text, thereby capturing Mr. Mad Bear's oral style.

He Goes Over and the Burning Log: A Wolf Story

1   tiítaku   ahá²at   tiihuurícawaatat   hi   ahaacawaátat.
    Here   he went   He Goes Over   and   he went over.
    There went He Goes Over, and he went over a knoll.

2   wiiruu²ahikíwahaahku   hi   ahahukaáta²iisat   hi   ahawáku²
    There was a pond   and   he went to the bank   and   he said
    There was a pond there and he went to the bank of it and said,

"aáka   táku²   asaahaáwari   tiiraskíwahaahku   ki²isiíra²
Oh my   someone   if you are in the water   you in this pond   come
"Oh my, someone, if you are in the water, you who are in the pond, you should come

hi   isuhaá²iirit.
and   see.
out and see it.

3 cáhiks   wiitatiíhaksa².
   People   a group is coming.
   A group of people is coming.

4 raaríksisu²   tiraáriisaat   tiítaku   rikuraáraara².
   Truly   there are many   Here   that is where they are coming.
   There sure are a lot of them who are coming here!

5 tiítaku   iritátiira²   rátkuwaaka   rataakuuhattaaríkaa²
   Here   I came   for me to say   for me to tell you
   I came here to say that—to tell

   sukstattahkatáhat   táku²   rikuuhastattaaraáwari².
   get out [of the way]   anyone   whichever of you are in the water.
   any of you who might be in the water to get away.

6 sukstattahkatáhat.
   Get out [of the way].
   Get out of the way.

7 hi   isiíra²   híruu   ituuhaaríkaa²   iriiraskuutaára
   And   come   then   I'll tell you   what you can do
   Come here and then I'll tell you what you can do

a   isiíkisit."
and   you'll be saved.
to be saved."

8   aáka   raáwiitakaaraahisu²   ahutpaksuúcaa²   hi   wiihiruu
    Oh my   all at once   a head stuck out of the water   and   here now
    Oh my, all at once a head stuck up out of the water, and now here

    ahí²   ícaas   icaáskucu².
    it was   Turtle   a large turtle.
    it was Turtle—a big turtle.

9   hi   ahuúta   wiiruu²ahaá²   ícaas.
    And   he did it   then he came   Turtle.
    And he did it: Turtle came up.

10 ahahukaáta²iisa².
    He came to the bank.
    He came to the bank.

11 híruu   ahawáku²   "kiruu riíhi² ?"
    Then   he said   Where is it.
    And then he asked, "Where are they?"

12 "tiítaku   taraára².
    Here   they are coming.
    "They are coming here.

13 wískucu²!"
    Hurry.
    Hurry!"

14 hi   tii'ahahácca   rákucu'.
    And   a log was lying there   a big log.
    There was a log lying there—a big log.

15 witahaákata.
    It was a hollow log.
    It was a hollow log.

16 híruu   ahawáku'   "sukskaá'at.
    Then   he said   Go inside.
    Then he said, "Go inside it.

    wískucu'!"
    Hurry.
    Hurry!"

17 híruu   ahakaá'at.
    Then   he went in.
    Then he went in it.

18 híruu   ahirahkaawarit   rattacápahtu'.
    Then   he put wood in it   fine chips of wood.
    Then [He Goes Over] put wood in the log—fine chips of wood.

19 híruu   ahiraarukáriwiis.
    Then   he covered it up.
    Then he covered the opening.

20 híruu   ahí'at   hi   ahahiíraraa'.
    Then   he went   and   he brought hay.
    Then [He Goes Over] went and got hay.

21 hawá   aharahkaáwarit.
    Also   he put the hay in it.
    He stuffed hay in it, too.

22 hi   caskí   ahuuhaáhcaakawi   hi   riiraruuraakítawi
    And   a little   it was sticking out   and   its being the reason
    A little amount of the hay was sticking out of the opening so that

    rihwícka?a   "aáka   kukaakíka.
    one'll think   Oh my   there is not anything in here.
    someone would think, "Oh, there is not anything inside this log here.

23 tiihuksiirahkaáwa   tiirutiírahcaakawi.
    There must just be hay growing there   this hay sticking out.
    There must just be hay growing here, this hay that is growing out of it.

24 hi   kukariiríka."
    And   there is nothing in there.
    There is nothing in there."

25 ráwa   hi   ahakaá?at   ícaas.
    Now   and   he went inside   Turtle.
    Now Turtle went into it.

26 hi   aharahkaáwarikusitit   rattacapáhtu?   hi   ahahiirahkaáwarit.
    And   he began putting them in it   fine chips   and   he put hay in it.
    And he [HGO] began putting the fine chips into it, and he put the hay into it.

27 hi   ahawáku?   "ráwa   tiiwiíraaraara?."
    And   he said   Now   here they are coming.
    And he said, "Now here they come."

28 ráwa   ahahaattícta²i   iriirahiírahcaakawi.
   Now   he lit the wood   where the hay stuck out.
   Now he lit the wood where the hay was sticking out.

29 "páhiitu²   kaásikaa.
   Still   you must be inside.
   "You must be still inside there.

30 tahaáwiskusku²   kira   hiítaku   kúsiiwu²."
   I am putting smoke here   so that   the other way   they will go.
   I am putting smoke here so that they will go the other way."

31 ruuwituuraahíwic   iirahaácca   ahahaákurictaahusitit.
   Then all at once   that log   the log began to blaze.
   Then all at once the log began to blaze.

32 kicí   witiratkií²aari²   hi   aharitpahkuskatuusítit.
   And   it was becoming night   and   the coals began to spread out.
   And now it was becoming night and the coals began to spread out.

33 híruu   ahiíku   ícaas.
   Then   he sat   Turtle.
   Then he was sitting by Turtle.

34 hi   ahuúta   ahakúsit   iiraáku   ícaas.
   And   he did it   he picked him up   that   Turtle.
   And he did it: he picked that Turtle up.

35 raaruuwitaaruúcaa²   hi   iiraáku   aáka   ruuwití²
   He just picked him up   and   that one   oh my   then he was
   He just picked him up, and that one, oh my,

kuuhaáras   ícaas.
he was cooked   Turtle.
Turtle was cooked.

36 iíka   kuuháras.
    Oh   he was cooked.
    Oh my, he was cooked.

37 híruu   ahiwaáwaahisitit.
    Then   he began to eat.
    Then he began to eat.

38 hi   ká²it   ahuuhaárihta.
    And   salt   he had [a bag of] it under his belt.
    And he had a bag of salt under his belt.

39 hi   ahuuta   híruu   ahawaáwaa   ahawaáwaa   ahawaáwaa.
    And   he did it then   he ate   he ate   he ate.
    And then he did it: he ate, he ate, he ate.

40 ahakaruuwaáhac.
    He ate things up.
    He ate everything up.

41 ruuraahkaruuwaáhac   ruu²ahiwáku²   "aáka   iriwitúraahi.
    After he ate things up   then he said   Oh   that is good.
    Then after he ate all of him up, he said, "Ooh my, that was good.

42 witatkaáwaki²it."
    I am full.
    I am full now."

43 híruu aharitpaahpíraa².
   Then he raked the coals.
   Then he raked the coals.

44 híruu ahikiistacákipu.
   Then he gathered the bones.
   Then he gathered the bones.

45 híruu ahiwáku² "tiítaku riiruutatikasáhista.
   Then he said Here I am going to lie on it.
   Then he said, "I am going to lie on them.

46 tiíraaku rikuriiriíwic tiítaku riruuriikusta
   This one   here then it is going to be
   These will be right here.

47 kusti²a rikukírikaara."
   I will eat it when I wake up.
   I will eat them when I wake up."

48 iíwiiraahku hi kuuhátkasitit.
   While he sat there and he went to sleep.
   While he sat there, he fell asleep.

49 hi kuuhátkasitit.
   And he went to sleep.
   He went to sleep.

50 hi kíci hawá rakuukíwira raáku²a kuhuútiirit.
   And but also a different one when he came he saw him.
   And now, there was another one, a different wolf came and saw him.

51 "ráwa   sukskiríkaa"   kuuhátkasitit.
   Now   wake up   he was asleep.
   "Now wake up!" but he was asleep.

52 hi   ahawaawaáhisitit   riícki.
   And   he began to eat them   intestines.
   And he began to eat the intestines.

53 "ruutuucíraa²u²   witatpaawaáhista   tiíraruuci.
   It is alright   now I am going to eat them   these.
   "Alright, now I am going to eat these.

54 iriwiitúraahi   ahaskuruuríwitka.
   It is good   that you saved it for me.
   It's good that you saved them for me."

55 ahakaruuwaáhac.
   He ate everything up.
   He ate up everything else.

56 híruu   ahiwícka²   "kira táku karariíraa²uuhu².
   Then   he thought   Don't let him blame anyone.
   Then he thought, "Let's not let him blame anyone for this!

57 táku karariíraspi²."
   Don't let him look for anyone.
   Let's not have him looking for anyone."

58 kítuu²u²   ahakstarahkicitkawaákaru².
   All   he greased his hands all over.
   Then he greased his hands all over.

59 híruu   ahúciʔa   ahítki   iirahaakarátawi   ahutuukúwarit.
    Then   he did it   fat   his mouth   he put it in his mouth.
    Then he did it: he put fat in his mouth.

60 ruuwituucícaaka.
    Then it was hanging from his mouth.
    Then the fat was hanging from his mouth.

61 hiruu   ahiruúcpaawu   kítuuʔuʔ.
    Then   he spread it all over   everywhere.
    Then he spread it all over everywhere.

62 witúciʔa   kirittaáririʔ   a   atkahaaraáririʔ   ahítki.
    He did it   on the eyes   and   on the ears   [with] fat.
    He rubbed it on his eyes and on his ears.

63 ruuʔahickákica   ahítki.
    Then his face was greasy   [with] fat.
    Then his face was greasy with fat.

64 híruu   ahiísa.
    Then   he lay there.
    Then he lay there.

65 ruuwituucícaaka   hi   ahihuukúrisa   ahítki.
    Then it was hanging from his mouth   and   he was lying with it in his mouth   fat.
    There it was, hanging from his mouth; there he was, lying with fat in his mouth.

66 hi   ahákirikaa   hiíraasa   kíci
    And   [when] he woke up   the other one lying   but
    And when the one lying there woke up,

ruuriwiikuúhat iirakaruuwaáhac haáwaꞏ.
he must have gone somewhere the one who ate everything up also.
he must have gone somewhere—the one who had eaten everything up again.

67 ahawáku? "aáka úh iíka hawaá kikií rasuúꞏut
He said Oh ugh oh also what is it
He said, "Ugh, oh my, what is this

tiíraaku tiíratuukúrisa?
this one that I have in my mouth.
that I have hanging in my mouth?

68 wikaakaatiriírarasku.
I have nothing to eat now.
I have nothing to eat now.

69 uu itkásiri? pitkusíhiri? tiihatuuhaáꞏit
Oh in [my] sleep twice I must have dreamed
Oh, in my sleep I must have dreamed twice

ratkuwaáwaꞏa itkásiri?.
that I was eating in [my] sleep.
that I was eating in my sleep.

70 tiihatuksitkaspaáwa.
I must have been eating in my sleep.
I must have been eating in my sleep.

71 kutuú kítuuꞏuꞏ kuuhatkaruuwaáhac.
It seems everything I must have eaten it all.
It seems that I must have eaten all of it.

72 ráwa   hawá   tiiriíku   ahítki   tiratuukúrisa.
   Now   also   here it is   fat   that I had in my mouth as I lay.
   Now, there is the fat that I had in my mouth as I was lying there.

73 kítu?   wititiihatkirittahpícistu?   a   itkahaaraáriri?.
   All   I must have greased my eyes   and   on [my] ears.
   I must have greased my eyes and my ears.

74 ráwa   hi   rikukírikaa."
   Now   And   I awoke.
   Well, then I woke up."

75 iiraá?a   wití?   ícaas   irakaawárika   iirahaácca
   When he came   he was   Turtle   that one he put in   that log
   When he came there, it was Turtle that he put in that log,

   rákucu?   ahahattarariíra?u   irii?ahaarásika   ícaas
   a big log   the log he burned   where he cooked him   Turtle
   the big log, the log that he burned and that cooked him—Turtle,

   irii?ahuuhuurícakat   ahaácatka.
   the one who was tricked   his being roasted.
   the one who was tricked and was roasted.

76 tiiwiirahaákawa?ac   tii?ahiíraa?.
   After he ate   this other one came.
   After he ate Turtle, this other Wolf came.

77 ahaá?   kici   iiwiirihkaruuwaáhac.
   He came   but   he ate everything all up.
   He came, and he ate up everything [that remained].

He Goes Over and the Burning Log   117

78 ahihkaruuwaahac.
   He ate everything up for him.
   He ate everything up for him.

79 iriwiiríriicu'at.
   Here the gut goes.
   Here the gut passes [goes].

A Pawnee Story

Narrated, translated, and introduced by Adrian Spottedhorsechief

This is the story that was told to me by my grandfather, and that was explained to him by various elders in our tribe. I am sure there may be other versions or translations of the song, but the story and the event were real. The Asakipiriru (Young Dog Dance) is an old ceremony that was done when the Pawnee were still living in Kansas and Nebraska. It is still practiced today, and this song is still sung during the ceremony. The translations of all songs will tell you about yourself and the history of our people. The songs tell about the way the people believed, the influences on them, their thoughts, their dreams, and their visions.

May our Pawnee culture, *ratarakuki* (our ways), always be here for those not yet here, our future generations.

Many years ago when the Pawnees were on the plains, their relationship with the Sioux was antagonistic. Many battles were fought among all the bands of Pawnee and the Sioux. A large part of the fighting was over the territorial rights to prime hunting lands, as well as to settle old scores. For some young Pawnee boys, to wage war and fight the Sioux was a rite of passage.

The last known Plains Indian war happened between the Pawnee and Sioux on August 5, 1873, in Hitchcock County, Nebraska. Approximately 350 Pawnee men and 350 Pawnee women and children were away from the main villages on their summer buffalo hunt. A combined force of 1,000 Oglala and Brulé Sioux warriors attacked the hunting party and, in the end, seventy Pawnee died.

Among the dead was a young man whose mother had a hard time having children. When she received the news that her only son had been killed, she was devastated. As any mother would, she had a hard time dealing with what had taken place and the loss of her child. She was inconsolable.

Then one night her son came to her in a dream and visited with her. He told her that he was fine and that he was in a good place, and not to worry about him. Tirawahut (God) came and took him. Her son told her to cry no more, and to go on living.

When she woke up, she was very happy. But although she felt better, there was still a small void in her life. She composed an Asakipiriru song. As the story goes, she went to this ceremony and approached the drum. She began to sing the song she composed, continuing until the men caught on and began to sing it.

They say the song's tune represents her crying and the words tell of her dream. *Hewerah* — Go on.

Pawnee Word List

Atius kasiwakuu 'Father (God) he tells me'
Utikees wekakirahe 'My son is no more'
Hewerah 'Go on'

SUGGESTED READINGS: PAWNEE ORAL TRADITIONS

Dorsey, George A. 1904. *Traditions of the Skidi Pawnee.* Memoirs of the American Folklore Society 8. Philadelphia: American Folklore Society.

——. 1906a. "Pawnee War Tales." *American Anthropologist* 8: 337–45.

——. 1906b. *The Pawnee: Mythology (Part I).* Carnegie Institution of Washington Publication 59. Washington DC: Carnegie Institution of Washington.

Fletcher, Alice C. 1903. "Pawnee Star Lore." *Journal of American Folk-Lore* 16: 10–15.

Grinnell, George Bird. 1893. "Pawnee Mythology." *Journal of American Folk-Lore* 6: 113–30.

——. 1894. "A Pawnee Star Myth." *Journal of American Folk-Lore* 7: 197–200.

Murie, James R. 1981. "Ceremonies of the Pawnee." Edited by Douglas R. Parks. Smithsonian Contributions to Anthropology 27, 2 vols. Washington DC: Smithsonian Institution Press. Reprint, Lincoln: University of Nebraska Press, 1989.

ARIKARA

The Race between the Horse and the Buffalo

AN ARIKARA NARRATIVE

Alfred Morsette (Paatú Kananuuninó, 'Not Afraid of the Enemy')
Transcribed and introduced by Douglas R. Parks

This narrative represents another genre of northern Caddoan oral traditions: accounts of the period right after humans appear in the world and they acquire their cultural institutions. Mr. Alfred Morsette Sr., who told this story, called that period in Arikara history the Holy Period, the time when human institutions and Arikara relations with their environment were being established. This story exemplifies how one feature of the world evolved: how buffalo originally attacked Arikara villages and ate their human inhabitants and finally how, as a result of a race, that situation was reversed and humans now kill buffalo. This narrative, like most origin stories, is based on a man's vision.

Mr. Morsette, who recorded this story in 1976, was reared by conservative grandparents who were monolinguals in Arikara and who lived in the conservative Beaver Creek district of the Fort Berthold Reservation in North Dakota. He was encouraged to learn traditional stories, as well as ritual and secular songs and Arikara ritualism. When the older ceremonial leaders conducted ceremonies in the first half of the twentieth century, they always wanted Alfred to sing for them because of both his knowledge and his voice. Throughout his life he was known on Fort Berthold Reservation for his prodigious knowledge of songs and traditional stories.

The Race between the Horse and the Buffalo

1 niiʔaNAsuxtaaʔuúʔA   AhnuxunuuwaáWI   wehnaahtakuwaʔá.
How it used to be   when they traveled around   when they came as a group.
Our people used to tell about things that happened when we were moving upriver.

2 nuu   naapakúhtuʔ   ništaaʔiitawaaWIhú   kanawituuNUxtaahé.
Long   long ago   what they used to tell   it was not good.
Long, long ago conditions were not good.

3 na   niiNAhkiitúhkUx   na   tanáhaʔ   noowiteeRAhwísaʔ
And   where a village was   and   the buffalos   then they came to it
The buffalo used to come to a village

weNAhkukhaanawiítIt   sáhniš.
when they smelled him   a human.
whenever they smelled humans.

4 niiʔAhnihwačeehUxukú.
What they used to say.
That is what they used to say.

5 noowituNAsaʔuúkUt   tanáhaʔ.
Then they attacked them   buffalos.
Then the buffalo attacked the people.

6 wewitatakuraakuNAhát   wenehkookawooruutíkA   wenehkuNAhunuúWI
Now they killed us   when they killed various ones   when they attacked it
They did away with us, killing many people when they attacked,

wenehkiitUhwirítkA   NAhkuuxitúhkUx.
when they knocked down the village   where the village was.
and tore down the village where it stood.

7   na   witiinakawooruútIt   na   tanáha⁷   witiinapa⁷á
     And   they killed many   and   Buffalos   they ate them
     The buffalo killed lots of people and ate

     sáhniš   weNAhku⁷iiníkUx   weNAhku⁷á   saNIškoótu⁷.
     human   when it had a dead body   when it ate it   a dead human.
     the bodies they obtained, eating the dead human beings.

8   tanáha⁷   nikuwitsúx.
     Buffalo   that is how it was.
     That is how the buffalo were.

9   witsuuxaanuuxuúku⁷.
     They used to do it.
     They used to do that.

10   na   witiRAsaawátAt.
     And   they moved away.
     [After they had attacked a village,] they moved off.

11   weNAhkuRAsaawátAt   noowiteeRAhwá⁷   na   niiNAhkuRAhčiiweešíkA
     After they had departed   then they came   and   the ones [people] who survived
     And after they had departed those people who had survived came back to the village

     nooWIšit'naaNIsá⁷us   weNAhkukoótU   wačéh   tanáha⁷
     then they put him on [a scaffold]   after he was dead   poor thing   buffalo
     and then put the remains of the dead, the poor things, on scaffolds

     wešinehkuxkakátkA   tanáha⁷   wešinehkuúxA.
     after they cut him up   buffalo   after they ate him.
     after the buffalo had torn up the bodies and eaten them.

12   natsú   wiináxtš   wewitUtpsiwá   nooxíni² na tšaápis
      And   a boy   he now had winters   sixteen
      Now there once was a boy going around who was

      weNAhkuwanú.
      when he would go around.
      sixteen winters old.

13   witikaapaátš   hi²áxti²   šáxti²   wešohnihkootíkA.
      He was poor   his father   his mother   their [du.] having been killed.
      He was pitiful after his father and mother had been killed.

14   na   wiináxtš   weNAhkučíkAt   weNAhkihtatata²aáhNA
      And   the boy   when he cried   when he went beside it
      The boy would go to the scaffold on which one of his parents

      niiNAhkuraaNAsáxA.
      where one lay on the scaffold.
      lay and would cry.

15   Wewit ͥNAhkiísA   weNAhkooweétA   weNAhkučíkAt.
      When he lay down   when he was tired   after he cried.
      Then one time he lay down after he had been crying and became tired.

16   nooWIšituútIt   pítkUx   wiítA.
      Then he dreamed of them [du.]   two   men.
      Then he dreamed of two men.

17   noowitiwaáko²   "wah   tAxtaRAhčíš   weNAxkučikAxwanú
      Then he said   Now   you're strong   as you go around crying
      One of the men said, "Now you are strong as you go around crying, here

tiweNAxkučíkAt.

as you've cried.

where you have been crying.

18 wah   nikuwešitatihwá²   číku² šinataakunuutaáNA

Now   we've come here   to do something for you

Now we have come here to do something for you

niit'noonahNAhuunuúku   tanáha²   t'naraapá²A.

after what they have been doing to you [pl.]   buffalo   their eating you [pl.].

because of what the buffalo are doing—because of their eating you people.

19 nawáh   wetAxiraaNAhtšíštA   štoh.

Now   you are going to be saved   again.

Now you people are going to be saved.

20 wah   štoh   kooxiRAhtšičiíta   niišakawooruutíkA.

Now   again   they will become alive   the ones who were killed.

Those who have been killed will come alive again.

21 haá²Ax   štoh   kooxuuteéRIt   na

Your father   again   you will see him   and

You'll see your father again, and

xáx   štoh   kooxuuteéRIt.

your mother   again   you will see her.

you'll see your mother again.

22 nawáh   wetAxúhtA   hináxtIt   niiNAxtaakitUhkákUx

Now   you are going to go   in the morning   where your village is in the woods

Now in the morning you are to go to your village there in the woods,

na   neešuutAhnaaʔiitawaáWI   wiiteešútš   wiítA."
And   you will tell them   young men   men.
and you'll tell the men and young men."

23   nooWIšitihnaaʔiitáWI   "taanikutuutuúʔIt   tⁱnátš.
      Then they told him   This is what they are like   bows.
      Then these two men instructed him: "This is what bows are like.

24   taanikuneešuúta   štáʔU   tⁱnátš.
      This is how you will do it   when you make it   a bow.
      This is how you'll make a bow.

25   na   kawíʔuʔ   niíšuʔ   neešikároʔ.
      And   arrowheads   arrows   you will make them.
      And you'll make arrowheads and arrows.

26   šuutAhnaaʔiitáWI :   'taanikukooxuútuʔ.'
      You'll tell them   This is the kind.
      You'll tell the men, 'This is the kind you should make.'

27   nawáh   neešiiwísWA   niinakuraaNIsáxA   niiháʔ.
      Now   you'll go to various ones   where he lies on a scaffold   there.
      Now you'll go to the different bodies lying on scaffolds there.
      <The flesh has not spoiled yet. It is still good.>

28   nootAxitawíʔIš   na   neešiwaákoʔ   'šuxčirikaʔá '   parúNIt!
      Then you touch him   and   you'll say   Wake up   quickly.
      Then you'll touch the body and say, 'Wake up quickly!

29   witⁱnakuunawireeríkA!'
      Fix yourself up.
      Fix yourself up!'

30 kooxeeRAhWIswá^ʔ.

They will all come.

Then they will get up and come back to the village.

31 'a   noowitiiširaakawireéhAs!'

And   then you all get ready.

'Now all of you must get yourselves ready!'

32 šuhnaakaaWIštaátA   AxtAhniškaroóku   na

After you [pl.] finish doing it   your [pl.] making [bows and arrows]   and

After you people have finished making the bows and arrows,

šuhnaakaaWIštaáta.

after you [pl.] finish doing it.

after you have finished doing it <we are going to a different world>.

33 wetiraahUhtačipiiruutíštA   niinoonakuú^ʔU   niinoonakuuraá^ʔU

They are all going to come together   the different ones   the different kinds

The different kinds of animals, the different kinds of us creatures,

nataraakunuuwaáWI.

we who go around [that is, are alive].

are all going to gather together.

34 wetⁱnaataruuwa^ʔóstA.

They are going to talk about it.

They're going to talk about different things.

35 wah   taanikuwetiraahiRAxá   niikohnuutAxitíštA

Now   this is what will be the first topic   whatever is going to happen

Now this is what will be the main topic: what is going to happen—

niinakuútA   tanáha⁷   t'naraapá⁷A   na   kananakuútA.

whether it will be   buffalo   their eating you   or   [whether] it will not be.

whether or not the buffalo will continue to eat you humans.

36   nawáh   nikuwet'naataruuwa⁷óstA.

     Now   that is what they are going to talk about.

     Now that is what they're going to discuss.

37   na   neešiitohnaa⁷iitáWI   niiwekohnuutáxtA

     And   we will tell you   this is what is going to be

     And we'll tell you what is decided—

     niiwenuutAxitštáWIt."

     what is going to happen.

     what is going to happen."

38   t'naákUx   wiiteešútš   nootí⁷At.

     This   boy   then he went.

     Then this boy went off.

39   nawáh   tsu   niiwenaraateehuúNU   wehninaateewaníkA

     Now   but   what was planned   when they planned it

     Now when the different animals—the buffalo,

     niinooNAhkuú⁷U   tanáha⁷   wáh   sčiríhtš   kuúNUx

     the different ones   buffalos   elks   coyotes   bear

     elks, coyotes, bears, the different ones—gathered

     niinooNAhkuú⁷U   wehnaraahUhtačipiiruútIt   xaawaarúxti⁷   noowitiwaáko⁷

     the different ones   when they gathered together   the horse   then he said

     together to plan how things on this earth would be, the horse said,

"wah   nikukoxtIhiRAxá   číku² nakuraa²iitawíhA."
Now   I will be the first one   to say something.
"Now I'll be the one who is first to say something."

40 t'naaríčI   xaawaarúxti²   noowitiwaáko²   "kaakat'nihnaaté²
     This   horse   then he said   I do not like it
     Then this horse said, "I don't like

     t'naaríčI   niit'nuutaánu.
     this one   what he is doing.
     what this buffalo is doing.

41 wah   čeésu²   saNIškaapaačíšu²   saNIščiraanarúhtu²
     Now   himself   the pitiful human   the weak human being
     After you abuse some pitiful human being,

     weNAxkuNAhuninoosiwaáhNA   nootAxikoótIt.
     when you abuse him   then you kill him.
     a weak human being, you kill him.

42 nootAxeeNAšítIt.
     Then you eat him.
     Then you eat him.

43 tsu   t'neekataahwá   niinaraateehuúNU   NAxkUhuhwaawá²A
     But   here is grass   which is the plan   that you should eat grass
     But here is grass, the thing that was intended for you to eat

     NAxkuwaawanú.
     that you should roam around.
     as you roam around.

44   tikaapaátš   sáhniš   tiNAxihkUhuunawiruuwaáhu."
      He is pitiful   the human being   now that you have cut his life short.
      The human being is helpless now that you have cut his life short."

45   noowitiwaáko?   tanáha?   "kaakí? táku? nakukunuhčitaátA
      Then he said   buffalo   No one is getting ahead of me
      Then the buffalo said, "No one is telling me what to do

      NItwaawanú.
      my roaming around.
      as I roam around.

46   nawáh   koosíhWA.
      Now   we will go.
      Now we'll race.

47   wah   inooškuutUhtaátA   na   IškoowíRAt.
      Now   if you beat me   and   you'll win.
      If you beat me, you'll win.

48   atsú   inoo?itootUhtaátA   wekukooxuú?Ut.
      But   if I beat you   it will be as it is.
      But if I beat you, it will be the way it is now.

49   wekukooxuhnaá?u?.
      It'll be that way.
      Things will remain the way they are now.

50   koxtiwa?á   sáhniš.
      I'll eat them   human beings.
      I'll eat human beings.

tat'nihnaaté⁷   sáhniš   NAtkutsaswaawá⁷A."
I like it   human   my eating flesh.
I like eating human flesh."

51 nikuwitiwaáko⁷.
That is what he said.
That is what he said.

52 "kaneeneetiihuunarúhtIt   niiNItkuWIská⁷A."
I'll have my way   as I think.
"I'll have my way, as I think it should be."

53 noowitiwaáko⁷   xaawaarúxti⁷   "wah   nikuneetuú⁷Ut.
Then he said   the horse   Now   I am that way.
Then the horse said, "Now I'm in agreement.

54 koosihwá⁷Ax."
We will race.
Let's race!"

55 nuu   wenaaríčI   tanáha⁷   áxkUx   noowití⁷.
There   when he stood   buffalo   one   there he was.
There was one buffalo standing out in front.

56 "wah   tačé nikunóxtA   nuunáxI?"
Now   who is going to be the one   his running.
He said to the other buffalos, "Now who is going to be the one to run?"

57 noowitaaxwaáta⁷   áxkUx.
Then he put his foot out   one.
Then one put his forepaw out.

58 čiití²Iš   wehnitapsiwaáhNA   nikuwití²   hukós   nakučipiriíNU.
    Four   one that had winters   he was the one   a bull   a young one.
    He was the one, a bull, a young one who was four winters old.

59 "wah   nikukoxtí².
    Now   I will be the one.
    "Now I'll be the one.

60 wah   nuukutAtkatarií²I.
    Now   I am fastest.
    I'm the fastest.

61 kaakí² táku² nakukusthunaáhWI."
    No one can equal me [lit., be close to me].
    No one can equal me."

62 noowitiraaninu²á.
    Then they became afraid.
    Then everyone became fearful.

63 wah   xaawaarúxti²   xaaNAhkatá   čiití²Iš   wehnitapsiwaahnuuxukú
    Now   a horse   a palomino   four   his winters were numbering
    Now a horse, a palomino, one four winters old, said,

    "wah   nikuneetuú²Ut.
    Now   I'll be the one.
    "Now I'll be the one to race him.

64 tAtkatarií²I.
    I am fast.
    I'm fast.

65   nikutatiikUxihnuúNAt   čiití²Iš   nakuuhaweéNA.
       I can run that long   four   its being days.
       I can run four days straight.

66   nikutatUstaRAhtšú²   nakuunáxI.
       That is the strength I have   to run.
       That is the strength I have to run.

67   nawáh   nikukoxtí².
       Now   I will be the one.
       Now I'll be the one.

68   koosihwá²Ax.
       We will run.
       We'll race.

69   t^{i}NAhunaanúhAt   hunaahčeeríškAt   nikuwetsehwaahíštA.
       This land that extends   on bare land   that is where we are going to come.
       On the land passing by here; on this bare land, is where we are going to race.

70   uu   kutiraáNIš   sihWIswáNA   niinatsteéhAt
       Oh   it is true   when we get there   where the edge of the water is
       Oh, the goal will be the edge of the water—

       niinatsteéhAt.
       where the edge of the water is.
       the edge of the water.

71   wah   škuutUhtaátA   wetAxkoowíRAt.
       Now   if you beat me   you will beat me.
       Now if you beat me, you'll win.

72 tsu   inookiitiWIsátA   iinatsteewaáhAt   wetataawíRAt."
    But   if I reach there   where the edge of the water is   I'll beat you.
    But if I reach the edge of the water first, I'll beat you."

73 nawáh   weWIšitiraateewáNIt.
    Now   they [du.] planned it.
    Now the two of them planned it.

74 wačéh   xaawaarúxti²   t'nawaaríčI   noowitiraaninu²á.
    Poor things   horses   these   then they became fearful.
    Then these horses, the poor things, became fearful.

75 tanáha²   kanawitiiwirooxuú²U.
    The buffalo   he was so strong.
    The buffalo was so strong.

76 nooWIšituhwá²Ax.
    Then they [du.] ran.
    Then the two raced.

77 nuuwešinawáNA   t'naaríčI   xaawaarúxti²   wenuunáxI
    Then when they [du.] went   this one   horse   when he ran
    When they went, this horse was

    kanawituhnaataRAhtščira²á   wešinawáNA.
    he was exceedingly fast   as they [du.] went.
    really fast when he ran on the course they took.

78 na   t'naaríčI   xaawaarúxti²   nootIhiRAxUhunítIt.
    And   this one   horse   then he got in the lead.
    And then this horse got in the lead.

79 nootIhiRAxUhunítIt.
Then he got in the lead.
Then he got in the lead.

80 tanáha²   nooteehUhtačeewií²a².
The buffalo   then he fell behind.
The buffalo fell behind.

81 nootiihUhtaawátAt.
Then he swerved to one side.
Then swerved to one side.

82 wah   nikunoowehnuutaáNA   noowiteewakaáhta²   sáhniš   čeésu².
Now   when he did that   then they yelled out   humans   themselves.
Now when the buffalo did that, the humans yelled out.

83 wehninaaničitawiítIt   nooWIšitiiNAhnuuwaawá²Ax   tanáha²
After they mounted   then they chased them   buffalos
Then they mounted the horses and chased the buffalo,

wešiniinapaníku   čeésu².
as they were shooting them   too.
shooting them, too.

84 wetsú   tⁱnaátA   xaawaarúxti²   nuu   nootí²At.
But now   this one going   horse   there   then he went.
Now the horse that was racing went on.

85 nootiwísAt   nii²AhnaraateehuúNU.
Then he arrived there   where it was planned.
Then he arrived at the goal.

86   tsu   tᶦnaaríčI   tanáha²   noowituhkúxAx   wehnuhkUxáxI
      But   this one   buffalo   then he ran away   his running off
      But this buffalo ran off, running away

      wešiniinawirátA   AhnuxwaákAhu   "táku² kaakí² nakukuutUhtaátA."
      after they beat him   after he had been saying   No one can outdo me.
      after he was beaten—after he had been saying, "No one can outdo me."

87   nawáh   nikuwitiraačítA   nataraahnaaničitáWI   xaawaarúxti²
      Now   that's the reason   our riding   horses
      Now this is the reason we ride horses:

      šiNAskuNAhnaáxI   nuuxunuuwaáWI   tanáha².
      for us to chase them   when they roam   buffalo.
      to chase the buffalo as they roam.

88   xaawaarúxti²   nikuwitanuunaateehuú²U.
      The horse   that is what his plan was.
      That is what the plan of the horse was.

89   nikuwiwituhnaateewáNIt.
      That is what he planned for himself.
      That was what he planned for himself.

90   nawáh   noowitiwaáko²   xaawaarúxti²   "wetateeričíšAt.
      Now   then he said   the horse   I have now saved you.
      Well, then the horse said, "I have saved you.

91   wetsú   tatská²   wačéh   NAxkukuraáhNA   tsu
      But now   I want it   poor thing   that you keep me   but
      And now I want you to keep me, poor me, and

weneetaraahníštA   nataakuhnaaNAxweekoóčI.
I am going to keep you   for me to look for things for you.
I'm going to take care of you, seeking out things for you.

92   niiNAxkuWIská[?]A   aataátA   na   tatariwísAt.
Wherever you want   'that I go'   And   I'll take you there.
Wherever you want to go, I'll take you there.

93   wah   tsu   tiihá[?]   kunaá[?]u[?]   wetAxkuhnanaahníštA   čeésu[?]."
Now   but   here   medicine   you are going to keep for me   too.
Meanwhile you are going to keep medicine for me here, too."

94   nikuwitanuhnaateehuú[?]U   xaawaarúxti[?].
That was the plan for him   horse.
This was the horse's plan.

95   nikukohniraačitáWI   xaawaarúxti[?]   šiNAsiiničitáWI
That must be the reason   Horse   that we rode it
That must be the reason we rode horses

natoxtaakunuuwaáWI   naapakúhtu[?].
when we lived   long ago.
when our people traveled around long ago.

96   siíno   tⁱneetohnaá[?]At   nataraahnaaničitawaáWI   xaawaarúxti[?].
Yet   we are that way   our riding them   horses.
We are still doing it, riding horses.

97   witiwaáko[?]   xaawaarúxti[?]   "wah   tsu   wetⁱnaatáRIt.
He said   the horse   Now   but   here I am standing.
The horse said, "Now I am standing here.

98   nikutatí⁷   xaakaatít."
       I am the one   the black horse.
       I'm the black horse."

99   tⁱNAhunásA   huukaawiraátA   nikuteéRIt.
       This earth   [in] the east   that is where he stands.
       In the east here on this earth is where he stands.

100   xaaNAhkatá   tuuhá⁷   hunaanapsíni⁷ ;   xaačiRAhpáhAt
       The palomino   there   [in] the south   a sorrel horse
       A palomino stands over there in the south; a sorrel horse,

       skaweéraa⁷u⁷ ;   xaačiišawatá   hunaahčeeríškAt   hunaahkoohaáhkAt.
       [in] the west   a white horse   on the bare land   [in] the north.
       in the west; a white horse, on the bare land in the north.

101   wah   tiihá⁷   nikuwetanuhwaawaáRIt   awaaháxu⁷
       Now   here   that is where they have their stations   the Powers
       Now there is where they have their stations among the powers

       neskoóhAt   šiNAsiinaanuuwaawanú   neešaánu⁷ tⁱnačitákUx   na
       in the sky   our asking for things [of him]   the Chief Above   and
       in the sky when we pray for things to the Chief Above,

       tⁱNAhunásA   niitⁱnataraakunuúWI   natakuraahnanaáhNA.
       [on] this earth   here where we live   the one who keeps us.
       the one who looks after us who are living here on this earth.

102   wah   tanikuwituhnaa⁷iitUxú⁷.
       Now   this is how the story goes.
       Now this is how the story goes.

103 nikutatuuNUxaakAtkookUxuúku²   atíka²   wenakunaa²iítI.
     This is what I used to hear from her   my grandmother   when she told it.
     This is what I used to hear from my grandmother when she told it.

104 na   atí²Ax   nuuNUxtaa²iitUxuúku²   haáwa².
     And   my father   he used to tell it   also.
     And my father used to tell the story, too.

SUGGESTED READINGS: ARIKARA ORAL TRADITIONS

Dorsey, George A. 1904. *Traditions of the Arikara.* Washington DC: Carnegie Institution.

Parks, Douglas R., ed. 1977. *Caddoan Texts.* International Journal of American Linguistics, Native American Text Series 2 (1). Chicago: University of Chicago Press.

———. 1991. *Traditional Narratives of the Arikara Indians.* 4 vols. Lincoln: University of Nebraska Press.

KITSAI

Coyote Frees Buffalo

Narrated by Kai Kai, Kitsai

Recorded by Alexander Lesser

Translated and introduced by Joshua A. Richards

The following story was told by a woman named Kai Kai, who was the last fluent speaker of the Kitsai language. She narrated this story to the anthropologist Alexander Lesser during summer fieldwork sessions carried out between 1929 and 1930.

Removed from their homeland in north-central Texas in the late nineteenth century, the Kitsai settled in Oklahoma among the closely related Wichita tribe. Most Kitsai people came to speak Wichita or, like Kai Kai, became bilingual in both Wichita and Kitsai. As she did not speak English, she had to first recite the story in Kitsai, so Lesser could write each word phonetically. Then she translated each word into Wichita so an interpreter named Tom Haddon could provide English translations. This circuitous method of telling and translating stories must have affected the natural flow and style of narration, perhaps resulting in a more halting and disjointed quality than might otherwise have been displayed. However, the stories collected during these sessions remain immensely important as they represent the only documented examples of Kitsai oral literature.

This particular story represents a widespread motif among trickster tales, in which missing game animals are released from an enclosure. In this variant Coyote transforms himself into a puppy and is taken by a young boy into the lodge of a man who is keeping the buffalo locked away behind a rock door in a bluff. Coyote then observes the man's secrets and succeeds in sneaking away while the man sleeps and releasing the buffalo, thus saving his village from starvation. This is an abbreviated version of the story, as the narrator later commented, and many of the details left out would surely have been familiar to any Kitsai audience. For example, though not mentioned in the telling of the story itself, Kai Kai added later that the man keeping the buffalo locked away was actually the mythical character Crow, whom she also refers to as Raven.

Coyote Frees Buffalo

1 uyatánu   táxku   ana:wi   katsnirawa:ki   uyatánu.
   Town is   coyote   there dwells   long time extends   village.
   There was a village where Coyote had lived for a long time.

2 itskunirawa:ki   nikairawa:t.
   Good time extends   they [pl.] finish plenty.
   After a while they ate up all of their food.

3 táxku   ayauknahyunaiwi.
   Coyote   along with children dwells.
   Coyote lived there along with his children.

4 niyakwawi:na.
   They [pl.] hunger them [pl.].
   They were all very hungry.

5 táxku   áktira.
   Coyote   goes round about.
   Coyote went all about.

6 hyaát   kúkuwa   kakúnyu   tánaha   ahuyaksa   (arahyuyakskwa:tira).
   Beyond   went   none is   buffalo   seeks   seeks them round about.
   Then he went far off but there were no buffalo, though he sought them all around.

7 tsáxka   nawitsu:hu   tsáxka   nuxtɛakwi:nata   tsáxka   a:ta
   Again   repeatedly arrive-comes   again   next morning   again   goes
   Again and again he came back and left the next morning to go

arahyuyáksa.
seeks them.
looking for them.

8   awítsku   "kinastikuna:su   tánaha.
Thinks   Somewhere I shall find them   buffalo.
He thought, "I will find the buffalo somewhere.

9   kyɛnyuku   kani:ha?"
How is it   isn't come.
Why don't they come?"

10   kakunihunasu:hu.
Repeatedly none finds.
But he never found any.

11   kúkuwa   Ayakánu   arakáwi   kúkuwa.
Went   woods is   knoll is   went.
Then he went into the woods to a knoll.

12   a:ta   a:ta   awaku:tawi   kúkuwa   kukuhuyárikya.
Goes   goes   [wind] blows   went   stopped standing.
He was going and going and as the wind blew he stopped.

13   kukinukutkayáha   nɛ:tana:s.
Somewhence came smell   meat.
The smell of meat was coming from somewhere.

14   táxku   nuitsuskánata.
Coyote   toward it his nose goes.
His nose followed it.

15 warasnihunánu   anínakawia   nɛ:tana:s.
   Bad place is   thence comes from within   meat.
   There was a bad place and the smell of meat was coming from inside it.

16 a:ta   táxku   aaka:ta   nirɛwa:tana.
   Goes   Coyote   goes in among   looks around.
   Coyote went in and looked around.

17 akusawi.
   House sits.
   There was a lodge.

18 uhuyárik   táxku.
   Stops standing   Coyote.
   Coyote stopped.

19 tsáxka   a:ta   akusawiunu.
   Again   goes   where house sits.
   Again he went toward the lodge.

20 kukuhuwítskwa   kukwawátsitikya   yauktski   tsutski:ki   kanikayáku
   There arrive-went   exited   infant   boy   immature
   When he got there a young boy,

   tikunihunikwiu.
   this tall is.
   about this tall, came out.

21 táxku   kuyakukiwinyátkya.
   Coyote   changed himself.
   Now Coyote transformed himself.

22 nɛninuxkusawiunu   nuyahyakaunu   tsutski:ki   nutakunyátskus
    Where their [pl.] house sets   in its doorway   boy   plays
    The boy was playing there in the doorway

    tiníni.
    at this place.
    of the lodge.

23 táxku   kuyakukiwinyátkya   kuyakurukya   irutsi   kaníkina.
    Coyote   changed himself   made himself   pup   small.
    Coyote transformed, making himself into a small pup.

24 tsutski:ki   anáana   nutsiari:ksana   irutsi.
    Boy   there goes about   becomes regardful   pup.
    The boy was going around when he noticed the pup.

25 kwanukuwa   tsutski:ki   kukukúsikya   irutsi   kuyakurikatéhuwɛ
    There went   boy   took up   pup   took in arms
    He went over and picked it up in his arms and the two of them

    kusukurahyukwa.
    [dual] went in.
    went inside.

26 kukuwakúkya   tsutski:ki   kukuwakúkya   "áas   natuna:su   irutsi."
    Said   boy   said   Father   I've found   pup
    The boy said to his father, "I've found a pup."

27 kukuwakúkya   nɛyuáas   kukuwakúkya   "a: kanyúk   irutsi.
    Said   his father said   Ah   is not   pup.
    His father said, "Ah, that is not a pup.

28 nikiwina."
Is different.
It's something else."

29 awáku   tsutski:ki   "húwa   irutsi   úk."
Says   boy   No   pup   is.
The boy said, "No, it's a pup."

30 awáku   nɛyuáas   "húwa   nikiwina.
Says   his father   No   is different.
His father said, "No, it's something else.

31 yahína   Isnawátsitiku   hyaát   isniyu."
Go on   exit [with] in-hand   that way   go [with] in-hand.
Go on and take it out of here!"

32 kanyátku   tsutski:ki   awáku   "astiyu:ku   irutsi."
Won't go   boy   says   Mine will be   pup.
The boy wouldn't go, but said, "The pup will be mine."

33 awáku   nɛyu:áas   "húwa   isnawátsitiku."
Says   his father   No   exit [with] in-hand.
His father said, "No, take it out of here!"

34 kanyátku   tsutski:ki.
Won't go   boy.
But the boy wouldn't go.

35 arátkyɛna   kukuwakúkya   wi:ta   "kaniai.
Becomes dark   said   man   Well, let's see about it.
When it got dark the man said, "Well, let's see about it.

36 isiya:hu.
Come [with] in-hand.
Bring it here.

37 kaniai   kaniwakníksu   kaniikuku   irutsi."
Well, let's see   is [it] truly spoken   let's see that one is   pup.
Let's see if it truly is a pup."

38 táxku   néi   úk   atkaráxkus.
Coyote   and   is   hears.
It was Coyote and he heard him.

39 táxku   úk.
Coyote   is.
It was Coyote.

40 awi:s   akiyak.
Much   fire burns.
There was a big fire burning.

41 nutasnayánikuk   iksini   tsáxka   arauráriki   akiaku:nu.
Grasps him by feet   by hand   also   is in hand foremost   where fire burns.
He took the pup's feet in his hand right in front of the fire.

42 tikwárana   arauráriki.
Thus does   is in hand foremost.
He held it right before the fire.

43 awáku   wi:ta   "kaniikuku   irutsi."
Says   man   Let's see that one is   pup.
The man said, "Let's see if that one is a pup."

44 kusixkuurárikya   táxku   néi   úk   táxku.
   Was [held] foremost by   Coyote   and   is   Coyote.
   Coyote was held up close to the fire.

45 tarahyúkuiyúsanya   awiús.
   Near way became   defecate.
   When he got close to the flames, he pooped.

46 kukuwakúkya   wi:ta   "áyi   ikuku   irutsi."
   Said   man   Yes   that is   pup.
   The man said, "Yes, that is a pup."

47 kukutunia:wa   tsutski:ki   irutsi.
   Gave him in hand   boy   pup.
   He handed the pup to the boy.

48 kukukúsikya.
   Took up.
   He took it.

49 kukuwakúkya   wi:ta   "yahína   isutkwaánu   nɛ:tana:s."
   Said   man   Go on   feed him   meat.
   The man said, "Go on, feed him some meat."

50 tsutski:ki   nunuk   nutkwaáni   nɛ:tana:s.
   Boy   does it   feeds him   meat.
   The boy fed him some meat.

51 nikayatu:hu.
   Repeatedly finishes much.
   Again and again he ate it all up.

52 kutskukutsiratkani:wa   kwixkwakunítkwia.
    Good [way] dark went [toward midnight]   they-them [pl.] settled to sleep.
    As it got toward midnight, they settled down to sleep.

53 táxku   kanihunítkwi.
    Coyote   settles not to sleep.
    But Coyote did not go to sleep.

54 nikíriku.
    Is awake.
    He remained awake.

55 kwi:s   niyakunítkwi.
    Soundly   they-them [pl.] settle to sleep.
    They were all sound asleep.

56 táxku   kuyakukiwatya   kukwawátsitikya.
    Coyote   undid himself   exited.
    Coyote transformed himself back and went out of the lodge.

57 táxku   kúkuwa   tiníni   nutatka:wi   nutsiakátata.
    Coyote   went   at this place bluff sits   is shut door.
    He went to a place where there was a bluff, which was a closed door.

58 kúkuwa   táxku   nutsiakatatu:nu   kukuhuwítskwa.
    Went   Coyote   where shut door is   there arrive-went.
    Coyote got to where the closed door was.

59 akwáts nunatewakaru:nu   tsáxka   ikúnutsia   nutsiakátata   kátanu.
    All   realizes them   again   thus is   is shut door   rock.
    Everyone already knew that it was a closed door, the rock.

60 kukuhuwítskwa   nutsiakatatu:nu   kukurixkúkya   "hyaát
There arrive-went   where shut door is   told   That way
He went up to the closed door and said to it, "Now,

isyutsiakatatu:ku."
open yourself.
open up!"

61 kuyakútsiakatatúkya.
Opened self.
It opened.

62 wi: kukurayawátsitikya   tánaha.
My!   [pl.] exited   buffalo.
My! The buffalo all came out.

63 kwanukwárikya   anáriki   táxku.
There stood   there stands   Coyote.
There stood Coyote.

64 akwáts   kukurayawatsitiksya:ta.
All   [pl.] finished exiting.
They all escaped.

65 kuyakwáha   táxku   kuyakuwi:tsa   uyatanikúnu   táxku.
Came   Coyote   arrive-came   where town is   Coyote.
Coyote arrived where the village was.

66 niráxkina   tánaha   a:kayu.
There are many   buffalo   spread out moving about.
There were many buffalo spread out, moving about.

67 akírikana   wi:ta.
   Wakens   man.
   The man awoke.

68 kuyakwiwiuksa   kúkuwa   awítsku   "túxka   tánaha
   Arose   went   thinks   Still   buffalo
   He arose and went there, thinking, "My buffalo

   natinuhyaxkárikyu."
   I've mine [pl.] inside standing.
   are still inside."

69 kakúnyu   nunuk   táxku.
   None there is does it   Coyote.
   But there were none there because of Coyote.

70 akwáts   tánaha   kukurayawátsitikya   táxku   nunuk.
   All   buffalo   [pl.] exited   Coyote   does it.
   All the buffalo had gotten out because of Coyote.

71 kukuhuwítskwa   wi:ta   aníni   kukutsiakatatúkya.
   There arrive-went man   at that place   opened door.
   The man arrived at the open door.

72 kakunikáriki   tánaha   akwáts   kakúnyu.
   None inside stands buffalo   all   none there is.
   There were no buffalo left inside.

73 kuyakwáha   wi:ta   warasnɛrikukúnu.
   Came   man   bad his feeling.
   The man came back feeling downhearted.

74 kukurixkúkya   tsutski:ki   kukurixkúkya   "ihyá   kanyúk   irutsi.
    Told   boy   told   All right   is not   pup.
    He told the boy, "Now, it is not a pup.

75 nikiwina."
    Is different.
    It's something else."

76 kukuwakúkya   wi:ta   "kakunikáriki   tánaha."
    Said   man   None inside stands   buffalo.
    The man said, "There are no buffalo left inside."

77 u'   táxku   uyatanikúnu   anayauknahyunaiwi
    There   Coyote   where town is   there along with children dwells
    There in the village where Coyote lived with his children,

    awáku   táxku   "ihyá   tɛsnakuyatánu."
    says   Coyote   All right   here you [pl.] [in] town.
    Coyote called out, "Now, all of you in this village . . ."

78 awáku   táxku   "kwatíya   u: tánaha   nakayu:ku."
    Says   Coyote   that I've come   there   buffalo   are spread out moving about.
    Coyote said, "Now that I've returned, there are buffalo spread out and moving about."

79 "ihyaá   isnákwihu "   kurawáknu   táxku   tanatsihunituw.
    All right   you [pl.] go after   sings   Coyote   "sings of himself."
    He sang, "Now, you all go get them," singing of himself.

80 kwixkuwiwa:wanya   akwáts   nihyunuwawa:tira
    They [pl.] went after   all   they chase round about [surround]
    The villagers chased after the buffalo, surrounding them all

nixkarawanák   tánaha.
they [pl.] kill [pl.]   buffalo.
and killing them.

81 nɛniriwitskwáwaa   tánaha.
    "They [pl.] in-hand arrive come"   buffalo.
    They all came back carrying the buffalo meat.

82 itskunixkatúnu   niwawa:waa.
    Good they [pl.] feel   they [pl.] eat.
    They felt good as they ate.

83 siniara:tasa   yatúnu   kírika   úk.
    Is same way [thing]   chief   person   is.
    Coyote was like a chief.

84 ikunútsia   táxku   nunuk.
    Thus is   Coyote   does it.
    It was because of Coyote.

85 niwawa:waa   uyatánu   akɛriwati.
    They [pl.] eat   town   saves.
    They ate and he saved the village.

86 táxku   wanyúk   yatúnu.
    Coyote   is like   chief.
    Coyote was like a chief.

87 akaniriku:ki   uyatánu   anáxka   nunuk   táxku.
    Are settled about   town   so   does it   Coyote.
    They were settled around the village because of Coyote.

88 anáxka   a:kayu   tánaha   nunuk   táxku.
   So   are moving about scattered   buffalo   does it   Coyote.
   The buffalo were here and there, moving around because of Coyote.

89 áksya   kaniyakwi:na   táxku   nunuk.
   By now   they [pl.] hunger them [pl.] not   Coyote   does it.
   They were no longer hungry because of Coyote.

90 katsnirawa:ki   uyatahu:ki   táxku   áwi.
   Long time extends   towns are   Coyote   dwells.
   For a long time Coyote dwelt there in the village.

91 akwáts   kírika   akiariwati   táxku   nunuk   anáxka.
   All   person   saves   Coyote   does it   so.
   Everyone was saved because of Coyote.

92 kikukutsiriáha   aníni.
   Thus happened   at that place.
   That's what happened.

93 itskinaniritkowákyu
   That's the story's end
   That's the end of the story.

WICHITA

Awa:hárikic: Hassí:ri:ha:stírih

Narrated and translated by Bertha Provost
Translated and introduced by David S. Rood

This very short Wichita text was dictated by Ms. Bertha Provost and recorded on tape in 1965. Bertha then repeated the story word by word so I could write it down, and she translated each word or sentence separately. Her glosses are the second line of the story presentation; I have supplied the free translation.

This story is not included in George A. Dorsey ([1904] 1995), *The Mythology of the Wichita,* and has never been published before. Besides its unusual brevity, it shows other earmarks of being a condensed version, such as the fact that the messenger makes his plea only twice, instead of the traditional four times, and some connecting events are left to the listener's imagination. For example we are never told of the consequences of the dove's gambling losses and are left to surmise that it was more important for him to try to recoup them than to pay attention to his family obligations. I suspect that one reason for this abbreviation was the fact that Bertha knew I could not understand what she was saying and thought I would be content with an outline. It is very difficult to tell a story well when there is no audience to appreciate the performance.

Nevertheless, there are also features that show skillful structural organization. The story both begins and ends with the salient fact to be explained (the dove is constantly mourning) and the basic explanation (he is a gambler). These opening and closing statements provide boundaries for the telling. After the initial summary Bertha gives us an introduction that sets the scene (the dove is gambling and losing). Once the context is established the word *ka:ʔa:ʔa:kó:kha:rʔa* signals a change of topic, and we are told of a pivotal event (his brother dies), a bad decision (the dove does not stop gambling), and the sad consequences of that bad decision (the messenger goes home without him and other people bury the deceased brother). We

161

are not told what triggers the next event, when the dove finally does pay attention to his responsibilities, but only that his action is too late and that to this day the gambling dove is suffering the consequences of his poor choice.

The function of a story like this is both to entertain and to teach values and proper behavior. Teaching is done by showing a bad example and the unfortunate consequences. There are at least two important lessons to be learned from the story: gambling can be an obsession, and one is obligated to honor a deceased relative. Because he ignored both of these lessons, the dove ends up mourning eternally.

Awa:hárikic: Hassí:ri:ha:stírih
(The Dove Who Is Constantly Mourning)

1 nahánthira:wa:híriskih né:riha:stíckih   has?á:?áki:ro:kháte?e awa:hárikic
   it is daylight many times he mourns constantly   he was a gambler dove
   Day after day he mourns.   The dove was a gambler.

2 has?a:?ákicá:ris,   kiyákic?aris hirí:skiwa:wáskih né:rih no:kháhkwe?ekih
   he gambled constantly he gambled he was losing   those his possessions
   He was gambling and gambling.   He was losing everything he had.

3 ka:?a:?a:kó:kha:r?a kíri?a:ká:ri   hinne:?í:ráskih i:ke?ekiwá:ri hirasa:?í:raskih
   then a time came   he died   his brother   he was told   your brother
   Then it happened that his brother died. Someone came to tell him, "Your brother

4 kíri?a:rá:ri   tatáchiri?as   a:ko:k?a   tó:kira:
   he died   I have come to chase you   he said   wait a while
   has died.   I have come to get you."   He said,   "Wait a while."

5 há:wah hiriwá:riskih   há:wah tó:kira: kiya?á:ki?iro:ckwa
   again he was told   again wait a while   he went outward
   When they told him again,   again he said, "Wait a while." So he [the messenger] left.

6 hiriwara:hissah nawississah   waʔí:keʔe:ki:kisks
 going along   arriving back where he started from they had already buried him
 He returned to where he had started, but   they had already buried him

7 hi:wéʔewakha:rʔa kíriʔé::ʔas hánne:ʔi:rásskih
 because   he didn't come his brother
 because his brother had not come.

8 na:hiʔincáwisʔaskih híriwah asskhah tackwah ro:kháraskih
 when he arrived then   later   big old time passing
 Then when he did arrive, later,   after some time had passed,

9 é:ka:ra:ki   i:keʔekiwá:ri   wáhitackisks
 where is he [inanimate] lying someone told him we already buried him
 he asked, "Where is he?" He was told, "We already buried him

10 kíriʔasí::ʔas   hira:wika: isah híriwa: tikitawí:tis tí:rasa:khírʔih
 you didn't come for a long time thus INSTR. it hangs it being this day
 because you didn't come for so long." That's why it is the case even today

11 awa:hárikic hassi:riha:stírih hi:wéʔewakha:rʔa hasʔá:ʔáki:ro:kháteʔe
 dove cries constantly   because   he was a gambler
 the dove is constantly crying: because he was a gambler.

Some Remarks about Wichita Literature

There are only two published collections of Wichita myths and stories, Dorsey ([1904] 1995), and Rood (1977). The Dorsey collection reports the history of the world from the nineteenth-century Wichita point of view. In his introduction (20–21), Dorsey explains the four periods of that history: creation, transformation, present, and future. After the initial creation of two people, a man and a woman, who wander the world in darkness, the man is able to call into being the contrast between day and night, and the second era (transformation) begins. Animals can talk and behave like people, and people often have special medicinal powers. At the end of their adventures the people often change into animals or celestial constellations. Gradually, however, people, plants, and animals develop in bad ways, so that the second era closes with a flood, which only two people survive. In the third era, the present, those two people procreate and their offspring interact with spirits and sometimes in supernatural ways with animals, but the animals are no longer able to speak. The future is a time of further loss, and will soon culminate in the end of the world and a new beginning.

Dorsey's texts are available only in English; he collected the stories through an interpreter or from a bilingual narrator. In contrast, Rood (1977) includes both English and Wichita versions of some of the same stories, mostly from the second era, but they are less elaborate and less well performed, for the most part, than the older versions. Bertha Provost provided a different, but compatible, typology for the stories in which she divided them into two groups. The first, *ksir?o:kha:r?a*, she called "fairy stories" in English, while the second was called "true stories." In the first category, animals talk and behave like people but, in the second, animals cannot talk although there is considerable supernatural activity. I think that the ksir?o:kha:r?a could correspond to Dorsey's second era, while the true stories belong to the third.

I find it difficult to decide whether this story is of yet another genre or whether it belongs to the second era (fairy stories). The dove is clearly acting in human ways, but the point of the tale seems to be to explain a present-day fact rather than to illustrate history. In either case the didactic values mentioned above (gambling can be bad, deceased relatives must be honored) are clear.

WRITING

There is no official or generally accepted writing system for Wichita besides what is used in my publications. Most of the letters I use have their English values. The colon (:) after a vowel marks the preceding vowel as long; two colons mark an extra-long vowel. The letter *r* is pronounced like the 'r' in Spanish (not English), and the letter *c* represents the sequence 'ts.' The glottal stop (?) is a complete closure in the throat, like the sound in the middle of the English word "oh-oh." In the sequences *ch*, *th*, and *kh*, both letters are fully pronounced somewhat like the *t-h* sequence in "white hat" or the *k-h* sequence in "lack heart." An accent mark (for example, *á*) signals a higher pitch or tone on that vowel. See Rood (1976) for a complete description of how to pronounce the language.

How the Language Helps Us Understand the Story

There are some linguistic and narrative features that the written version of the story conveys poorly, and some that require some elaboration in the translation. Here are a few comments about them.

Wichita has no indirect speech construction; instead, speakers report speech directly. This is illustrated in lines 3–4, which tell how the gambler was informed of his brother's death. It is not "He was told his brother had died," but "He was told, 'Your brother has died.'" Another consequence of using direct quotation to report conversation is the difference in the two words for "he died" in lines 3 and 4. When the narrator is reporting this event, in line 3, she uses the tense marked with $-k$-; when the messenger actually tells the dove the news in line 4, however, he uses a tense that is marked with $-r$-.

In the free translation of the story, I have inserted "he asked" in line 9. There is no equivalent to that in the Wichita. Instead, the narrator paused, then changed the pitch and speed of her pronunciation, taking on a different "voice" when the character, rather than the narrator, was speaking. Something similar was done at line 5 with "he said." All the utterances that I have put in quotation marks have this kind of voice change in the spoken Wichita narrative.

Although Wichita does not distinguish gender in the pronouns (there is no difference between "he" and "she"), the dove in this story is unambiguously male. This is made clear in the choice of the word for "brother," which means "brother of a man." A different word is used for "brother of a woman."

Moreover, these words for "brother" are verbs, not nouns. The forms for "brother of a man" are always either dual or plural (in this story only the dual is used), and their structure depends on the grammatical context. There are two examples in line 3 and one in line 7. The first one, in line 3, uses an indefinite subject pronoun (the *l* after the initial *h*) and a definite article. It means "brother of the dove" because the dove is the main character at this point, and the brother is new information. The second one in line 3, "your brother," does not have the definite article, but it does have a reflexive object pronoun. Literally it means something like "one such that you two are brothers to each other." The third example has initial *ha-* instead of *hi-* because now the subject is definite. This one means "brother of the deceased man." English would have to work hard to make the distinction between "brother of the dove" and "brother of the deceased man" clear, and instead uses "his brother" for both of them, letting the listener sort out the difference in reference.

Awa:hárikic   165

REFERENCES

Dorsey, George A. 1904. *The Mythology of the Wichita*. Washington DC: Carnegie Press. Reprinted 1995 by the University of Oklahoma Press.

Rood, David S. 1976. *Wichita Grammar*. New York: Garland Publishing.

———. 1977. "Wichita Texts." In *Caddoan Texts, edited by* Douglas R. Parks, 91–128. Native American texts series vol. 2, no. 1. Chicago: University of Chicago Press.

PART FOUR

Iroquoian Language Family

CHEROKEE

Diary

Translated and introduced by Durbin Feeling

"Diary" is the story of a woman who has lost her two sons and their father. The woman floats on water with papers upon which she has written about how she feels about her loss. She believes nobody cares how she feels. This story reflects the depression and despair experienced by those in mourning.

ᎠᏂᏍᎬᏘ	31ne	1927	ᎯᏒᏍᎩ
May	31st	1927	a few
ᎢᎧᏁᏥ	ᏓᎪᏪᎳᏂ	ᎪᎯ	ᎢᎪᎯ
words	I will write	this	day
ᎠᏆᏓᏂᎳᏉ	ᏱᏕᏗ	ᎠᏎᏉᏉ	ᏱᏂᏥᏪᏎ
I am just ill	if I say	no reason	I would be saying it
ᎥᏝ	ᎩᎶ	ᎰᏩ	ᏰᎦᏴᏔ
no	someone	truth	he would not think
ᎠᏋᏌᏉ	ᎾᏆᏛᎾᏕᎦ	ᎥᏋᏕᏨᏉ	
I am just alone	condition	I have just been abandoned	
ᏥᏙᏩᏕᎦ	ᎠᏫᏄᏣ	ᎠᏋᏕᏥᏄᏉ	ᎾᏆᏛᎾ
I am standing around	young man	he has just abandoned me	I am in that situation
ᎾᏉ	ᏑᏕᏘᏴᏓ	ᏑᏓᎵᏃ	ᎢᏯᏅᏙ
now	one year	and six	months
ᎬᏋᏕᏨᎯ	ᎠᏉᎯᏳᏗ	ᎤᏁᎳᏅᎯ	ᏗᏆᏓᏂᏒᏤᏒᎯ
since he abandoned me	I trust	God	He accepted him
ᎨᏒᎢ	ᎠᎵᎮᎵᏍᏗ	ᏗᎨᏒ	ᏫᏒᏛᏅ
has	happy	at the place	he is there
ᎠᏉᎯᏳᏗ	ᏧᏅᏟ	ᏧᏩᏛᏛ	ᎨᏒᎢ

I trust	his brothers	he has found them	has
DᏤ·ᎭG	Dơ	OᏕᏴᏒᏝ	OᏀᏁᏁ
I trust	and	his parent	he has found
ⱶRT	OᏟᏤ·	OᏓᏝG	ᏬᏘᏒᎤWᏝ
has	much more	worse off	he would have been
ᎤᏗᏒR	ᎤᏝᎩᏁ	OᏕᏒᎤᏝ	TGᎤᏝ
I	a little bit	stronger	like

Syllabary

DᏂᎤEᏝ 31Ꮧ 1927 ᏰᎤᏓ TᎤᏝⱶ ᏝᎪWᏂ AᏠ TAᏠ DIᏝᏂWᏤ· ᏬᏕᏝ D4Ꮴ·Ꮴ·
ᏬᏂⱶᎪᏘ iᏝ ᎩG ⱶᏀ ᏴᏕᏰW ᏐIᏁᏝᏕᏕ DᎬᏌᏤ· ᏐIᏁᏁᏕᏕ iᎬᏕᏟᏤ· ⱶVᏁᏕᏕ DᏐᎢᏟ
DᎬᏕⱶᎤᏤ· ᏐIᏁᏐ ᏐᏤ· ᎨᏕᏝᏴᏝ ᎨᏝᏒᏃ TᎤ᎐Ꮴ ᎬᎬᏕᏟᏠ DᏤ·ᎭGᏝ O᎐ᏁWO᎐
ᏝᏤᏂᏘᏤᏘᏠ ⱶRT DᏒᏒᎤᏝ ᏝⱶR ᏐᏘᏁᎤ DᏤ·ᎭGᏝ Ꮷ᎐Ꮯ ᏟGᏁᏁ ⱶRT DᏤ·ᎭG
Dơ OᏕᏴᏒᏝ OᏀᏁᏁ ⱶRT OᏟᏤ· OᏓᏝG ᏬᏘᏒᎤWᏝ ᎤᏗᏒR ᎤᏝᎩᏁ OᏕᏒᎤᏝ
TGᎤᏝ TᏕᏝ᎐ᏝᏝᎤAT

English

May 31, 1927. I am going to write a few words on this day. There is no reason for me to say that I am ill because no one would believe me. My life is worthless because I am all alone with no one to stay with me. A young man has left me. It has now been a year and six months since he left me. I have faith that God has accepted him. I have faith that he is in the "happy place," that he has found his brothers. I have faith that he has found his parent. When I think about it he would have suffered if I had left him first. Then I feel a little better.

I Shot It, You Shot It

Transcribed and translated by Durbin Feeling

The story allows us to see the results of bragging. The man with a gun has no intention of including anyone in this sport until he realizes he is in *utan* ('big') trouble.

Agidoda	jigesv	kanohesgo	kilo	unohiselv	gesv.
my dad	who was	he tells about	someone	who told it to him	it was

My [late] dad tells about a story someone had told him.

Anita'li	anisgaya	Aninohalidohe	ahwi	dunihyohe.
two	men	they were hunting	deer	they were looking for them

Two men were hunting for deer.

Sagwuno	asgaya	galogwe	ganehe	So'ino	tla.
and one	man	a gun	had a gun	and the other	not

And one man had a gun and the other one didn't.

Nahno	galogwe	ganehi	udlvgwisati	gese.
and the	gun	one who carried	a braggart	he was

And the one with a gun was a braggart.

gohusdino	yudvnela	adlvgwisge.	anaisvno	gohusdi	wunigohe
and something	when he did	he bragged	and as they walked along	something	they saw

When he did something he bragged about it. And as they walked along they saw something

Dotsuwa'itlv.   "ni.   ahwi,"   udvhne   na galogwe   ganehi.
in the bushes   look   a deer   he said   the gun   carrier
in the bushes. "Look. A deer," said the one with the gun.

kilagwu iyv   widusdayotle   osdagwu   nuksestanvna   iyusdi   ayohihv.
immediately   he shot at it   just good   without observing   what it was   he was shooting
Immediately he shot at it without observing what he was shooting at.

doyuhno   wunigohe   gohusdi   eladi   ganvgv.   "ahwi
and for sure   they saw   something   down on ground   it falling   deer
And sure enough they saw something fall to the ground.

eniyo'a"   udvhne   na   galogwe   niganehvna.   "tsiyo'ega!"
we shot it   he said   the   gun   not carrying   I shot it
"We shot a deer," said the one without a gun. "I shot it,"

udvhne   na   galogwe   ganehi,   adlvgwisgv.   na'vhno
he said   the   gun   carrier   as he bragged   and close
said the one with a gun, bragging.

wunilutsa   unigohe   sogwili   gana'v   eladi.   nahno
they arrived   they saw it   a horse   lining   on ground   and the
And when they got close they saw a horse lying on the ground. And the

uyohlv   nogwu   usgasdanele.   "sogwili   eniyo'a,"   udvhne.
shot it   then   was getting scared   a horse   we shot   he said
one who had shot it then became afraid. "We shot a horse," he said.

"Hiyo'ega!"   Agosele.
YOU shot it   he was told
"YOU shot it," he was told.

SENECA-CAYUGA

Minnie Thompson Stories

Narrated by Minnie Thompson
Recorded and transcribed by J. W. Tyner

At the time of the interview Minnie Thompson was eighty years of age. Mrs. Thompson has lived in the community of Turkey Ford, Ottawa County, Oklahoma, all of her life. She was the official caretaker of the Seneca-Cayuga meeting grounds. All of her education was obtained at the Wyandotte School.

Mixing Tribal Languages

Cayuga and Seneca, you know
Now Seneca some of their language I don't understand their words
But the Cayuga I can understand nearly everything they say
They said we speak the same language not much of Seneca
They're mixed up
—speak it now
There's a woman trying to reach 'em, but she can't reach 'em
She don't know too much of it herself
You can't learn
You got to speak it from baby on up
Everyday, too
Forget
And you can't just say it right off
Right quick
Wyandotte school
They've even got maids up there
Call 'em grandmother
They call 'em

Children Indian Schools

Kids don't even have to work
Those grandmothers take care of 'em
Well, there's just not very many Senecas going
Only Cherokees and different tribes
They're from broken homes

Grist Mills

It was down south of Tiff
Tiff City
Just Buffalo
They used to have a mill there
People took their corn
Had it ground into meal and flour
When it thrashed we'd haul our wheat
And get flour, you know
Start off in the morning and
Wouldn't get back till night
Twelve or thirteen miles
That's a long ways to drive
A horse
No, no it wasn't
Winding roads

Foods and Clothing in Early Days

Calico was so cheap that you could buy
Enough to make you a dress and
Get a package of coffee, little package
Of sugar
You had your own meat
People, you know, neighbors butcher
A cow and then go around and peddle it
Buy meat
Put up your own hogs
Fatten them

Salt it down in the fall
And winter, you know
Still have meat and lard away
In the summer
Somehow meat don't keep
Anymore
No
They raise tobacco
In their fields
In their garden
I lost a real nice-looking garden
I don't plant anymore
I used to have a corn patch
And I used to dry corn every year
We made bread from fresh corn grated
Put in the pan, dough in the pan like
And then back it
When it's done just crumble it up
And dry it in the sun
Well you can boil it and cut it
Off the cob and dry it
Soup corn
You can buy that now
Yes, you can buy it in the stores
Fifty cents a can about this size

Medicines Were Made By Indians

They learned that from the Indians
No, they didn't make that either
And mullein
And he makes—cotton—horehand [horehound?]
Make syrup out of it
Makes a good cough syrup
She used to use on her children
Not me

Turkey Ford Country

In the Turkey Ford country of Ottawa County is Bassett Grove, the principal meeting grounds of the Seneca-Cayuga Indians. Within the some ten acres within the fenced area of the meeting grounds are the several houses surrounding the Long House. Also there are many camp lots of individual Indian families that they maintain themselves. The home of Minnie Thompson is in this fenced area and she is the official caretaker of the grounds. Adjoining the meeting grounds on the west is the Bassett Grove Cemetery, one of the two burial grounds used by this tribe.

Bassett Grove was named for Joe Bassett, an early-day Indian whose land joined the meeting grounds. The area that is known as Turkey Ford was named for Mandy Turkey, a Seneca of long ago who lived at the crossing, or ford, on Elk River (sometimes called Cowskin River).

Of the many Indian tribes to be moved to Indian Territory, the Seneca-Cayuga were among the first. It is recorded that they first came to Oklahoma in 1832. On a historical plaque beside a highway north of the Seneca country it tells: "SENECA AGENCY. About 12 miles south. Established July 4, 1832 near Buffalo Creek for Senecas, Cayugas, Shawnees and remnants of six other tribes that came from Ohio over a Trail of Tears as the United Nation. They signed first treaty on December 29, 1832, made by U. S. commissioners Henry Ellsworth and John Schermerhorn, on Indian Territory. Ex-Governor Stokes, North Carolina, headed the Commission and was U. S. Agent for these tribes in 1836–37." This brief account of an event in history tells much more than a first observance reveals and brings on many questions: How many Indians of each tribe? Who were the chiefs and leaders, and who were the "remnants of six other tribes"? Why did there have to be a "Trail of Tears"? Is the historical marker a memorial to the three white men and their deeds or the epitaph of a race of people? There is no longer a Seneca-Cayuga Nation—the white men have taken care of that. But in a brief period of time in the history of the world these people did live, and it is of this span that Mrs. Thompson speaks.

Before the coming of Grand Lake, the formation of Cowskin Bay, and the great invasion of white people and foreigners, the Seneca-Cayuga had another meeting ground on Elk River just south of Bassett Grove. She says that there used to be many Indians living in that part of the old Seneca Nation, but most of them are gone now. They were concentrated along the Neosho River, Elk River, and Buffalo Creek and east to the Missouri line.

She reflects on many things of the past. One of her very close friends was Berta Cedar, who was the daughter of Mandy Turkey. Another lifelong friend was Mamie Long. She and these two older Indians were among the last who knew the woods and streams and the wealth of nature-provided plants, herbs, bark, and other things that were used for Indian medicine. From revered Indian doctors they learned much, and through their lives they preferred the old-time remedies to the more modern shot in the arm or a vial of pills. Along with the changing times, the Indians now "want to get well quick," like the white man, and the waiting rooms of Indian hospitals, clinics, and doctors' offices are crowded today. When the older Indians of their generation pass on, so will the great store of knowledge of the sources of most present-day medicines, for today the synthetics, chemicals, and related materials have replaced the use of medical plants and herbs. There was a time long ago when the herb gatherers, in the early morning, would kneel by the healing plants and offer "sacred tobacco" and chant a prayer. The "civilized" Indian has forgotten, or never knew, much of the bountiful spread nature provides. Other than the older Indians few could go out and gather one of the snakeroots, yellowwood, puccoon, mullein, horehound, wild ginger, or any of the hundreds of plants beneficial to man.

Most of the old location of Turkey Ford settlement is now under water, but there was at one time a trading post there and from 1905 to sometime in the 1950s a post office functioned for the area. All the places of the olden days are gone now. No longer can the Indian hunt the squirrel or fish in unpolluted waters. For few are the places along the hundreds of miles of lakeshore that are not private property, and woe be unto any Indian who would trespass. The attitude of the owners of the lakeside cabin lands has perhaps changed little from the days of the mid-1800s, when Indians were shot down for walking across a white man's land. Minnie says, "I get sick of it sometimes," referring to the way the white man has invaded and taken over the Indian country. Looking to the future as regards the Indian, she says, "I don't want to be here then." She adds that the time will come when the Indian will be past being an Indian, and there will no more be any Indian country: "It will be Indians with no country as they have taken it away from us."

In the days of the Indian Territory a few of the many Indians who lived in the Turkey Ford area included the Balls, Spicers, Whitecrows, Splitlogs, Bee, Crow, Chateau, Whitetree, Charloe, Peacock, White, Cedar, Long, Thompson, Williams, Logan, Bassett, Bearskin, Young, Birdsong, and Whitewing.

Minnie Thompson tells that across the river south of Bassett Grove is a place known as Cayuga. In the old days Mathias Splitlog, who was of mixed Seneca, Cayuga, Mohawk, and Tuscarora blood, became a very wealthy Indian. Mathias Splitlog lies at rest in the little Cayuga cemetery in the courtyard of the beautiful tone church that he built for his people.

Minnie Thompson tells that her people were Seneca-Cayuga, and that most of the language spoken was basically Cayuga. As time has moved on the Seneca and the Cayuga languages have somewhat become one. She speaks what she refers to as the Cayuga language, and although the Seneca language is intertwined, she says there is some of the original Seneca that she does not understand. She states that the tribal language is being preserved in the families, as well as classes being conducted at different places in Ottawa County. To the Seneca-Cayuga it is important that their young people have knowledge of their language and heritage. To have full command of the language, or any Indian language, one almost has to speak it from time of baby, and speak it every day.

Mrs. Thompson's education was all obtained at Wyandotte Indian School, which was in the years before World War I. She says much has changed in the schools since her attendance. She says now they have "grandmothers" at the schools to take care of the kids and see to their needs and guidance. In her school days the children were "on their own" for whatever education they got. Nowadays, she says, the children at Indian schools "don't even have to work."

In the days of the Indian Territory there were few stores or trading posts in the Seneca Nation. She remembers that Turkey Ford was the first store her folks went to for trading. Later there was the Hensley store farther up on Cowskin River. She says Grove was just a little place with only one store when she was a little girl. Tiff City, Missouri, located on the state line, is a very old settlement, and in early days many Indians traveled there to trade and get their corn ground. However, the grist mill was on the Indian Territory side of the line on Buffalo Creek. In later years there was a grist mill at Seneca, Missouri, where many went to get meal ground and to trade. She says Tiff City in its early days was a bad place, as killings and whiskey peddling and other unpleasant things took place there. She still remembers traveling in a wagon some fourteen miles over almost non-existent roads from their home to Seneca, Missouri. She tells that the family used to buy calico cloth for six to ten cents a yard. Somehow they would manage to buy some sugar and coffee, which were very much the luxury staples of that time. At home they always had plenty to eat as there was wild game everywhere and fish in all the streams. Some neighbor was always butchering beef and distributing it among the community. Very little "store tobacco" was purchased in the old days, as most families grew their own in their gardens. Now less than half a dozen people grow any tobacco in her country. Some of the tobacco still raised is the "sacred tobacco" used in rituals and ceremonials. The sacred tobacco is used at funerals, dances, naming of babies, prayer time, and so on.

Corn has always been the "stuff of life" to the Indian, and she tells about the different ways it can be used. In what she calls the "dough time" of the green corn (roasting ear stage), there are many ways it is used and cooked as stew, soup, dumplings, and even as a bread. As the corn matures it takes on other uses such as poaching, grinding to make a beverage, meal, and so on. At a certain stage in the growth of young corn it is gathered for "soup corn."

Talking again about plants and herbs, she says many have disappeared with the clearing and development of the land by white men. One plant still to be found and used is what the Indians call *nun-ka-ga-na-yont,* or 'strong medicine.' It is used to "clean you out" when the winter months have passed. It is very bitter and will make you sick for a while, but take three doses and the white scalps hanging high will take on a new beauty.

WYANDOTTE

History of the Wyandotte Indians

Donna Elliott Vowel interviewed by J. W. Tyner

The history of the Wyandotte Indians fits well into that of the great area of central North America, for it tells of a once-great nation of some 20,000 people in the mid-seventeenth century whose numbers had been reduced to only 222 by 1872, then living in the Indian Territory. In the early history of the Wyandottes, they occupied all of what is now Ohio, a part of Indiana, and perhaps a part of the southern portion of Ontario, Canada. Demands by a growing white nation, a government that opposed the existence of Indians in general, diseases introduced by foreigners, loss of lands and hunting grounds, and other factors through the years now show, at this point in the twentieth century, what has become of a minority group.

After the government took the Wyandotte lands in the north-central United States these Indians were forcibly moved to an area that now includes Kansas City, Kansas. Perhaps the Wyandottes were more fortunate in their removal than some of the other Indian tribes, as they were transported on flat boats. On arrival at their new designated land, in about 1840, the Indians spent the winter on the east side of the Missouri River. The following spring they moved across the river and settled in what became Wyandotte County, Kansas. These tribespeople were known as good agriculturalists and at once adapted themselves to a new and fertile land. Hardly had they become settled and established when the black cloud of white invasion again caught up with them. Demands of white settlers were heard by the government men in Washington, and again, what remained of the Wyandotte Nation was uprooted and moved to Indian Territory around 1857. The Indians were convinced that "might was right" in their circumstance. For most Indian tribes across the country there was a piece of land set aside by the government when they were moved. But not in the case of the Wyandottes—they were simply moved to and "dumped" across the Kansas line into Indian Territory. The Seneca Nation came to their assistance and gave them a tract of land across their own northern reservation.

A recent census is not available, but in 1940 the tribe numbered less than one thousand members. By now it is doubtful that there is a full blood Wyandotte living, for at that time there were only three full bloods counted in the census, and nearly seven hundred had less than one-quarter Indian blood.

In a treaty of 1855, the government did set aside three acres for a Indian tribal cemetery in Kansas City, which was established when the tribe was moved from the Ohio region. The tribe still claims these three acres, now in the middle of the downtown business area of Kansas City, Kansas, although somehow it has been reduced to 1.9 acres. What will eventually happen there at 7th and Minnesota Streets is not certain, but if Indian graves are respected the same as white people's graves, it will remain a long time.

Beginning at the time when the Wyandottes left Ohio under the leadership of their chief, Francis A. Hicks, the tribe has had many able leaders. Some of those chiefs were Loren Zane, George Long, and Little Tom Spicer. Chief Leonard Cotter is their able leader at present.

The early settlement of the Wyandotte families was along Lost Creek and Sycamore Creek, from the area of Wyandotte town northeast to the Missouri [state] line. The valleys through which these streams ran were and still are fine farming land. The wooded hills afforded needed timber and excellent hunting grounds. Some of those Indian original settlers included Zane, Spicer, Walker, Elliott, Lofland, Harris, Wright, Hodgekiss, Brown, Peacock, Sarahass, Long, and Cotter.

About 1893 the government made allotments of land in severalty of the Wyandotte Reservation to some 241 Indians, thus ending an area that was the Wyandotte Reservation. Adults got 160 acres of land, and minors got 40 acres. Very few of the Indians still own any of the land that was originally allotted. Descendants of the Elliott family still have their land. Mrs. Vowel has the original deed on which 160 acres was allotted to her father, Isaac Elliott, in 1892.

Mrs. Vowel says that most of the early-day Indians did not understand any of the treaty matters, and certainly none of the removal actions. She says that the Indians were told that they were being moved to a new and better land that would be theirs forever. Many of the Indians held to the thought that they could continue living their own way of life for hundreds of years.

As evidence of the fact that the Wyandottes are a diminishing tribe is that they held their last Green Corn Dance in 1936. The old tribal stomp grounds was located at the foot of the hill by the present Seneca Indian School.

Of the many Wyandottes who contributed to the welfare and strength of the tribe, one B. N. O. Walker is frequently mentioned. He was born in 1870 at Kansas City and was buried in the family cemetery on Lost Creek in 1927. For many years he was chief clerk in the Quapaw Indian Agency. He was also an accomplished musician, singer, and poet. Writing under his Indian name, Hen-toh, he recorded history and stories [blank space] . . . sincere effort is being made to preserve the Wyandotte language. Because these Indians have intermarried with other tribes and the white race most of their customs, beliefs, and ways of life have disappeared. However, some of the recipes for their native Indian dishes have been preserved and are still used.

She [Mrs. Vowel] recalls her older folks tell that in the early days the Wyandotte Reservation was thinly settled, primarily because there were very few of their people. She tells that an uncle used to ride for miles to visit the next neighbor. To most of the Indians the trips to Seneca, Missouri, for buying and trading also afforded an opportunity to visit with friends of their own and other tribes of this part of Indian Territory. Their neighboring tribes included the Seneca-Cayugas, Eastern Shawnees, Modocs, Peorias, Quapaws, and Ottawas.

Life on the reservation in the olden days was one of nearly complete self-sufficiency. The families provided for their every need, as it was a matter of necessity. They were good farmers and woodsmen, as well as hunters and traders, and there was little else they had need of. In comparison, the Wyandottes were a peaceful and industrious people, and they lived in a sincere attitude of thankfulness and reverence of their Creator.

Mrs. Vowel relates that Christianity did not come to the Wyandottes until early in the nineteenth century. After a missionary had been killed, the Christian way of life was brought to them in the form of an orphaned Negro boy.

PART FIVE

Kiowa-Tanoan Language Family

KIOWA

Ją́:mátàunhè̀:jègà (Star Girls Story)

Narrated, transcribed, and translated by Parker P. McKenzie

Retranslated and introduced by Gus pànthại:dê Palmer

"Ją́:mátàunhè̀:jègà" (Star Girls Story) is among the oldest stories in the Kiowa oral tradition. No one knows the author of the original story. I have heard many versions of the Star Girls Story. The one I retranscribed and retranslated was by Kiowa linguist Parker P. McKenzie (1897–1999). I accomplished this utilizing the writing system invented by McKenzie. Linguist John P. Harrington, who compiled the first in-depth study of Kiowa, was an acquaintance of McKenzie at the Anadarko Area Office, where McKenzie worked. Harrington, assisted by McKenzie, published *Vocabulary of the Kiowa Indians* in 1928.[1] The volume first appeared as a bulletin in the series of annual reports published by the Bureau of American Ethnology (originally, Bureau of Ethnology). The BAE was established in 1879 by an act of Congress for the purpose of transferring archives, records, and materials relating to the Indians of North America from the Department of the Interior. John Wesley Powell, founding director of the BAE, headed up the bureau for many years. Other early field-workers associated with the BAE were Franz Boas, Frank Hamilton Cushing, Alice Cunningham Fletcher, Francis La Flesche, Clark Wissler, James Mooney, and James Owen Dorsey, to name a few. These ethnographers were among the first field-workers responsible for the documentation of many American Indians of North America.

At the center of the Star Girls story is Xoa:dàu, 'Rock Tree,' commonly known as Devils Tower, and how it came to be. Devils Tower itself is a great igneous monolith that juts out of the earth in northeast Wyoming. Declared a national monument in 1906 by Theodore Roosevelt, Devils Tower is an important site to Plains tribes, who also tell their own versions of how Devils Tower came to be. Tribal delegations often visit the site to pray and conduct ceremonies significant to them.

According to Kiowa legend, there were seven girls playing bear when suddenly one of them turned into a bear. For Kiowas, who venerated and even feared bears, such an act was high-risk, perhaps even treasonous. At best it is a story of great daring, almost heroic. For such an act of daring, one might suspect the original story implied a certain kind of personal disposition against tribal beliefs, that at center it was meant to confront a long-held taboo, to discourage or change it. We don't know this but we get the idea that this might be the case. Great literature holds many such elements to provoke thought.

In this story the children are all girls. In other, older versions they are boys or a combination of boys and girls.[2] Like most stories, each telling changes according to the storyteller. In *The Way to Rainy Mountain*, Kiowa poet and painter N. Scott Momaday writes, "Eight children were there at play, seven sisters and their brother" (1969, 8).

The Star Girls Story is a magical tale. The transformation of the girl into a bear is a hallmark of magical realism, much in the manner of storytelling by South American novelist Gabriel García Márquez, and North American novelists Gerald Vizenor, Louise Erdrich, and Sherman Alexie, to name a few. Other examples of surrealism in the story include the flat rock that transports the children into the heavens; the great bear, scoring the side of the monolith with steel-like claws to reach the children; the children forming the constellation Pleiades; and, finally, the transformation of the flat rock into Devils Tower itself.

Storytellers take liberties when telling stories because it suits them to. Cherokee novelist Thomas King writes, "I've heard this story many times, and each time someone tells the story, it changes. [He is referring to stories generally, not the Star Girls Story.] Sometimes the change is simply in the details. Sometimes in the order of events. Other times it's the dialogue or the response of the audience . . ." (1992, 1). Indeed, stories change every time they are told. Stories evoke the deepest human emotions, dreams. In a recent interview N. Scott Momaday informed the interviewer that he occasionally turned into a bear. It was his way of conveying the essence of a bear taken on by the writer. The implication is an animal, even a bear, can be manifested in a man at the behest of the man himself. We are of course assured of this metamorphosis when we read Momaday's novel *The Ancient Child*; or when we read Franz Kafka's *Metamorphosis*, where the main character, Gregor Samsa, transforms into an insect; or in Homer's *Odyssey*, where Odysseus's crew turn into swine; or in John Keats's poem "Lamia," where the transformation of a serpent into a woman occurs. I find these notions of transformation of objects and people exceedingly powerful and useful in oral tradition as well as in writing. Even the most skeptical of readers finds satisfaction in the realm of the metaphysical in literature. In Kiowa storytelling, the Star Girls Story carries the notion of medicine, magic, and power in the most classical way.

Parker McKenzie transcribed "Ją:matàunhè:jègà" in the writing system he invented around 1920. The Star Girls Story is but one of many traditional Kiowa stories McKenzie transcribed and translated during his lifetime. Parker was fond of telling stories and then transcribing them into his system of writing. He would include voluminous notes about the structure of Kiowa, explicating lexical and syntactic forms that occur in storytelling, as well as tribal myths, history, and cosmology. He liked to talk about the connection of the Kiowa people to the cosmos. In this particular story he offered much detail about how the stars were connected to the Kiowa people in the earliest accounts of Kiowa origins. He believed there were many symbolic images and meanings in stories and that they helped to explain many wonderful things about the world, people, and life. I took a few liberties in spelling some Kiowa words, for instance in marking vowel features. For example I do not mark high tones for vowels nor do I capitalize the initial word of sentences or proper names. I also replace the macron or overscore with a colon (:) to mark vowel length. These were convenient methods for calling attention to the sound elements of spoken Kiowa. The standard typewriter was the extent of technology available to McKenzie when he was assembling his orthography. The young linguist substituted other English letters for distinctive (phonemic) sounds noted in the writing system below.

In this story I have tried to stay as close in spirit to the original story told long ago and handed down in spoken Kiowa.

Kiowa Writing System

CONSONANTS

There are thirty-two consonantal sounds in Kiowa. While there are fourteen consonants that are the same in English, the remaining eight are variations of /p/ /k/ /t/ and /c/, what Parker McKenzie called the "distinctive" Kiowa sounds. The first group is unaspirated /p/ /t/ /k/. These so-called soft consonantal sounds McKenzie lists as *f* /p/, *c* /k/, and *j* /t/, respectively. Such sounds occur in words as the soft 'p' sound in 'spot,' the soft 'k' sound that occurs in 'Scot,' and the soft 't' in 'stop.' These soft or unaspirated sounds are generally unnoticed in English because they do not occur in word-initial position, as in many Kiowa words.

Kiowa also has so-called hard or ejective consonant sounds. They are listed in the McKenzie system as *v* /p'/, *q* /k'/, *th* /t'/, *ch* /c/, and *x* /c'/. Like the soft consonants, these sounds can be easily pronounced with practice just like their consonantal counterparts in the Kiowa alphabet. All the remaining Kiowa consonants are equivalent to English sounds.

THE PALATAL GLIDE /Y/

In Kiowa when the consonants /c/, /g/, /k/, and /q/ precede the vowels /a/ and /ai/, there is a 'y' sound, so *ca* is pronounced 'cya,' *ga* is pronounced 'gya,' *ka* is pronounced 'kya,' and *qa* is pronounced 'qya,' respectively. Although the McKenzie system does not mark the glide in the environment where it occurs, it is understood to be there nonetheless.

Some Kiowa words where the palatal glide occurs are:

KIOWA WORD	PRONOUNCED	ENGLISH
qá:hî̱	k'yá:hî̱	'man'
kâi:gùn	khyáy:gùn	'jump'
Câigù	kyâygù	'Comanche'
cúngà	kúngyà	'dance'

While many young Kiowa writers include the glide in their transcriptions, I eliminate its use as described by McKenzie.

VOWELS

There are ten vowel elements in Kiowa. Six of these are vowels and four are diphthongs; they are sounds made like those in English. When they are combined with consonants and given qualities of tone, length, and nasality, the vowels and diphthongs become sounds that are characteristically Kiowa.

The ten-vowel inventory comprises the following symbols and sounds:

i pronounced 'ee' as in 'feet'
e pronounced 'ay' as in 'day'

a	pronounced	'ah' as in 'f**a**ther'
u	pronounced	'oo' as in 'b**oo**t'
o	pronounced	'oh' as in 'b**oa**t'
au	pronounced	'aw' as in 'c**au**ght'
ai	pronounced	'ahy' as in 'wr**i**te'
ui	pronounced	'ooy' as in 'ph**ooey**'
oi	pronounced	'owy' as in 't**oy**'
aui	pronounced	'awy'

Tone

All Kiowa vowels possess tone. Tones can be high, low, or high-low. Tones are indicated by markers over the vowel. High tones may be found in such words as *fái* ('sun'), *són* ('grass'), and *fígá* ('food'). Low tones are found in words like *hàu:* ('yes'), *gàu* ('and'), and *nàu* ('but,' 'I,' 'me,' 'my,' 'our'). High-low tones are found in such words as *chê* ('horse') and *zêbàut* ('arrow'). In my writing I have dropped the use of the high tone marker, hence *fai, son*, and *fi:ga*, as readers will note in the transcription below.

Length

Vowels may also have length as a contrasting element in pronunciation and meaning. In the McKenzie system length is noted by a macron or overscore over the vowel, while I incorporate a colon (:) in mine. Importantly length indicates a drawn-out vowel pronunciation. Such words as *xó:* ('stone') and *já:* ('star') have a high tone and length. There are many Kiowa words where length is a critical factor in denoting the meaning of words.

Nasality

Many Kiowa vowels are nasalized. Accordingly the nasal marker is indicated by a line drawn underneath the vowel, as in words *chê* ('horse'), *fí:gá* ('food'), *háu:tò* ('axe'), *páò* ('three'), *pái* ('dirt'), *kó:gí* ('grandfather'), *tá:cí* ('maternal grandmother'), and *jógá* ('speak,' 'word,' 'language'). Conversely the elimination of the high tone marker for the same lexical items would appear as *chê, fi:ga, hau:tò, paò, pai, ko:gi, ta:ci,* and *jo:ga* In diphthongs, the first vowel is underscored although the entire diphthong is sounded as one nasal unit.

Pronunciation Table

The following table lists the American Phonetic Alphabet (APA) and corresponding Parker McKenzie Kiowa orthographic symbols and descriptions for consonants and vowels.

Consonants

STOPS	UNASPIRATED	ASPIRATED	GLOTTAL	VOICED
Labial	p	ph	p'	b
Parker McKenzie	*f*	*p*	*v*	*b*
Dental	t	th	t'	d
Parker McKenzie	*j*	*t*	*th*	*d*
Velar	k	kh	k'	g
Parker McKenzie	*c*	*k*	*q*	*g*

AFFRICATIVES				
Dental	c		c'	
Parker McKenzie	*ch*		*x*	

The remaining consonants are the same as they are in English and include: *h*, *l*, *m*, *n*, *s*, *w*, *y*, and *z*.

VOWELS	*i*	*u*
	e	*o*
	a	*au* [ɔ]
DIPHTHONGS	*ai*	*ui*
	oi	*aui*

Tone	high (*a*)	low (*à*)	high/low (*â*)
Length	colon	(:)	
Nasalization	underscore	(a̱)	

Já̱:mátàunhè̱:jègà (Star Girls Story)

1 habe cauigu a ci:dê nàu sā̱:dàu maun et yai:à̱u:mè. "het, be àunha:dé yàiàum, fa matàun," ø jo̱:nê, ne matàun setàlmà kau:dêdè haun ø a̱u:nâuhèl. bôt maun gà fe:lê. haun àn châu em yai:à̱u:mè cauigu.

The Kiowas were once camping when some children began to play. Directly one of the little girls said, "Let's play bear," but one girl who was called Bear-Chasing-Woman objected because it was taboo. Kiowas did not play such games.

2 "dè ci:gòp," ø jo̱:nê. "a̱u:gàu be caunyàiàum," ø jo̱:nê. Betàu gà îldą̀u:mè. e yài:sètàumdèthàu: nàu haun ø cò:doą̀u:nàu:hèl.
"I am fearful," she said. "Play yourselves." Apparently such things were forbidden. They had asked her to play bear but she protested seriously against it.

3 ha:bêl e bò:jàu:yì: nègau hègau ha:òi ø alaumdehèl gàu ø jo̱:nê, "dè ci:gòp. bà jo̱:gà 'ha̱u:né' ne haun bà thau:yâu nàu dè kosètą̀umjàu: nàu hègau haya gà dau:thau:. bà ha:be:," ø jo̱:nê.
They persisted until finally she accepted. "All right, all right. I'm fearful. I said no but you all wouldn't listen so I'm going to pretend I'm a bear and we'll see what happens. All right? You all are too much."

4 avì:jè syaunhèldè hègau ø je:lê, "dè kosetàumjàu: nàu e̱ jau:bè haiò̱:dè. [Aside:] hau hègau haiò̱:dè yan hai:gadàu:, hą̀u?"
Then she warned her little sister, "When I make myself into a bear, keep a close watch on me. [Aside:] You understanding this clearly?"

5 "jôi à he:bèthàu: gàu dè tonkùljàu: nàu haiò̱:dè e̱ jau:bà. [Aside:] hau hègau èm thau:dâu:?"
"Observe closely when I enter the tipi and when I exit. [Aside:] Are you listening to what I'm saying here? Are y'all understanding anything clearly?"

6 "hayatjò à obòisètàumjàudè," ø jo̱:nê."
"I might truly change into a bear."

7 "dè yaugùtònkùljàu:chè̱: hègau hayatjò setmaunxo̱ e̱ qia:dàu:thàu:," ø jo̱:nê."
"I might come out of there next time with bear claws coming out of my hands, you know."

8 "dè pa̱òkùljàu nàu mauncù haiò̱:dè bàt bo̱:," ø jo̱:nê."
"When I exit the third time, look closely at my hands," she said.

9 "hayatjò mauncù emgàu ne dau:chèm pau:ga y<u>a</u> qia:dàu:thàu: nègau bàt càuetà:ài."
"If I have furry hands, run for your life."

10 "ch<u>ê</u>h<u>ì</u>ì:còmjò: bàt dôn gàu bàt t<u>a</u>u:jau: gìgau au:hyàu: èm he:bè. fòi èm kîthàu, maunsepmà:," ø j<u>o</u>:nê. "haun àn èm thau:yâu," ø j<u>o</u>:nê.
"Seek out a mother dog's den and enter it. Do not come out either, you wild girl," she said. "You never listen."

11 "Hègau ha:òi à âuichànthàu gàu èm kaumjau, nègau ôihyàu èm kî."
"Eventually I'll return and call out to you. That's when you can come out."

12 <u>a</u>:kô, hègau setàlmà èm yaisèt<u>a</u>u:mè gàu hègau mat<u>a</u>u:dàu: e a:lê.
With that, Bear-Chasing-Woman pretended she was a bear and began chasing the little girls.

13 nègau matàun avì:jè augàu je:lêdèchò hegáu ø jahòtg<u>ù</u>:yì:.
And so her little sister did as she was told and kept an eye on her.

14 am ø j<u>o</u>:nêdèchò èm p<u>a</u>òkùlhèl gìgau màuntal:âugì:fè hègau ø pau: a qià:d<u>a</u>u:mè: nègau gà càuetà:ài:hyèl gìgau am àn c<u>a</u>umè:dèchò ch<u>ê</u>h<u>ì</u>:ìcòmjò gà j<u>o</u>:âihèl.
Just as she had told her, the third time she exited all along her hands fur was growing and she [the little girl] ran for her life just like she was told and looked for a mother dog's den.

15 gà t<u>a</u>u:hêl gìgau au:hàu: ø he:bèhèldèòi hègau avì:jè s<u>a</u>dàu e holê fan:y<u>a</u>.
She found one and crawled inside, for by then her sister had killed the others one by one.

16 <u>a</u>:kô, avì:jè hègau ø k<u>a</u>umè nègau ø kîhèl.
And so she called out to her sister and she exited.

17 betàu àunsôifà ø gu:fêd<u>a</u>u:mè.
She had apparently been wounded on the foot.

18 gàu avì:jè ø fàuhihèl gàu jo:h<u>î</u> gà ethêldéè<u>e</u>: hègau ø fàu:he:behèl gàu men màuho:gaihyèl nègau, ø j<u>ó</u>:nê: "à tau:h<u>ê</u>mà. èm ba gàu câul pòl<u>a</u>:yì à hô gàu à bau:" ø j<u>o</u>:nê.

She took her sister to the large tipi and led her into it and when they were settled, she said, "I am hungry. Go and kill a rabbit and bring it back here."

19 nàu hègau e̱:dè ø e̱:bà:hèl haya augàu avì:jè an ca̱u:mîdèchò gàu kâun ø au:lyî. máun cholhàu ø au:lyî nègau maun aja̱u:dàu tàlyop è é̱:tòyà gàu e qàujèhèl gìgau e chà:lê, "náuhâundo èm autto:yà?" è jo̱:nê.
And so this one went hunting just like she was told and was crying. Apparently as she was crying her brothers, who had been out hunting, were returning to camp and asked why she was crying.

20 "matàunyàul ø seta̱umga gàu je: èm àutâun. náu a̱u:gàu gà ki:bo̱:. e̱:gàu jau: nau a̱u:. 'háun pola̱:yi à ho:lîjàu: nàu èm holjàu,' ø jo̱:gà dò à màucauàut:tò:yà."
"Crazy woman turned into a bear and annihilated everybody, and I am the sole survivor. She gave me this rabbit-killing club and said, 'If you don't kill a rabbit and bring it back, I'll destroy you,' she said, and that's why I'm wandering about hopelessly."

21 nàu aja̱u:jè augàu ø etha:dè ø jo̱:nê, "het jau: à báu:."
And so her big brother said, "Let me have that rabbit-killing club there."

22 nàu jau: a a̱u:hèl nàu èm a̱u:zonhêl gàu pòla̱:yì ø bo̱:hêl sondo̱:gà.
She gave him the rabbit-killing club and he went off and saw a rabbit in the grass.

23 nàu hègau jau: ø jo̱:ta:hèl gàu ø jo̱:nê, "pòla̱:yì augàu ø qau:dè gàu qi:jàu nàu fê:dè bàt ai gàu ga gu:fâ kô:va̱uigà," ø jo̱:nê.
And he told the rabbit-killing stick, "That rabbit lying there, I'm going to throw at it, so fly straight for it and hit it right in the middle."

24 gìgau jau: ø qi:hèl nàu pòla̱:yì a gu:fâ gàu ø holhèl.
And so he threw, hit the rabbit, and killed it.

25 "jau: gàu pòla̱:yì mèn kohì:," aja̱u:jè ø jo̱:nê. "gàu alfi:jáu: nàu bat jemdètà:ài:. "hau hègau haio̱:dè: yan hai:ga:dàu?"
"Take the rabbit-killing stick and rabbit," her brother said. "If she disputes you didn't kill it, blare it out of there. Do you understand clearly now?"

26 nàu e̱:dè hàu:, ø jo̱:nê.
And this one said yes.

27 nègau matàun pòla̱:yì ø hau:hèl gìgau avì:jèè̱: ø câunhèl.
And so the girl took the rabbit and brought it to her sister.

28 nègau avì:jè setàlmà ø cha:lê, "hau: a̱u:gàu à oboihol, ha̱u?"
And so her sister, Bear-Chasing-Woman, asked her, "Did you truly kill it by yourself?"

29 nàu matàun ø jo̱:nê, "hàu:, a̱u:gàu gà hol."
The girl said, "Indeed. I did kill it myself."

30 nàu e̱:dè, "nàu het ai à xo: gàu da̱u:àise̱:gà ga gu:fê," ø jó̱:nê, setàlmà.
This one said, "So put it on a limb and hit it right in the wound of it."

31 nègau jau ø hau:hèl gìgau pòla̱:yì ø qi:hèl gàu ø jo̱:nê, "semàunzàigù bàt âi gàu ga gu:fe!"
And so she took the rabbit. She threw it, saying, "Hit it right in the center of its business."

32 à:kô, cholhàu hègau a gu:fâhèl gàu ø ki:bo̱:hèl. [Aside:] "hau hègau tha:gà èm thau:dâu:?"
And so that's exactly how she hit and killed it. [Aside:] "Do you hear me clearly?"

33 "nàu hàu:," ø jo̱:nê. hègau habêkì: matàun maun ø fi̱:òbàjàubà:hèl gìgau aja̱u:dàu é âuiqàujèhèl, a:dòmgà.
"Well, all right," she said. One day the little girl went looking for food and met her brothers in the woods again.

34 nègau augàu ø etha:dè ø jo̱:nê, "e̱:gàu èm a̱:che̱: chô̱:gau gàu qâugàu gàu autcàu gà se:beha:dè:àl bàt jo:je gàu bàt hî:. bàt hi: gàu daumgu bàt sau: jo:hi̱chàtcà."
Then the big brother said, "As you come along, gather awls, knives, and any sharp-pointed objects and carry them to the tipi and stick them with the sharp-pointed end out of the ground, just outside the door."

35 "à:kô, be qi:he:be, nègau amàn chatkòpcàut èm to̱:a̱umthàudèjàuchè̱ qi: àunsotài â vèl gìgau sauidè bè kûl."

"Now, build a fire, and when she stretches her legs toward the door as she customarily does, spill the wood on her foot and beat it out of there."

36 "tau:chò èm jembeà: gàu èm chanthàu: nègau bagî kòbèài, cap."
"Beat it this way and when you arrive here, we'll all take off in the opposite direction."

37 nègau e̱:dè qi ø jojehèl gàu jo:hî gà sauldeè̱: ø qihe:behèl.
Thereupon she gathered wood and she took it to the tipi.

38 augàu avì:jè ø a̱:gàdee̱̱̱ ø ba gàu hègau qi àunsotai a vetjehèl.
Where her sister was sitting she brought the wood and dropped it on her foot.

39 setàlmà èm ciàutà:dèhèl. "saupôl! hègau àunsôi e̱ àunzo̱̱i!"
Bear-Chasing-Woman cried out, "Fool! You've smashed my foot!"

40 hègau avì:jè èm tonkùlhèl gìgau chatca èm yaldahà:hèl gìgau autcàu matàun ø dau:hi:hèldeèm ø qau:ba:heà:lè.
Her sister pursued her out the door, racing crazily after the girl and tripping as she raced along.

41 gìgau èm se:behèl augàu cho̱̱:gáu gàu qâugàu gà sauldeè̱.
And so she stabbed herself on the awls and knives that were set out.

42 nègau matàun aja̱̱u:dàu augàu è au:dè:deèm gà âihyèl.
So the girl ran to where her brothers waited.

43 nàu emchò avì:jè setàlmà ø tona̱̱:hèl, gàu gà zelbehêl.
And over here her sister, Bear-Chasing-Woman, chased her, and it was awful.

44 matàun gàu aja̱̱u:dàu cap et càuetà:àihèl.
The girl and her brothers scattered in the opposite direction.

45 habê gà da̱u:mêe̱ gôm et bo̱:hèl nàu hègau o:gâu ø ve:dèhèl àunha:dè.
Every so often they glanced backward and shortly the bear appeared.

46 hegau sâuiàumgàhe̱̱: àunhadè edê qaujeà:hèl nègau ôihyàu et ci:àuthà:dèhèldècàu:gàu haunde tho:ga sondo̱̱:gà an jo̱aunhèl.

And so the bear chased them, closing in on them as they cried out fearfully, whereupon something made a noise under the grass ahead of them.

47 "tau:chò! tau:chò! emchò bà a̱:! haòbà gà chaimethau:àl yi:câdò au: qobe bedê ai gìgau tai bedê gun gàu bà jo̱i, 'mai! mai bàt ai, xo:êl!'"
"Come this way! Come this way! This way you all come! No matter how much time it takes circle me four times and jump on top of me and shout, 'Up! Rise up, Big Rock!'"

48 nègau yi:câdò e màugùihyèl gìgau tai edê pa̱u:hèl nègau è jo̱:nê, "xo:êl, mai bàt ai! mai bàt ai!"
So they circled four times and jumped on top, shouting, "Big Rock, rise up! Rise up!"

49 nàu e̱:dè xo:êl yàugutjè mai èm tonkì:fèhèl.
And predictably Big Rock rose without haste.

50 nàu e̱:gàu gomga àunha:dè ø chandehèl gàu èm kai:gùnhèl, ne haun tai ø a̱umdehèl. maun xo:êl còdomàmchò a̱umdehèl.
And so behind the bear gained on them and jumped, but he did not reach the top. The rock must have risen very high up.

51 gàu e̱:gàu sa̱dàu pànmai è chande a̱:hèl.
Now here the children arrived in the heavens.

52 ha:òi mamgàu maun è aumga gàu hègau be sepfa:àu:dèhèl.
When they finally arrived they had difficulty disembarking.

53 nàu aja̱u:dè etha:dè ø jo̱:nê, "hadàljè còdomàmgàu bà a̱umgá. het opchò bà kohìl, pànmâ."
The big brother said, "Obviously we reached very high, so why don't we just go on, skyward."

54 nègau je è ala̱umga gàu è hi:hèl panba.
All agreed and so they proceeded into the sky.

55 augàu jogúl etha:dè ø jo̱:nê, "dè tautjèjàu gàu o: haòi zêbàut nau haunthàudeòi hègau bà pa̱ui:de."
And so the big brother said, "I'm going to shoot and wherever the arrow hits, we'll go stand there."

56 nàu "hàu:," è jo̱:hêl.
   And so "yes," they all agreed.

57 châu hègau èm tautjèhèldècàugàu è hi:hêl cholhàu gàu o: panba è chanhèl.
   ja̱:mata̱u:dàu hègau è a̱umga.
   That's how he shot and at the same time they climbed and they reached
   the heavens. They became the Star Girls.

58 a̱:kô, obàhàu. [Aside:] hau cholhàu?
   That's all now. [Aside:] Is that agreeable?

NOTES

1. Parker was fond of talking about working with Harrington, noting Harrington's pen-
   chant for secrecy about his language work. Referring to Harrington as a "wizard," Parker
   became aware of Harrington's enormous abilities to figure out how languages worked.
   Harrington also made the first claim that Kiowa was affiliated with the Tanoan languages
   of the Southwest. That claim has stood ever since.
2. There has always been disagreement among Kiowa storytellers over whether the constellation the little girls became in the story was Canis Major (the Big Dipper) or the
   Pleiades. That the action took place at Devil's Tower has been undisputed among Kiowas
   down the years. In North America alone, the Cheyennes, Lakotas, Cherokees, and many
   other Indian tribes have similar stories based on the Pleiades constellation.

REFERENCES

King, Thomas. 1992. *All My Relations: An Anthology of Contemporary Canadian Native Fiction.*
   Norman: University of Oklahoma Press.
McKenzie, Parker P. *Ja:matàunhè:jègà* [Star girls story]. 1980s conversations, recordings &
   interviews.
Momaday, Scott N. 1969. *The Way to Rainy Mountain.* Albuquerque: University of New Mex-
   ico Press.
Wikipedia. "Bureau of American Ethnology." Updated January 13, 2018. https://en.wikipedia
   .org/wiki/Bureau_of_American_Ethnology.

FURTHER READING

Boyd, Maurice. 1981. *Kiowa Voices.* Vol. 1, *Ceremonial Dance, Ritual and Song.* Fort Worth:
   Texas Christian University Press.
———. 1983. *Kiowa Voices.* Vol. 2, *Myths, Legends and Folktales.* Fort Worth: Texas Christian
   University Press.

Harrington, John P. 1928. *Vocabulary of the Kiowa Language*. Washington DC: U.S. Government Printing Office.

Kiesel, Helmuth, ed. 2002. *Kafka's Metamorphosis and Other Writings*. New York: Continuum.

Kozak, David L. 2013. *Inside Dazzling Mountains*. Lincoln: University of Nebraska Press.

Marriott, Alice. 1945. *The Ten Grandmothers*. Norman: University of Oklahoma Press.

———. 1947. *Winter-Telling Stories*. New York: Thomas Y. Crowell.

———. 1963. *Saynday's People*. Lincoln: University of Nebraska Press.

Momaday, N. Scott. 1969. *The Way to Rainy Mountain*. Albuquerque: University of New Mexico Press.

———. 1989. *The Ancient Child*. New York: HarperCollins.

Mooney, James. 1896. *Calendar History of the Kiowas*. Washington DC: U.S. Government Printing Press.

Palmer, Gus, Jr. 2003. *Telling Stories the Kiowa Way*. Tucson: University of Arizona Press.

Parsons, Elsie C. 1929. *Kiowa Tales*. New York: American Folklore Society, G. E. Stechert & Co.

Watkins, Laurel J. 1984. *A Grammar of Kiowa*. Lincoln: University of Nebraska Press.

PART SIX

Siouan Language Family

PONCA

A Ponca Ghost Story

Narrated by Francis La Flesche
Originally transcribed and translated by James Owen Dorsey
Reanalyzed and introduced by Sean O'Neill

Introduction

This story, as recounted here, was dictated to the linguist James Owen Dorsey in the late nineteenth century, as a sample of Ponca oral literature. Even though the narrator, Francis (Frank) La Flesche, mostly spoke Omaha growing up, his father, Joseph La Flesche, was a leader in the Ponca community during his youth and was thus an authority on the language and oral literature of the Ponca people—a legacy that he eventually passed down to his son, Frank. Though we hear Frank's voice in this short text, he was in his way attempting to channel a much earlier tradition when he passed this text on to Dorsey for the sake of posterity.

During the early nineteenth century, when this story appears to be set, the Native peoples of the Plains were in crisis, having been hunted down and relocated repeatedly by forces within the U.S. government. These horrific events, amounting to genocide, all unfolded rather suddenly and violently in the aftermath of the Louisiana Purchase in 1803, which quickly transformed life on the Plains. During this violent period the Native peoples of the Plains found their homelands increasingly circumscribed by these outside invaders. This vast region, which was then teeming with massive herds of buffalo, was also home to the people who passed this story on to Dorsey, including the many speakers of the Siouan languages, which encompass the tongues now known as Lakota, Dakota, and Omaha, among the northern members of the group, and Ponca, Otoe, Quapaw, and Osage, whose speakers now reside in the southern Plains. Yet before being driven to the Plains by the westward expansion of the United States, these Siouan-speaking peoples appear to have inhabited the region around the Great Lakes, where they probably lived a more sedentary way of life before adopting the nomadic lifestyle of Plains Indians, with tipis, horseback-riding, and buffalo-hunting. The Poncas, for their part, have many stories in their oral tradition; they were situated further east, with many names in their vocabulary for the places there that their ancestors once knew well, such as the Ohio Valley and even Niagara Falls. There are also stories placing their ancestral home in the Smoky Mountains of present-day North Carolina and Tennessee.

As lands passed from one "territory" to another—including the "Dakota" and "Nebraska" Territories of the mid-nineteenth century—these diverse peoples of the Plains were quickly rounded up and placed on semi-permanent reservations, often far from their original homelands, with "treaties" that were quickly drafted and just as swiftly abandoned. The "divide-and-conquer" mentality of these reservations meant that rival tribes were often situated nearby, with tensions escalating under the intense stress of being forced to settle into an unfamiliar, sedentary lifestyle. The Poncas, for their part, soon entered into ongoing conflict with their fellow Siouan-speaking neighbors, the Lakotas and Dakotas, during their reservation days in the north, when the groups were placed alongside one another along the border of the Dakota and Nebraska Territories, despite preexisting tensions. The story recounted here echoes the tense relationship between these tribes, who were also distant kin, with a ghostly visitor from the Dakota Tribe making an appearance at a Ponca camp, which was on the brink of warfare during this eerie visitation. In this sense the story directly confronts the trauma of the times, with themes of warfare, bloodshed, death, funerals, subsequent ghostly visitors, and the lingering memories of war.

After years of strife on the northern Plains, the government began a campaign in 1877 to relocate the Ponca yet again—this time to a land then called Indian Territory, in the north-central part of what is now known as Oklahoma. Like many of the other tribes that were forcibly removed to Indian Territory, the Ponca Tribe experienced its own "Trail of Tears," as it was forced at gunpoint to relocate to a foreign homeland, with many members of the tribe dying on the way. Chief Standing Bear, the leader of the Poncas, even lost his daughter, Prairie Flower, along the way. With bitter irony the state was opened up to outsiders in 1889 during the so-called Land Run, a little more than a decade after the arrival of the Poncas in 1877. In 1907, just two decades after the arrival of the Poncas, Oklahoma was inaugurated as a new state, formally ending the era when the land was set aside strictly for displaced indigenous peoples, such as the Poncas, alongside thirty-eight other tribes.

It was during these turbulent times that the missionary James Owen Dorsey first came to know the Ponca and Omaha peoples, living among them and learning their language well enough to preach in Ponca (and Omaha) on a regular basis. Dorsey is still fondly remembered today within the Omaha and Ponca communities, as much for his advocacy and compassion as for his mastery of the languages, which few outsiders (before or after) have managed to grasp. The La Flesche family, who served as his chief consultants, were not spared the intense separation, betrayal, and agony of the late nineteenth and early twentieth centuries, instead finding themselves very much at the center of this vast storm. While Joseph, the father, was born into the Ponca Tribe during its reservation days in the north, he and his son, Frank, were eventually separated from their Ponca kin during a period of tremendous social upheaval for the Native peoples of the Plains, coming to live instead among their closely related linguistic brethren, the Omaha, in Nebraska. In the words of Dorsey (1890, 1–2):

> Joseph LaFlèche [sic] is a gentleman to whom I am indebted . . . I regard him as my best authority. By birth he is a Ponka, but he has spent most of his life among the Pawnees, Otos, and Omahas. He has acquired a knowledge of several Indian languages, and he also speaks Canadian French. While Frank, his younger brother, has remained with the Ponkas, and is now reckoned as a chief in that tribe, Mr. LaFleche has been counted as an Omaha for many years. Though debarred by Indian law from membership in any gens, that did not prevent him receiving the highest place in the Omaha governmental system. He has some influence among the Pawnees, and when the Yankton Dakotas wished to make peace with the former tribe, it was effected through the instrumentality of Mr. LaFleche, who accompanied Struck-by-the-Ree to the Pawnee village. Mr LaFleche is the leader of the "citizens" party among the Omahas. The names of two of his children, Susette (Bright Eyes) and Frank (Wood-worker, or Carpenter), are familiar to all who have read of the Ponka.

Frank, the narrator here, was primarily an Omaha speaker, though he was doing his best in telling this story to provide a faithful sample of the oral traditions of his ancestors, the Ponca people. The two languages are in fact intimately related—to the point where they are sometimes counted as mere "dialects" of the so-called Ponca-Omaha language. This view is not shared, however, within the Ponca and

Omaha speech communities, which have been politically and linguistically distinct for many centuries, despite their considerable mutual intelligibility. As a consequence of their long-standing separation, the two groups have drifted apart, leading to a number of fundamental differences in the areas of pronunciation, grammar, and vocabulary, even as these overlapping communities have come in and out of contact during reservation times, as witnessed in the case of the La Flesche family, who were keepers of Ponca oral history even as they were integrated into Omaha society. The Omaha and Ponca today have independent governments and isolated speech communities, while the groups themselves insist that they speak different—though mutually intelligible—languages. In this sense there are parallels to the languages of New Guinea or even Scandinavia, which are often mutually intelligible to a considerable degree but socially and politically distinct (see Romaine 2000, 1–17). Frank was apparently fluent in English and adept at writing his Native tongues (Dorsey 1890, 2) and was doing his best here to represent the Ponca storytelling tradition. He tells the story masterfully, giving vivid imagery in a fairly measured way, with about four to five lines for each scene, while opening with a one-line introduction and closing with a one-line conclusion, revealing only at the very end of the tale, very dramatically, that the ghostly visitor was a Dakota, ostensibly killed in battle long ago.

Pronunciation Guide

The Ponca language bears many of the hallmarks of the close-knit Siouan language family to which it belongs, while also sharing some general regional characteristics with the languages of the neighboring peoples of the Plains, such as the Kiowas and Plains Apaches, whose languages have many of the same types of sound, despite their structural differences.

The basic vowel positions, as notated here, are similar to those of Spanish. The letter *a* is pronounced as in the English expression 'ah' [a], while it is often reduced to something like the vowel sound in English 'but' [ʌ] when short. The letter *e* is close to the sound found in English 'bet' [ɛ] when short (*e*), though closer to English 'bait' [beɪt] when long (*ee*); however, in Ponca, the vowel quality remains constant, unlike the two-part vowel (or diphthong) in English 'bait.' The letter *i* signifies two related sounds, much as it does in Spanish. When long (*ii*) it remains high, as in the English word 'heed' [hīd]; when short (*i*), it is often reduced to [ɪ], as in English 'hit' [hɪt]. The letter *o* in Ponca is similar to the sound of English 'boat' [boʊt], though sustained when long (oo), rather than shifting like the second part of the English diphthong [oʊ] in 'boat.' There are other subtle vowel distinctions in Ponca, though none that occur in this particular text.

Like many languages of the Plains and Southwest, vowels can be marked for tone, length, and nasalization, sometimes simultaneously; this much is true of both the Siouan and Athabaskan tongues of the Southwest and may reflect distant historical contact. Dorsey, for his part, marked high tone with with an acute accent (á), which is reproduced in the text given here; like the Apaches and Navajos today, Dorsey left low tone unmarked, which is also reproduced here. In the current Ponca orthography, however, which Louis Headman created, low tone is sometimes marked with a grave accent (à), leaving a third, middle tone unmarked (a). Dorsey did not make these distinctions, and the editor has chosen to leave the text in Dorsey's notation.

Following the current tribal orthography among the Ponca, nasalization is marked herein with a forward-pointing descending hook (ǫ), much as it is in the unrelated Athabaskan tongues, which share this feature. Dorsey, in contrast, marked nasalization with a raised-n character (aⁿ). The effect is similar to the nasalization of the vowel a, when isolated from the English word 'wand' [wãnd].

Long vowels are indicated with a doubling of the vowel in question (aa); short vowels, in contrast, only appear once (a). Dorsey sometimes notated the long vowels, especially in final position, with a plus sign (a+). Any of these markers that alter the quality of the vowel can also be combined, giving rise to high tone with nasalization, for instance, in both long (ą́ą́) and short instantiations (ą́).

A handful of consonants require explanation. One of the most noticeable sounds in the writing system is the d with the slash through it, in both the lower and upper case. For many speakers today this is simply a voiced interdental fricative [ð], much like the 'th' sound in English 'that,' though with slightly less voicing; this is not to be confused with the separate 'th' sound in English 'thing,' which is voiceless [θ]. On the other hand, fluent speakers, both past and present, tend to release this sound off the sides of their tongues, while also pushing the sound through their teeth, making the articulation quite complex. To approximate the sound in English, start with the quiet (voiceless) 'l' of words like 'clean' [l̥] (as opposed to 'lean') or 'slow' (as opposed to 'low'), then combine this voiceless 'l' with the 'th' [ð] of 'that' or 'these.' The combination of these sounds approximates the slashed d of Ponca, which is really a lateral fricative with interdental release [ɬð], in terms of the technical jargon of linguistics.

Several of the stops—that is, *t'*, *p'*, and *k'*—bear an apostrophe, which indicates that they are glottalized, meaning that they are released with a sharp popping sound that some people find almost metallic in quality. Physiologically this effect is created by suddenly releasing a burst of pressure that is built up in the mouth, activated by closing the vocal cords (technically called the glottis when closed) and raising them up momentarily like a plunger, using pressure from the lungs (and abdomen) beneath them. No exact equivalent exists in English, except for the occasional articulation of some voiceless stops in final position.

A Ponca Ghost Story

I. EPIC BATTLE STAGED

Nudą'aðá-biamá	To war went-they say
níaðįga'	person(s),
áhigi	many
p'ą'k'a-biamá	Poncas-they say.

It has been said that a great many Poncas went on the warpath.

II. CAMPFIRE WITH COMMUNAL MEAL

Ki'	And
aðá-b	they went [it is said]
egą'-aít'i-biamá	having-camped for the night.

As they went along their way, we hear, they camped for the night.

Néða-biamá	They kindled fire, they say.
hą'dą-amá	[at] night time-they say.

As night fell, they kindled a fire.

Ki'	And
néðexti	kindling a bright fire
gðį'-biamá	they sat-they say.

And then they sat [for a while] kindling that bright fire.

P'éde	Fire
te	the [object]
náhegaji'xti	to burn very brightly
gáxa-biamá	they made it-they say.

They made that fire burn very brightly, it has been reported.

Gíđeqti	Rejoicing much
wađáte	eating,
gđį'-biamá	they eat-they say.

Rejoicing together, they ate, it is reported.

III. MYSTERIOUS SINGER CALLS GROUP TO ARMS, CALLS FOR SILENCE

Sabájiqti	Very suddenly
niashįga	person
wį'	one
waą'-biamá	sing-they say.

Suddenly, some [unknown] person began to sing, it is said.

Xđáji	"Speechless"
Á-biamá	said [one]-they say.

Someone spoke up and said, "Go silent, stop talking."

P'éde	"Fire
šéte	yonder
Ába'úi-ga	cover with earth."

"Push the ashes over that fire, cover it with earth."

Xđíáji	"Speechless
man'de	how
gđízai-ga	take ye yours."

"Keep quiet, and arm yourselves [that is, take up your bows]."

IV. GROUP SURROUNDED

Ki' wą'giđe   And—all

man'de   how

gđíza-biamá   took their-they say.

Suddenly, everyone took up [their weapons, their bows], it is said.

Ki' égaxe iđą'đ   And—[to] surround them

ađá-biamá   they went, they say.

They began to surround [the ghostly intruder], it is said.

Égaxe iđąđa-bi   They surrounded them, they say.

They surrounded him, it is said.

Gą'   So,

ubísande   in close quarters

ađį'   they had him

átiáđa-biamá   they began at once, they say.

They moved in on him at close proximity, it is said.

Ki' gą'   And still

waą'   singing

najį'-baimá   he stood, they say;

šeđeshtewa'ji   he did not heed at all.

He stood there singing, without moving or taking notice.

V. GHOSTLY APPARITION: PILE OF BONES

Égiđe   At length

xđabé   tree

te'di   by the

K'ą'ge   near

ađá-biamá   they went-they say.

Finally, after a while, they gathered near a tree.

Ki'	And
k'ą'gexchi	very near
ahí-biamá	they arrived, they say
k'i	when
đashtą'-biamá	he stopped singing, they say
waą'-aká	he sang-he who.

When they drew near, [the intruder] stopped singing.

Ki'	And
xđabé'	tree
te'di	by the
ahí-bi	they arrived they say
K'i	when
wahí	bone
te	the [obj.]
gą́'te	had lain there some time
amá	they say.

When they reached the tree, all they saw was a pile of bones that had been there for some time.

Xđabé'	Tree
hidé	the bottom
te'dí	by the
wahí	bone
te	the, there
ededí-amá	they were-they say
níašįįga	human
wahí	bone
te	the.

That is, at the base of the tree, there was a pile of human bones, it has been said.

VI. SIGNATURE OF GHOSTLY VISITOR: DAKOTA FUNERARY PRACTICES

Cháą	Dakota
amá	the (sub)

Ubátihéwađe-hną-biamá	they hang up the bones-regularly-they say
níašįiga	persons
t'ai	they die
k'i	when.

When a person dies, the Dakotas normally hang the bones horizontally in a tree.

BIBLIOGRAPHY

Dorsey, James Owen. 1890. *The Dhegiha Language*. Washington DC: Smithsonian Institution and Bureau of American Ethnology.

———. 1891. *Omaha and Ponka Letters*. Washington DC: Smithsonian Institution and Bureau of American Ethnology.

Romaine, Suzanne. 2001. *Language in Society: An Introduction to Sociolinguistics*. Cambridge: Cambridge University Press.

OTOE-MISSOURIA

Introduction to Otoe-Missouria

Sky Campbell

The Otoe-Missouria Language Department is currently working to revitalize the Otoe-Missouria language with the ultimate goal of having it spoken conversationally in the tribal community. As part of our language revitalization efforts, we gather and study any information available on the Otoe-Missouria language. One source contains a large amount of language information, thanks to the efforts of an individual named Reverend James Owen Dorsey.

In the late 1800s Dorsey collected anthropological material from many tribes. This material included information on history, language, tribal traditions, clans, and more. One of these tribes was the Otoe-Missourias. Of the Otoe-Missouria stories that Dorsey collected, Rabbit is featured the most and plays several critical roles in the survival of the human race. It is these stories that we are including here.

The stories presented here are adaptations of the ones originally collected by Dorsey. Dorsey's orthography has been transliterated into our own and his English translations have been adjusted to a more English-friendly version and, where necessary, adjusted to give the reader a better idea of the context of the Otoe-Missouria being used.

To help readers we are including a small key to our writing system. Our writing system is relatively straightforward as far as how the letters are pronounced in English. There are a few sounds that do not really exist in English and are hard to describe on paper. These have been shown with their pronunciation in a language that uses them. Special characters are described in the table below and nasal vowels (indicated with a "tail") are pronounced the same as in the table below but are also nasalized.

Writing System

a as in 'father'	*e* as in 'hay' or 'jet'	*i* as in 'feet'	*o* as in 'note'
u as in 'food'	*b* as in 'boy'	*ch* as in 'chair'	*d* as in 'dog'
ð as in 'they'	*g* as in 'give'	*h* as in 'horse'	*j* as in 'judge'
k as in 'kid'	*m* as in 'mother'	*n* as in 'no'	*ng* as in 'sing'
nk as in 'think'	*ny* as in 'canyon'	*p* as in 'pie'	*r* (rolling 'r')
s as in 'sky'	*sh* as in 'short'	*t* as in 'table'	*th* as in 'think'
w as in 'west'	*x* (guttural German 'ch')	*y* as in 'you'	*zh* (French 'j')

The Otoe-Missouria Language Department
Sky Campbell
Kennetha Greenwood
Shawna Littlecrow
Olivia Buffalohead
Jade Roubedeaux

The Rabbit and the Grasshoppers

AN OTOE STORY

Collected by Rev. James Owen Dorsey

Ange nanthaje china iyą ida nąnge. Ange Wakąnda wą'shige ranyi wok'ų. Eda nanthaje brogesji ranyi wą'shige wagiruðe gųnra. Shige Mayą ewaną, "Hįntagwa, nanthaje china hįwįnre to. Rijega ranyi Wakąnda wok'ųsge, nanthaje broge wana-she ki. Arechi hįwįnre to."

"Hųnje," e Mischinge. Eda Mischinge ikų gratogreną iwarawi. Eda nanthaje china ida hiwi. China chejeda hiwi.

Shige, "Hįntagwa, tųnt'ų 'ų isrugrąsge igų, 'ų re," e hina'shinge. Eda Mischinge hotų. Hotųsge, mayą broge rahuhuðe.

Eda nanthaje, "Wa! Wakąnda pi skunyi dąnra iyą ji ke. Senawawahi hnye ke," e. Eda nanthaje dotąhą nąha ranyi tų ruðeną, Mischinge uk'ų. Eda ikų ugrak'ų. Eda hina'shinge nąha wosa ugrayu.

Eda shige inuhą hotų. Shige mayą eta rahuhuðe.

Shige, "Ho! Pi skunyi danyi ke! Ranyi shige ithge uk'ųwi re." Shige nanthaje dotąhą nąha ranyi tų ruðeną, Mischinge ithge uk'ų.

"Ho! Hįnkųnyi, uda je are ke. Ruðe re. Womąnkenye hnye ke." Shige'sų hotų. Shige hotųsge, mayą etasji rahuhuðe.

Shige, "Ho! Pi skunyi dąnranye ke! Asgisji ajinye ke! Ho! Ithge wok'ųwi re," anye. Shige nanthaje ranyi tų ruðeną Mischinge uk'ų.

Eda, "Ho! Hįnkųnyi, womąnkesjinye hnye ke," e. Shige uda je are ke, ranyi." "Ho, hįntagwa, gasųsji ki," e. Eda ruðe ke, ranyi.

Shige inuhą hotųsge mayą broge etasji rahuhuðe. Eda nanthaje nąha broge git'ąnye, mąngrida. Nanthaje ranyi uda i 'ų uyunyeną git'ąnye. Areną ranyi rasgige ithgesji. Eda i etawe ðithewethgesji axewenye. Ranyi ruðeną mayą ida u'era be, hina'shinge. Eda thu broge axewe. Eda mayą axewe.

Gahedą.

There was a grasshopper village. And Wakąnda had given tobacco to the people. All of the grasshoppers wanted to take the tobacco from the people. Earth said, "Grandson, let's go to the grasshopper village. When Wakąnda gave tobacco to your uncles, the grasshoppers took it all away from them. So let's go."

"Yes," said Rabbit. And Rabbit and his grandmother went to the village of the grasshoppers.

When they arrived at the outskirts of the grasshopper village, the old woman said, "Grandson, whatever you decide to do, do it." And Rabbit cried out and the entire earth shook.

And the grasshoppers said, "Wa! A bad god has arrived! He will destroy us!" And the grasshopper leader took some tobacco and gave it to Rabbit. Rabbit gave it to his grandmother. The old woman put it in her sack.

And again, Rabbit cried out and the earth shook very much.

Again, the grasshoppers said, "Oh! It will be bad! Give him tobacco again like you did before." Again, the grasshopper leader took some tobacco and gave it to Rabbit.

"Well, Grandmother, here is the rest. Take it," said Rabbit. "It will be easy to get the rest." Again Rabbit cried out and the earth shook even worse than before.

The grasshoppers said, "Oh! They are very bad! They have come very close! Give it to them again!" Again, the grasshopper leader took some tobacco and gave it to Rabbit.

And then Rabbit said, "Well, Grandmother, it will be very easy to get the rest."

"Well, Grandson, that will be enough," she said and took the tobacco.

Again, Rabbit cried out and the earth shook repeatedly and all the grasshoppers flew away. The grasshoppers put some tobacco in their mouths as they flew away. And so just like if they chewed tobacco, something dark-yellow comes out of their mouths.

Then the old woman took the tobacco and scattered it across the land. And all the seeds grew on the earth.

The end.

The Rabbit and the Mountain

AN OTOE MYTH

Narrated by Joseph La Flesche
Collected by Rev. James Owen Dorsey

Mayą hina'shinge are ke. "Wą'shige brogesji mįtawe, mį watų ki," e. Ange "Wą'shige hinage rihų arenye ki," hina'shinge Mischinge ige ke. "Wange nąha rijega arenye ki," e.

Shige eda aheri xąnjesji iyą idąnge. Eda aheri i yaweda wą'shige broge ahunyeną, i broge ugwesdą 'ų̧nye. Waraxesesdą 'ų ke. Eda wą'shige mayąda dokira udanye, broge raxesenyechi.

Hina'shinge nąha ga e ke, "Hįntagwa, aheri ga'e iware skunyi re," e.

Ange Mischinge wirugrą. "Hįnkunyi, dagure 'ų̧ną iwaaje skunyi?" e.

Eda, "Re skunyi re. Pi skunyi dąnra ki. Sresge, riraxese hnye ki," e.

Eda Mischinge, "Iwaaje hnye," irugrą. Eda, "Hįnkunyi, iwaaje hnye ke."

Eda shige "'Re skunyi re,' ihe ki. Rihų rijega hedą rohą waraxesenye ki. Sresge, inuhą ragri skunyi hnye ki," e.

Eda, "Hįnkunyi, hakinąngra haje ke," e Mischinge. Eda Mischinge iware, aheri. Eda aherida hi. Wą'shige ida hi skinąnye, Mischingesdą ida hi. "Ho, Aheri Warashruje, įnrashruje re!" e. Aheri i yawe skunyi. Eda th'isji gasų 'ų manyi. Ange aragrąnda miną Mischinge.

Wą'shige rohąsji asgi ahunyeda, Mischinge wada ke. Ange aheri i yawe. I yawe woxąnje wą'shige rohą dąnra i ugwenye, Mischinge woyuge.

Rodada hi, woxąnje aheri grahi skunyi. Eda Mischinge igrewe. Wą'shige igrewe skunyi Mischinge isdąsji igrewe. Eda shige aragrąnda ida miną Mischinge.

Ange sų th'isji ida miną Mischinge. Arechi wą'shige rohąsji ajinye shige i yawesge i ugwanye shige Mischinge ugwe.

Eda grewe gųnra, nų'a aheri rush'age ke. Mischinge nyixa rodada hi. Nyixa rodada hisge, washį rohą ada manyi. Nąnje washį hedą ada, nąnje hedą ada. Adasge, shige wą'shige rohą wada. Th'isjida ugwe nąha wahu etawe wada. Iroxre ugwe nąha wahu, xuha, ką orath'į wada. Shige agitagi ugwe nąha ch'e ithgesji wada. Shige agitagi ugwe nąha ugisigenye wada ke. Shige go'o ugwe nąha ugisige skunyi wada ke.

Shige ga se e ke, Mischinge, "Wa! Dagure 'ųną rixranyi rach'e ramanyiwi?" e. "Je warajiwisge, pi nų'are," e. "Je washį nąnje hedą waruje pisjinye ke," e. Warajiwisge, pi nų'are," e.

Shige wą'shige, "Hinyego, je nąnje aheri etawe are ke. Aheri nąnje etawe ruje pi skunyi je?" e.

Ige, "Ruje pi dąnra ke," e.

"Hįnąngwewi ke," wą'shige anye.

Eda ga se e, "Mįnrethgare hįnranąngwe skunyiwi? Aheri ranąngwewi," e. "Hįnkunyi washį ninge. Washį hegrak'į hagre hnye ke."

Shige mithu mahi 'ųną, Mischinge gruðe. Gruðeną nąnje are bagrųnje. Nąnje unąngeną bagrųnjesge, gasų bagrųnjesge aheri, "Hų! Hų! Hų!" e manyi ke. Nąnje bagrųnjesge aheri ch'e. Ahe xąnrage ke. "Hų! Hų! Hų!" Eda ch'e. Eda ewak'į ruse.

Mischinge washį rohą dąnra ruðeną, "Washį je hįnkunyi hegrak'į hagre hnye ke," e.

Eda wą'shige brogesji ix'ąnye nąha, "Mischinge wangegihi hį'ųta hnye!" anye.

Shige Mischinge, "Ja! Mį'e wangegihi hagųnda skunyi," e. "Mayą tąndowarajiwithge iwagrawi re," e. Eda wą'shige brogesji tąndowajinyethge agranye. Eda Mischinge gre. Washį k'į gri. Hina'shinge gri.

Mischinge, "Aheri Warashruje ch'eha ke," e.

Hina'shinge, "Hįntagwa, tąnda Ahe Warashruje ch'era israyį? Waxobrį dąnra ki," e.

"Hinyego, ch'eha ke," e. "Washį hak'į hagri ke," e. "Ada re."

Hina'shinge washį ada. Iwahunge. Nąnje rodada Mischinge dagure 'ų iwahunge, nų iwahunge skunyi gųnðe. Hina'shinge, "Hį! Hįntagwa, gasųngi wasrupi dąnra ki," e. "Rijega rihų hedą ix'ąnye hnye ki," e. Eda gasų.

The Earth was an old woman. "All the people are mine. I gave birth to them," she said. And the old woman said to Rabbit, "Human women are your mothers. The men are your uncles."

And there was a very big mountain. When the mountain opened its mouth, all the people who had gone there went into its mouth. It did nothing but devour people. And there were very few people remaining on the Earth, because all were devoured (The old woman was the Earth, and she wished to save humankind, but the mountain was not part of the Earth).

The old woman said, "Grandson, do not go to that mountain."

And Rabbit thought for a moment. "Grandmother, why shouldn't I go?" he asked.

"Don't go. It is very bad. If you go, it will devour you," she said.

"I will go there," thought Rabbit. And then he said, "Grandmother, I will go there."

"I said don't go. Many of your mothers and uncles have been devoured. If you go, you will not come home again," she said.

Rabbit said, "Grandmother, I am going hunting." And then Rabbit went to the mountain. No people arrived there. Only Rabbit arrived there. "Ho, Aheri Warashruje! Devour me!" said Rabbit. The mountain didn't open its mouth. And so it was for a long time and Rabbit sat close by.

When many people came near, Rabbit saw them. Then the mountain opened its mouth. As soon as it opened its mouth, the people went inside and Rabbit went with them.

As soon as Rabbit got inside, the mountain did not like it and vomited Rabbit up. The mountain did not throw up the people. He only threw up Rabbit.

Again, Rabbit sat close by for a long time. Therefore when many people arrived again and the mountain opened its mouth, they entered and so did Rabbit.

The mountain wanted to vomit again, but could not. Rabbit reached the stomach inside. When he arrived inside the stomach, he saw a lot of fat as he walked. He also saw the fat around the heart. He also saw the heart. When he saw it, again he saw many people. Those who had entered a long time ago, he saw their bones. Those who entered next he saw their bones with skin and muscle hanging from them. And those who arrived after them, he just saw them as dead. And those that had entered after them, he saw that they were sick. And those that had just entered, he saw that they were not sick.

And Rabbit said to them, "What? Why do you continue starving to death? If you would eat this, it would be good. This fat and heart are very good food. If you ate them, it would be good."

The people replied, "No, this is the mountain's heart. Isn't the mountain's heart bad to eat?"

Rabbit said to them, "It is very good to eat."

"We are afraid," the people said.

Rabbit replied, "You don't fear me like that, do you? You fear the mountain. My grandmother doesn't have any fat. I will take some fat home."

Using a flint knife, Rabbit seized it. Seizing it, he cut at the heart. Holding the heart as he cut it, while he was cutting it like that, the mountain kept saying, "*Hᶙ! Hᶙ! Hᶙ!*" While [Rabbit was] cutting the heart, the mountain died. The mountain groaned, "*Hᶙ! Hᶙ! Hᶙ!*" Then it died and fell open.

Rabbit, having taken a great deal of fat, said, "I will take this fat to my grandmother."

All the people who were alive said, "We will make Rabbit chief!"

Rabbit replied, "What? I don't want to be chief. Go back to where you came from." Then all the people returned to their lands. Then Rabbit went home. He took the fat home and returned to the old woman.

"I have killed Aheri Warashruje," said Rabbit.

The old woman said, "Grandson, why do you think you killed Aheri Warashruje? It is very sacred."

"No, I killed him," said Rabbit. "I brought some fat home. Look at it."

The old woman saw the fat. She knew. In her heart she knew what Rabbit did, but she pretended she did not know. "Why, grandson, now you have done a very good thing. Your uncles and mothers will live."

The End

PONCA OMAHA

Ponca Omaha Letters Dictated and
Taken by James Owen Dorsey

Introduced by Vida Woodhull Stabler

We will talk of men, men of importance to our people, who spoke for our people, the leadership of days past. I am an Umóⁿhoⁿ teacher, and I find myself in a place where every day I have an audience of students who are more than children sitting in my classroom. They are my relatives. We are related by blood, clan, or division. We are related by a shared history.

I want our relatives to know of the life and struggles of those ancestors who gave much thought to the future of our people. They wanted a better life for we Umóⁿhoⁿ that are living today. Dúba-Moⁿthiⁿ was one of these men. He lived at a time in our history of continued change. He was a young man, already impacted by so much change. So much change that he spoke of wanting to "leave [his] Indian ways behind and never look back" and "pushing them away." These words are beyond *hurtful* to read. How can I understand the depth of desperation he must have felt in order to say these things? I tell you, though I may not have lived at this time, the fact is I still live at a time where our people continue to experience great change. Case in point: the loss of our fluent speakers looms within reach. Is that not similar to what it must've felt like to our people to know there would be no more buffalo hunts, or earth lodges, or ceremonies?

How do we take the historical trauma of our past and deliver it to our children in such a way that we can tell a "true" story of what happened? What if we use something that was so negative in our history as a means, a road, to reclaim our power from the past to give our children a more solid road to walk? Understanding our history is important to me as a teacher. It is important that we develop materials and teach from a place of heart. I believe our relatives, whether they are students, parents, or community members, all have an innate need and hunger to retain our uniqueness as Umóⁿhoⁿ people.

Dorsey, in his work with our people way back, tells the stories of Umóⁿhoⁿs from our past. Our students, our children sitting in my classroom today, *it does relate* to the Umóⁿhoⁿ of today. My hopes are that this material will be used to expose our children to that history, and that they understand, in their own way, the relationship.

Ebé oⁿthíⁿ, edádoⁿ oⁿgáxe ("Who Are We and What Did We Do?")

We are two different language workers from very different backgrounds. Vida Woodhull Stabler is an Umóⁿhoⁿ teacher from the Woodhull family and of the Thátada people. She has worked among her people at Umóⁿhoⁿ Nation Public School for seventeen years. Her interest lies in the belief that Umóⁿhoⁿ people are the best resources to teach the children. She enjoys working with the community to document and develop teaching materials with the intent that these materials will be used by the people wherever there are Umóⁿhoⁿ people.

Bryan James Gordon is a linguistic anthropologist and got into language reclamation work eleven years ago, in part as a commitment to Póⁿka relatives. He has worked as a consultant for the Umóⁿhoⁿ Language and Culture Center since 2008 and recently came to work here full time. His motivation for this work is repatriation of materials that have been largely useful to non-community members and getting the word out in Umóⁿhoⁿ and Póⁿka communities about the cultural and historical value of these materials, the need for retranslating and transliterating them, and the methods involved in this work, so that it can be continued by more Póⁿka and Umóⁿhoⁿ people, healing and strengthening their people.

We present a retranslation and transliteration of a letter dictated by Dúba-Moⁿthiⁿ, Káxe-Thoⁿba, Óⁿphoⁿ-toⁿga, Maxéwathe, and Páthiⁿ-Noⁿpazhi, taken by James Owen Dorsey, and sent to the progressive newspaper the *Cincinnati Commercial* in the late summer or early fall of 1879 and later published by Dorsey in *The Ƈegiha Language* (1890, 755–62). Today, *The Ƈegiha Language* is available for free on Google Books and has been circulated for decades among linguists in searchable electronic formats, including the two recent conversions from Rankin (2008) and Gordon (2005). Yet accessibility is still a huge problem. These and other documentary materials were physically inaccessible to all or most Póⁿka and Umóⁿhoⁿ people for decades and were recorded in a stylistically inaccessible way, intended for non-Umó^{n}ho^n and non-Pó^{n}ka audiences, and never "translated" in a collaborative way that would have bridged these gaps. For these reasons in 2014 we still find ourselves in the position of needing to "repatriate" Dorsey's documentation piece by piece, while the bulk of it is as inaccessible as ever.

A special thank you goes to Rufus White, an elder at the Umó^{n}ho^n Language and Culture Center who helped us select a good spelling for some words where we were unsure of Dorsey's transcription. We are grateful for the helpful observations and suggestions of Assiniboine historian Dennis Smith and of the attendees who heard our sharing at the SSILA (Society for the Study of the Indigenous Languages of the Americas) meeting in Portland this winter (Gordon and Stabler 2015). We acknowledge the work of linguists, anthropologists, and historians before us, both Umó^{n}ho^n and non-Umó^{n}ho^n, who have struggled with Dorsey's work or with our understanding of the era that Dorsey shared with Umó^{n}ho^n and Pó^{n}ka people like this letter's authors. Umó^{n}ho^n historian Dennis Hastings merits particular acknowledgment, as does anthropologist Mark Awakuni-Swetland. We preface the remainder of our introduction with a sketch largely built from their work.

Brief Historical Sketch

In February 1832 Dr. Johnston Lykins reported that John Dougherty believed more than four thousand Pawnee, Otoe, Omaha, and Ponca people had died of *díxe* ('smallpox') (Hastings and Coffey 2007). The 1831 sickness was the third time smallpox had hit the Umó^{n}ho^n people, and set the stage for the theft of land and sovereignty that followed over the next few decades via the treaties of 1830, 1836, and 1854; the forced sale of land to establish the Ho-Chunk (Winnebago) reservation in 1864–65 (Hastings and Coffey 2007); and the long-term leasing of unallotted lands to white farmers beginning in the 1880s (Hastings and Coffey 2007; Awakuni-Swetland 1994, 222–32). Disease continued to sweep Umó^{n}ho^n communities even at the time of the letter we present. Although smallpox was no longer the biggest problem at that time, it was a continuing issue, as we can see by reading letters like Mo^{n}chú-No^{n}ba's, dated April 3, 1879, in which he advises his Yankton relative Wiyákoi^n, "Thiádi mo^{n}kó^n iwó^{n}xe-k^{h}ithá-ga" ("Have your agent ask for medicine [vaccines]") and says he will do the same (Dorsey 1890, 731).

The letter we present, which as best we can guess was dictated between August and October 1879, comes in the immediate aftermath of another calamity for Umó^{n}ho^n people besides disease, land theft, occupation, and spiritual warfare. The winter of 1876 had seen the last buffalo hunt, a historic event that the Umó^{n}ho^n Nation Public School commemoratively retraced in 1999. By the fall of 1879, then, there had been three winters without a hunt. The annual hunt was like a glue that held together Umó^{n}ho^n people's settlement patterns, religious practices, calendar, traditional scientific knowledge, and clan roles and prohibitions. Many Umó^{n}ho^n words specifically describe or distinguish between buffalo- and buffalo-hunt-related activities and concepts. But this "glue" was abruptly dissolved by the extermination of the herds from the Plains. Awakuni-Swetland suggests that anticipation of the extermination of the buffalo encouraged participation in the first round of Umó^{n}ho^n land allotments in the early 1870s; he describes the following years as the "Decade of Disillusionment," characterized by the end of the hunt, the removal of Pó^{n}ka people, rumors of Umó^{n}ho^n removal, and the discovery that allotment did not come with legal title (1994, 213–14).

For a few decades up until the smallpox outbreak at the turn of the nineteenth century, Umó^{n}ho^n people had had a permanent village called Tó^{n}wo^n-to^{n}ga-tho^n ("Big Village") near what is now Homer, Nebraska, where Omaha Creek emerges from the bluffs onto the floodplain of Nishúde-k^{h}e ("The Smoke River"), the Missouri River (Hastings and Coffey 2007). During the first half of the century, Tó^{n}wo^n-to^{n}ga-tho^n was inhabited off and on while Umó^{n}ho^n people traveled around more southern lands, west of Wat^{h}é-k^{h}e, the Elkhorn River, and down to what is now Council Bluffs, before returning to Tó^{n}wo^n-to^{n}ga-tho^n again by 1839 (Hastings and Coffey 2007). By 1851 Umó^{n}ho^n people left Tó^{n}wo^n-to^{n}ga-tho^n and had villages near what is now Bellevue as well as the lower Little Sioux River during this time (Hastings and Coffey 2007). The village near Bellevue was called Pahé-tho^n Áto^{n}wo^{n}gtho^n ("The Village on a Hill") and is described by Dorsey (2015) as situated on an "isolated flat-topped hill" and by the artist Frederick Kurz (quoted by Jenkins 1940, 63) as between Nishúde-k^{h}e and Papillion Creek above and south of the Fontenelle bluffs.[1]

Yet another catastrophe was division along lines created by colonial policy. The 1854 treaty established the Umó^{n}ho^n Reservation, and in 1855 Umó^{n}ho^n people left Pahé-tho^n Áto^{n}wo^{n}gtho^n and established three villages on the reservation lands: Bik^{h}úde ("Lodged under the Snow"), a mile or two south of present-day Macy on the southern branch of Blackbird Creek; Wi^{n}jáge, near the mouth of Horsehead Creek north of Macy; and Zho^{n}thát^{h}e ("Wood Eaters"), on Wood Creek north of present-day Decatur (Awakuni-Swetland 1994, 203–5). Wi^{n}jáge was situated close to the Presbyterian mission where the reservation's only school operated from

1856 to 1868 (Hastings and Coffey 2007), before three day-schools were established (Awakuni-Swetland 1994, 210).

Nearly all of the Umóⁿhoⁿ people who worked with Dorsey were members of the "citizens" and "young men" parties associated with the Wiⁿjáge village (1890, 1–4). Dorsey also worked with Húpethoⁿ, who "refuse[d] to join either political party," and two members of the "chiefs'" party associated with Bikʰúde: Moⁿchú-Noⁿba and Shóⁿge-Ska (Dorsey 1890). These two men's letters are silent rather than dissenting on most matters relating to the progressive ideals and actions that predominate in most of Dorsey's documentation. Moⁿchú-Noⁿba does chide his Jíwere (Otoe) relation for what he perceives as willingly agreeing to removal to Oklahoma:

> Moⁿzhóⁿ-thoⁿ úmoⁿkʰa shkáxe tha'óⁿnai-tʰe íⁿtha-mazhi. ("I'm sad that you are giving up your land too easy / too cheap.") (Dorsey 1890, 689)

After a mishap in which other chiefs refused to feast visiting Yankton people (Dorsey 1890, 714), he tells his Yankton relative Matʰó-Maza:

> Íye oⁿwóⁿha-mazhi oⁿthóⁿwoⁿkʰegai. ("They have sickened me by not listening to my words.")

But another Umóⁿhoⁿ person who contributed to Dorsey's work, Moⁿxpíya-Xaga, speaks more forcefully than anybody else in Dorsey's documentation. He shares with his Pawnee friend:

> Umóⁿhoⁿ-ma móⁿzeska thizá-bazhi shóⁿshoⁿ íⁿtʰoⁿ. Pahóⁿga-gedi móⁿzeska thizé shoⁿshóⁿi, éde íⁿtʰoⁿ thizá-bazhi, wa'í-bazhíxtioⁿi. ("The Umóⁿhoⁿ are not receiving their annuity payments anymore. We always used to receive them before, but not anymore, they don't give them to us at all.") (Dorsey 1890, 644)

In a letter to the Póⁿka leader Maⁿchʰú-Naⁿzhiⁿ, Moⁿxpíya-Xaga voices his displeasure with progressive ideals and behaviors:

> Umóⁿhoⁿ-ma íⁿtʰoⁿ wazhíⁿ-xidá-awáthe, níkashiⁿga-bazhi góⁿthai-tʰe, ádoⁿ wazhíⁿ-xidá-awáthe. ("Some Umóⁿhoⁿ people, I've run out of patience for them, because they want to become non-Indian, that's why I've run out of patience for them.") (Dorsey 1890, 486)

In the notes to this letter, Dorsey says, "Maqpiya-qaga had been a member of the young men's party, but he joined the chiefs' party prior to sending this letter. Notwithstanding his bitter feeling against his former friends, he was a good farmer, and was making considerable progress in civilization" (Dorsey 1890, 486).

These words are among the few in the documentary record challenging the image of Umóⁿhoⁿ people that white philanthropists worked to create. Awakuni-Swetland notes:

> Certain 'progressive' elements of the Omaha Nation can be identified because they produced written records, letters and petitions. As well, some of these individuals were favorably mentioned by name in reports and letters from Indian agents, missionaries, and Fletcher. On the other hand, Omahas who opposed allotment and assimilation were often lumped together as an amorphous 'other.' Fletcher reported that about one-third of the tribe resisted allotment. They were led by twelve unnamed traditionalist families banded together as 'the Council Fire.' They were rounded up by Indian police and forced to take allotments (Mark 1988). (1994, 219)

It should be pointed out that these factional divisions were imposed on Umóⁿhoⁿ people by settlers and their foreign colonial government, through violence, deceit, poverty, threats, extortion, and other mechanisms both "legal" and "illegal" under their own foreign colonial law. It should also be pointed out that some of the relevant factions were made up of white people, not Umóⁿhoⁿ: see Awakuni-Swetland's discussion of the conspiratorial manipulations of the "Pender faction" (1994, 223–26), for example. (Despite an adverse but narrow ruling by the U.S. Supreme Court in *Nebraska v. Parker*, entered March 22, 2016, merchants in Pender continue to oppose specific aspects of tribal jursidiction.) It should also be noted that many Umóⁿhoⁿ people besides Moⁿxpíya-Xaga changed their minds about so-called progress, progressivism, and assimilation during and after this period. Bernd Peyer reports, "At the thirty-third annual meeting of the Lake Mohonk Conference of Friends of the Indian in 1915, for instance, [Francis] La Flesche called upon those in control of Indian affairs to protect the remaining Indian land base" (2007, 292). Yet we have no doubt that all Umóⁿhoⁿ leaders during, before, and after this period, in and across all factional divisions, were doing what they thought best for the healing and strengthening of their people.

Method of Retranslation and Transliteration

Our goal was to "update" this letter from Dorsey's orthography to the contemporary Macy Standard, and from Dorsey's 135-year-old translation to a style more easily understandable by contemporary community members. Dorsey's orthography is idiosyncratic. Compare it with the Macy Standard for this line from the letter, in which Káxe-Tho^{n}ba wonders whether the president would like it if he took justice into his own hands:

Dorsey: Kǐ éga^n wama$^{n'}$¢a^n áakíb¢a ӽi, I̧íga^n¢aí aká úda^n e¢éga^n te éska^n enéga^n ă.

Macy: K^{h}i égo^n wamó^{n}tho^n áak^{h}ibtha-ki, Itígo^{n}thai-ak^{h}a údo^n ethégo^n-tésko^n enégo^n-a?

Translation: Do you think the president would like it if I retaliated against the thief?

Dorsey's transcription has symbols unfamiliar to community members (like ¢, ӽ, and ҙ), complex vowel gradations (like ă and ǐ) and accent marks, and puts spaces and hyphens in different places than the Macy Standard. His transcription sometimes doesn't match contemporary conventions, especially the glottal state of stops. There is a regular tendency for Dorsey to have aspirated (for example, t^h) or ejective (t') stops where today's speakers use a tense stop (t). This is sometimes due to Dorsey's mistranscription and other times due to changes in the language over the past 140 years. For example although the contemporary future/potential marker te would have been transcribed ҙe by Dorsey, he transcribes it te, which corresponds to t^he in the community orthography.

The Macy Standard orthography we use at the Umó^{n}ho^n Language and Culture Center is a work in progress and represents more an attempt to standardize the relationship between sounds and letters than the spellings of words. For instance we don't have a "standard spelling" for words whose pronunciation varies, like the word for "five," which is usually sáto^n but sometimes the more conservative sát^{h}o^n in our documentation. We see this as a good thing, since to insist on a standard spelling would send the message that only one pronunciation is correct. This message is related to the message that other pronunciations are harmful to the language or the result of English influence, but in fact both speakers and learners have different pronunciations of the same word, even different conjugations of the same verb, and very often these different pronunciations and conjugations are all equally traditional, even if one is newer than another.

The second part of our goal—"updating" the translation—ran the risk of getting away from the literal meanings of the words. So we cross-checked five sets of documentary material to triangulate literal meanings as closely as possible: Dorsey's free translation (1890); Dorsey's glosses (1890); Mark Awakuni-Swetland's *Umónhon Íye of Elizabeth Stabler* (1977); Dorsey's slip-file lexicon (2014); and Umónhon Language and Culture Center materials (1999–present).

Dorsey's free translation and glosses typically translate words in only one sense, while the two lexicons (Awakuni-Swetland 1977; Dorsey 2014) gave us hints to a wider range of meanings for many words and helped us detect cases where Dorsey's choice of words has shifted meaning in the last 140 years.

It would be misleading to suggest that these five helpful resources are "enough" to be sure that our retranslation really is as close to the original meaning as possible in a twenty-first-century English style. A large part of the methodology is subjective and comes from spending hundreds of hours with Dorsey's work, figuring out the patterns in his representations of Pónka and Umónhon meanings and words. It would be better if many Umónhon and Pónka people were in a position to do this kind of work as a team, discussing and improving the transcriptions and translations and building a culturally based understanding that would not be impacted by our particular biases. This has not yet been possible, but it is a goal that we hope is furthered by our work.

Subject Matter

We have something else to discuss before we present the words of Dúba-Monthin, Káxe-Thonba, Ónphon-tonga, Maxéwathe, and Páthin-Nonpazhi: In what ways can these words be understood in today's cultural and historical context? How have these words been understood before, and what can we do to improve that understanding? Ultimately, how can we move away from colonial understandings and toward an Umónhon understanding?

A powerful story has been told about the genocide and robbery of Native peoples, a story in which blame is "shared" with Native leadership, culture, genes, or technology. Among the tribes of the Plains, Umónhon culture and history in particular have been distorted by this libel. Because of the presence of some powerful white progressive figures in Umónhon country before and after the turn of the twentieth century (including Dorsey and Alice Fletcher), some Umónhon people adopted some outside ideas and in return were given labels like "good Indians," "progressive," "civilized," or "docile." As Awakuni-Swetland (1994, 202) points out, it was "success or failure at emulating white culture" on the part of only two of the several groupings of tribal members at the time that "was interpreted as an example of the attitude of all Omaha people." While their white "allies" saw these Umóⁿhoⁿ people's work as a sign of "civilizing" Indians, and used it to support nationwide allotment policy via the Dawes Act (Awakuni-Swetland 1994, 202), it's unlikely that these Umóⁿhoⁿ people had the same idea in mind about what they were doing and what it meant for their people.

Another powerful story has been told, one in which Native people are seen as powerless victims whose voices and choices have no role in the story at all. Truth is not so much in between these two racist narratives as outside of them entirely.

It is also important to remember that Dorsey was only able to work with those Umóⁿhoⁿ people who were willing to work with him. In April 1879, the Póⁿka leader Maⁿchʰú-Naⁿzhiⁿ, contemporary of this letter's authors and friend and relative to many of them, said, "In every tribe of Indians there are two parties. First, those who understand that it is necessary, if the Indians are not all to be exterminated, to go to work, to learn to read and write and count money, to be like white men. . . . Then there are always some who believe in the old traditions, who think the Great Spirit will be displeased with them if they do like white men" (translated and quoted by Tibbles [1880] 1995, 51; see Awakuni-Swetland 1994 for details on the factionalization of Umóⁿhoⁿ communities in the period leading up to allotment). What is important to mention is that the words we present do not represent late nineteenth-century Umóⁿhoⁿ leadership as a whole, and Umóⁿhoⁿ people were neither as monolithic nor as factional as some have suggested.

We hope that the teachers, students, and community members who are our intended audience will struggle as we have struggled with the challenging words of these five Umóⁿhoⁿ leaders and critically resist ideological stories that distort Umóⁿhoⁿ history.

To the Cincinnati Commercial, *from Several Omahas*

Part 1, written by Dúba-Moⁿthiⁿ

My friend,

I heard[2] the letter you sent here to us Indians, us Umóⁿhoⁿ people. You asked me what I thought, so I'll tell you. I have this land here. It is my land. And I've seen the people around here who are always busy.[3] I want to leave my Indian ways behind and never look back. I'm pushing them away. These white people

I see, I think their ways are really good, so I hope to do what they do. Indian ways are the reason we are afraid to leave the camp; this is why I want to leave them behind, push them away. All day long I try to provide for myself.[4] As far as I can see, your ways are the only ways anybody can provide for anybody.[5]

I've looked at these people, and I've looked at myself, and I think I've got strong arms and legs just like them. I've planted wheat, potatoes, onions, cabbage, corn, beans, pumpkins, apples, cherries, turnips, red beets, tomatoes, lettuce, and watermelon. I have cattle, horses, a wagon, a harness, and chickens. My friend, we hear that these people, who are friends of yours, live in houses that are just full of things. And all of them think the way I think.[6] It's like I'm traveling a totally new road—and I'm not even close to tired of walking it. Next year I hope to raise even more crops than I just told you I've raised so far.

My friend, these friends of yours do not all run the same distance. It's like they are following each other. It's like they are following the leader.[7]

Kʰagéha,

níkashiⁿga thé óⁿgathiⁿdi, Umóⁿhoⁿ óⁿgathiⁿdi, wabágtheze-wiⁿ tʰíthathe-tʰe anóⁿʼoⁿ. Wéthigthoⁿ-tʰe oⁿthóⁿthamoⁿxe-tʰe uwíbtha-tamiⁿkʰe. Moⁿzhóⁿ-thoⁿ théthoⁿ agthábthiⁿ. Moⁿzhóⁿ wiwíta. Kʰi níkashíⁿga-ma théma shkóⁿ moⁿthíⁿ-ma watóⁿbe-ha, iⁿshtá wétoⁿbe. Níkashiⁿga shkóⁿ wiwíta-kʰe agíyoⁿbtha kóⁿb-tha háshi-atáthishoⁿ; agítoⁿba-mázhi. Agípaznu théathe. Kʰi wáxe théama watóⁿbe-tʰe shkóⁿ eyóⁿi-tʰe údoⁿ ínahi ebthégoⁿ, éskoⁿ égimoⁿ kóⁿ-ebthégoⁿ-ha. Níkashiⁿga ukéthiⁿ shkóⁿ-tʰe náxixitha-tʰe kóⁿbtha-mazhi-ha, háshi-atáthishoⁿ agípaznu théathe, é-áwakʰe. Óⁿba itháugthe edádoⁿ oⁿthóⁿgiudoⁿ-tʰe uwákigth-ixíde-ha. Égithe shkóⁿ thithíta-tʰe enóⁿ ígiudoⁿwathe-tʰe tóⁿbe-ha.

Níkashiⁿga-ma watóⁿbe-tʰe wíshti ákitoⁿbe: shóⁿ edádoⁿ úgaxetha íwashkoⁿ eyóⁿi-tʰe wíshti égimoⁿ-átʰoⁿhe-de, ebthégoⁿ-ha. Wamúske uwázhi, nú uwázhi, moⁿzhóⁿxe, waxthá, watʰóⁿzi, hiⁿbthíⁿge, watʰóⁿ, shé, nóⁿpa, núgthe, pʰóⁿxe-zhíde, tomato, lettuce, sákathide. Téska wábthiⁿ, shóⁿge, zhoⁿthínoⁿge, shóⁿge-wéʼiⁿ, wazhíⁿga-zhíde. Kʰagéha, níkashiⁿga thikʰáge théma tí-tʰe ugípixti-óⁿ gthíⁿ oⁿnóⁿʼoⁿi. Kʰi wéthigthoⁿ ebthégoⁿ wóⁿgithexti ethégoⁿi. Kʰi wagáshoⁿ íⁿshte tégaxti bthé égoⁿ-ha. Moⁿbthíⁿ oⁿthóⁿbthoⁿ-mazhíxti-móⁿ. Kʰi edádoⁿ óⁿbathe bthízhutʼoⁿ uwíbtha-tʰe, éskana umóⁿthiⁿkʰa ázhi-ki, átʰa bthízhutʼoⁿ koⁿbthégoⁿ.

Kʰagéha, thikʰáge-amá théama ukíxthaxtha-bázhi-ha. Íⁿshte kigthíxe-
ama égoⁿi-ha. Pahóⁿga-thiⁿ gthíxe-ama égoⁿi-ha.

Part 2, written by Káxe-Thoⁿba

My friend, and all of you who are like him,

We were very glad when we heard word from you. We are very willing to
work. But even though we are always working for ourselves so gladly, we
feel afraid whenever we think about the president's servants.[8] It seems
they aren't helping us at all. We hope you'll let a whole lot of people hear
about these words you wrote[9] here to ask from us. We hope to meet with
lawyers.[10] We hope you'll give us a very firm deed to the land. If you do,
we won't need to be afraid of misbehaving white people.

My friend, I want to tell you something even though you didn't ask me
for it. Whenever we sell any of our produce, it weighs in very light, but the
storekeepers tell us theirs is very heavy when they sell to us.

Kʰagéha, níkashiⁿga thíegoⁿ-máshe,

íye oⁿthínoⁿ'oⁿi-de wéthexti-óⁿi. Wathítʰoⁿ oⁿthóⁿnahiⁿxti. Wéthexti
oⁿwóⁿkigthitʰoⁿ oⁿmóⁿthiⁿ-shtewóⁿ, Itígoⁿthai-thiⁿkʰe wagáxthoⁿ etá-ama
sabázhixti oⁿsíthe-nóⁿi-thoⁿdi, oⁿthóⁿkuhe-nóⁿi. Óⁿshte uwáwagikoⁿ-
bazhíxti-thoⁿkʰá. Éskana íye thaná tʰíthathe níkashiⁿga áhigixti unóⁿ'oⁿ-
wathákʰithe kóⁿ-oⁿthóⁿthai. Éskana moⁿzhóⁿ-thoⁿ waxíⁿha sagíxti wathá'i
kóⁿ-oⁿthóⁿthai. Edíhi-ki, wáxe wáspa-bazhi-ma oⁿthóⁿkuha-bázhi-etʰégoⁿ.

Kʰagéha, íye óⁿthamoⁿxázhi shóⁿ uwíbtha. Edádoⁿ waxtá
oⁿthízhut'oⁿi-ge weóⁿthiⁿwiⁿi-tʰedi, háhadoⁿxti-egoⁿ-nóⁿi, shi edádoⁿ
etái-ge skígexti wegáxe-nóⁿi, úthiⁿwiⁿ-tí athíⁿ-ama.

Part 3, written by Óⁿpʰoⁿ-toⁿga

I'm writing[11] to tell you the things that are hard on me in my heart. We Indians want to make something good for ourselves, but the only thing the Indian
agents ever do is fail to help us. My friend, people like you are the only people
we can talk to about these acts that are hard on us.[12] The president truly thinks
the things that are hard on us are not hard on us. He apparently only ever
thinks the people he has look out for us—Indian agents—are doing us good.

So I hope to do the things the people do for themselves. I want to be a good person on the land; I don't even want to look at my Indian ways. I want all of you to help me get the land strong enough to support us. Each of you, since your hearts are in the right place:[13] When you report to each other,[14] please help us so we can stay on our land as we wish.

Shóⁿ nóⁿde-thoⁿdi iⁿdádoⁿ íⁿtexi-ge uwíbtha shuthéathe. Níkashiⁿga ukéthiⁿ-ma edádoⁿ údoⁿ kikáxe góⁿtha-améde, ithádithai-ama uwágikoⁿzhi-ama-noⁿ. Kʰagéha, níkashiⁿga thiégoⁿ-mashé-noⁿ, úshkoⁿ wétexi oⁿthóⁿguthikiye-étai. Itígoⁿthai-thiⁿkʰe edádoⁿ wétexi-ge wétexi-bázhi ethégoⁿxti-nóⁿ, wákʰihide-wákʰithai-ma, ithádithai-ma, íⁿshte wáthiudoⁿ-bi ethégoⁿ-noⁿ gthíⁿ-tʰe.

Ádoⁿ níkashiⁿga-ma edádoⁿ kikáxai-ge égimoⁿ koⁿbthégoⁿ. Shóⁿ moⁿzhóⁿ-thoⁿdi níkashiⁿga údoⁿxti kóⁿbtha-ha; níkashiⁿga ukéthiⁿ agítoⁿbe-shtewóⁿ kóⁿbtha-mazhi. Moⁿzhóⁿ-thoⁿdi áwoⁿzhixti níkashiⁿga-mashe bthúga iⁿwíⁿtha-koⁿi kóⁿbtha. Níkashiⁿga-mashe, nóⁿde údoⁿ ithóⁿthathe-mashe, wóⁿgithe, uthákigthai-ki, uwáwathakóⁿi-ki, moⁿzhóⁿ-thoⁿdi oⁿmóⁿthiⁿ oⁿgóⁿthai.

Part 4, written by Maxéwathe

My friend who sent me a letter,

I tell you I am writing to ask something from you. I'm very happy, my friend, that you wrote a letter here to tell me that you want to help me. We don't know anything about your ways, yet we really love them. We hope you'll search hard and find what is best for us. These Indians who came here with a paper you made for them[15] are very happy; your friends' hearts are good. None of our ways provide us any amount of sustenance, we have nothing at all. No matter how much we search, we don't find sustenance. Only your ways can sustain life.

My friend, be kind to us.[16] All day long we constantly pray to survive.

Kʰagéha, waxíⁿha tʰi-óⁿthakʰithe-niⁿkʰéshe,

wíbthahoⁿ théathe, shéhe-ha. Éskana iⁿthéwashkoⁿ shkóⁿna, kʰagéha, waxíⁿha tʰi-óⁿthakʰithe, íⁿthexti-móⁿ. Shkóⁿ thíta oⁿthóⁿbahoⁿ-shtewoⁿ-bázhi shóⁿ xtá-óⁿthexti-óⁿi. Éskana wéyudoⁿ-ethégoⁿ uwáwathaginixíde kóⁿ-oⁿthóⁿthai. Shóⁿ níkashiⁿga waxíⁿha wethéshkaxe tʰí-ma wéthexti-óⁿi, nóⁿde gíudoⁿxti-óⁿi thikʰáge-ma. Úshkoⁿ oⁿgútai-kʰe ínitawathe gáthoⁿska-

shte edíthoⁿazhi, wathíⁿgexti-óⁿi. Ínitawathe oⁿgúthixide-shtewoⁿ
oⁿthóⁿtha-bazhi-noⁿi. Shkóⁿ thithíta enóⁿxchi ínitawathe-ha.

Kʰagéha, tha'é-áwagithai-ga. Oⁿníta oⁿgóⁿthai-egoⁿ oⁿkíwahoⁿ'e-noⁿ
shóⁿshoⁿ oⁿthíⁿ óⁿba itháugthe.

Part 5, written by Páthiⁿ-Noⁿpazhi

The storekeeper on our land is trying to kill us. It's hard for us, because
we want to get rid of him, but the president himself helps him. Whenever
I yield a crop, he always abusively takes advantage of[17] me by grabbing up
more than I owe him, so we hope he won't be here anymore by next summer. I hope you'll tell the president about this.

Moⁿzhóⁿ théthoⁿdi úthiⁿwiⁿ-ti athíⁿ-akʰa t'éawathe góⁿthaxti-óⁿi. Oⁿgíoⁿtha
oⁿgóⁿtha-shtéshtewoⁿ Itígoⁿthai-akʰa-noⁿ uwíkoⁿ-tʰe wétexi-ha. Edádoⁿ
akígthizhut'oⁿ-tʰe íxtaxti óⁿthiⁿ átʰashoⁿ íⁿnashe-nóⁿ shóⁿshoⁿ, ádoⁿ éskana
umóⁿthiⁿkʰa thé mashté óⁿmoⁿ-tʰetá-hi-ki, théthu noⁿzhíⁿ íⁿgoⁿtha-bázhi.
Éskana Itígoⁿthai-thiⁿkʰe unóⁿ'oⁿ-thákʰithe koⁿbthégoⁿ.

Part 6, written by Káxe-Thoⁿba

My friend,

You wanted to know how we're all doing, so we'll write to you and tell
you. Things are very hard for us in this land, and we have nobody to help
us. The president moved some Hocąk Indians next to the land we live on.
It's very hard on us having these foreigners settle so close to us. The Hocąk
stole three hundred horses from us, Umóⁿhoⁿ horses. The Indian agents
knew the whole thing, but they never want to lift a finger for us. We told
them to tell the president about it, but I don't think they ever sent any
letter. And so I conclude that the president never finds out.

When white people lose even a tiny thing it is hard on them,[18] but we
are sad that the president doesn't work on our behalf even when we lose
a whole lot. Do you think the president would like it if I retaliated against
the thief? The reason I haven't yet is that I've thought it was better not
to, so far. But since the president has done nothing to help me, I'm sad. I
thought he'd definitely give me some Hocąk money, but though I thought
he'd pay me from their funds, he hasn't. Clearly he hasn't paid me because

the president wants me to do wrong and retaliate.[19] I hope you send those words in a letter to the president.

Go^n edádo^n, k^{h}agéha, eyó^n o^{n}mó^{n}thi^n-ge watháno^n'o^n shkó^{n}na, ádo^n ó^{n}gu-wi^{n}thitha shúthe-ó^{n}the-tó^{n}gat^{h}o^n-ha. K^{h}i mo^{n}zhó^n théthuwadi úshko^n wétexi héga-bazhi éde, uwáwako^n wathí^{n}gai. Itígo^{n}thai-ak^{h}a níkashi^{n}ga ukéthi^n Húto^{n}ga dúba mo^{n}zhó^n o^{n}gthí^{n}i-tho^{n}di eshó^n ithó^{n}wathai. K^{h}i uk^{h}ít'e wétexi héga-bazhi níkashi^{n}ga eshó^n wégthi^n-t^{h}e. Shó^{n}ga Húto^{n}ga-ak^{h}a gthébo^n-hí^{n}wi^n thábthi^n wémo^{n}tho^{n}i, Umó^{n}ho^n etái. K^{h}i ithádithai-ak^{h}a wébaho^{n}xti-ó^{n}i éde, wéthit^{h}o^n-shte gó^{n}tha-bazhi-no^{n}i. Itígo^{n}thai-thi^{n}k^{h}e ithádithai-ak^{h}a unó^n'o^{n}k^{h}ithe wó^{n}gagazhi-shtewó^n wabágtheze-shtewó^n giáxa-bazhi-no^{n}i, ebthégo^n. Ádo^n Itígo^{n}thai-thi^{n}k^{h}e no^n'ó^{n}zhi-no^n-t^{h}é-ha.

K^{h}i wáxe-ama edádo^n zhi^{n}áxchi-shtewó^n uwíxpathai-ki, gítexi héga-bazhi-no^{n}i, k^{h}i edádo^n to^{n}gá héga-bazhi uwáwagixpathai Itígo^{n}thai-thi^{n}k^{h}e wéthit^{h}o^n-bázhi wétha-bazhi. K^{h}i égo^n wamó^{n}tho^n áak^{h}ibtha-ki, Itígo^{n}thai-ak^{h}a údo^n ethégo^n-tésko^n enégo^n-a? K^{h}i áakibtha-mazhi-t^{h}edi, é údo^n éskó^{n}bthégo^n-ego^n áak^{h}ibtha-mazhi thó^{n}shti. K^{h}i Itígo^{n}thai-ak^{h}a í^{n}thit^{h}o^{n}zhi-ego^n, í^{n}tha-mazhi-ha. K^{h}i edádo^n wawéshi Húto^{n}ga-ama o^n'í-tat^{h}e ebthégo^n thó^{n}shti. Edít^{h}o^n o^n'í-tat^{h}e ebthégo^n-tho^{n}zha, o^n'íazhi Itígo^{n}thai-thi^{n}k^{h}e. K^{h}i píazhi-t^{h}égo^n áak^{h}ibtha í^{n}go^{n}thego^n Itígo^{n}thai-ak^{h}a, ádo^n wawéshi-t^{h}e o^n'íazhi-t^{h}e-ha. Shó^n wabágtheze-tho^{n}di Itígo^{n}thai-thi^{n}k^{h}e édi hí-thák^{h}ithe ko^{n}bthégo^n íye gát^{h}e.

NOTES

1. It's hard to tell what Dorsey might have meant by "isolated," as the hills above these bluffs are connected by ridges and deep ravines. What he likely was referring to was one of the several hilltops between adjacent branches of Big Elk, Mud, and Papillion Creeks, or possibly the flat promontory below those hilltops at the southern end of the bluff that now borders Offutt Air Force Base. There are multiple sites known to contemporary tribal members.
2. These letters were dictated and transcribed, then read aloud at the other end.
3. This sentence could be translated as "And I've seen that the people around here are always busy." Here the idea of "busy" comes from the words *shkó^n mo^{n}thí^n*, literally "to walk and do things"; the idea of "always" comes from the idea of "walk." *Shkó^n* is a very important word culturally, meaning not only "do things" but "exert" or "make an effort"

and more. This word is the root of other words like *úshko^n* "ways" or "deeds" and *washkó^n* "try hard" or "do your best," as well as *washkó^{n}to^{n}ga* "strong."

4. Literally, "All day long I search on my behalf for that with which I do well," or "for that with which things are good for me," or "for means of self-improvement."

5. Literally, "the only things that make one do well."

6. The word Dúba-Mo^{n}thi^n uses for thinking here is *wéthigtho^n*, which refers to decision-making, planning, and leadership. By comparing white with Umó^{n}ho^n "ways of thinking," his words show us today how U.S. colonial violence was psychological as well as physical.

7. This passage is difficult to translate, and for Dorsey, too. The first sentence, literally, is "My friend, these friends of yours do not *ukíxthaxtha*." To not *ukíxthaxtha* can mean "not run the same distance" or "not pass each other" or even "to be of unequal length or height." In his slip files, Dorsey says the word was often used to describe unequal lines. At very least we can be sure that Dúba-Mo^{n}thi^n is pointing out that not all white people are alike, in order to make a point by comparison about Umó^{n}ho^n people. In his translation of this letter, Dorsey glosses *ukíxthaxtha-bázhi* as "they run unequal distances" and interprets this as referring to unequal distributions of "improvement" and "success" among white people.

But using another definition from his slip files it might have literally meant that they do not all succeed in "passing" each other. Dorsey chooses the interpretation that, in his words, "seems" to make most sense to him. It is important to bear in mind while reading this letter that the closest white allies that Umó^{n}ho^n people had at the time were persons like Dorsey, who were obsessed with the "improvement" and "success" of Indians. Another thing Dúba-Mo^{n}thi^n and his peers are often preoccupied with in their letters is being lumped together with "bad Indians." Umó^{n}ho^n people had settled down and agreed to government terms, but were still targeted by racist Nebraska governments for expulsion along with all other Indians. This must have been quite confusing to Umó^{n}ho^n people like this letter's authors, who had built close relationships with white allies, who told a story of progress, salvation, and fair treatment that was constantly being falsified by "westward expansion."

Whether or not we take Dorsey at his word, we can conclude that Dúba-Mo^{n}thi^n is writing reactively. He is responding to the racist slander of Native people as lazy and backward. Much of his text reads as a narrative of "improvement" and "success," which coincidentally happens to be the narrative of white allies.

8. The Umó^{n}ho^n Íye word for "president" is, literally, "fictive/adoptive grandfather," or "one who is made a grandfather." Similarly the word for "Indian agent" is literally "fictive/adoptive father."

9. Literally, "sent."

10. Literally, "adviser" or "counsellor."

11. Literally, "sending."

12. Because *téxi* means "mean" as well as "hard," *úshkoⁿ wétexi* could conceivably be translated as "acts of aggression towards us."
13. Literally, "you people who place your hearts in a good way."
14. Dorsey interprets this as referring to a meeting of Congress. This is highly plausible, and suggests that the letter writers had been led to believe the *Cincinnati Commercial* had somewhat direct influence over congressional acts.
15. Ho-Chunk refugees.
16. Although Dorsey translates *tha'éthe* as "take pity on," it is often used in contexts where "be kind to" would be appropriate, and may not carry the heavily hierarchical connotations of "pity." Tha'éthe definitely connotes action in addition to emotion; Maxéwathe is asking for help, not sympathy.
17. The word *íxta* has a range of meanings, from "take advantage of" to "abuse" to "rape." It connotes maliciousness (or, in Dorsey's terms, "wantonness"). My translation, "abusively takes advantage of," attempts to capture more of this range of meanings than Dorsey's "wantonly."
18. Dorsey translates this "But when white men lose even a very small thing, it is always regarded as a great wrong." Here Dorsey reaches far from the literal meaning, but this reach may be justified. Umóⁿhoⁿ Íye truth claims have a different set of criteria and procedures than English truth claims. In the Umóⁿhoⁿ evidential system the unmarked form (which is what occurs here) entails that the truth of the claim is directly known—in this case not by Kaxé-Thoⁿba but by the hypothetical white property owner who suffers loss or theft. Such a person's report of their experience of hardship would be accepted as true by others unless the speaker was disreputable. To report hardship and be ignored or disbelieved does not fit well within this system.
19. Or "wants me to retaliate for the sake of evil." Dorsey translates this as "wishes me to repay the Winnebagos with injury for injury."

REFERENCES

Awakuni-Swetland, Mark, and Elizabeth Stabler. 1977. *Umóⁿhoⁿ Íye of Elizabeth Stabler*. Macy: Nebraska Indian Press.
——. 1994. "'Make-Believe White-Men' and the Omaha Land Allotments of 1871–1900." *Great Plains Research* 4: 2.
Dorsey, James Owen. 1890. *The Ȼegiha Language: The Speech of the Omaha and Ponka Tribes of the Siouan Linguistic Family of North American Indians*. Contributions to North American Ethnology 6. Washington DC: Government Printing Office.
——. 1891. *Omaha and Ponka Letters*. Bureau of American Ethnology Annual Report 11. Washington DC: Government Printing Office.
——. 2014. *Omaha & Ponca Digital Dictionary*. Administered by Center for Digital Research in the Humanities, University of Nebraska, Lincoln. Available at omahaponca.unl.edu.

Gordon, Bryan J. 2005. TXT versions of Dorsey (1890; 1891) in multiple orthographies. Available on request from B. J. Gordon at linguist@email.arizona.edu.

Gordon, Bryan James, and Vida Stabler. 2015. "Back Off the Library Shelf: Repurposing Umóⁿhoⁿ Íye Documentation for Umóⁿhoⁿ People." Paper presented at the annual meeting of the Society for the Study of the Indigenous Languages of the Americas, Portland OR.

Hastings, Dennis, and Margaret Coffey. 2007. Omaha timeline through history. In *Omaha History, Culture, Language: A Workbook for the Faculty and Staff of the Umóⁿhoⁿ Nation Public Schools*, edited by Dennis Hastings and Margaret Coffey. Macy: Omaha Tribal Historical Research Project.

Jenkins, Genelle. 1940. "Introduction to the Ethno-history of the Omaha." Unpublished MA thesis, University of Nebraska.

Peyer, Bernd C. 2007. *American Indian Nonfiction: An Anthology of Writings, 1760s–1930s*. Norman: University of Oklahoma Press.

Rankin, Robert L. 2008. PDF version of Dorsey (1890). Provided as searchable versions of Dorsey's texts. Unpublished but available on request and freely distributed.

Tibbles, Thomas Henry. 1995. *Standing Bear & the Ponca Chiefs*. Originally published as *The Ponca Chiefs: An Indian's Attempt to Appeal from the Tomahawk to the Courts*. Boston: Lockwood, Brooks, 1880. Lincoln: University of Nebraska.

KAW

Two Accounts of a Battle between the Kaws and Cheyennes

Narrated by Zhóhiⁿ Máⁿyiⁿ and Paháⁿle Gáxli

Collected by Rev. James Owen Dorsey

Retranscribed, retranslated, and introduced by Justin T. McBride

For most of the nineteenth century, the Kaw (also known as Kanza or Kansa) people lived in numerous semi-nomadic bands scattered along the rivers and streams
of present-day Kansas—a state that derives its name from the Kaws' name for
themselves and their language, *Kaáⁿze*. This was a very difficult time for the tribe;
indeed, the Kaw chief Alíⁿk'awaho called the early 1870s "the darkest period in our
history" (Parks 2014, 6). The tribe had begun the century with territories stretch-
ing from what is now western Missouri to eastern Colorado, with a population
of perhaps 1,500 (Unrau 1971, 25, 108), only to ring in the twentieth century on a
nearly 150-square-mile reservation in what is now north-central Oklahoma, with
a little over two hundred tribal members, less than half of whom were full-bloods
(Unrau 1975, 68–69). In the hundred-year interim, the tribe faced wave after
wave of social and economic upheaval, epidemic disease, Native and non-Native
encroachment, forced removal, starvation, and, of course, warfare.

Perhaps it is not a surprise then that the few surviving examples of oral literature collected from Kaws during this time so often involve the violence and horror
of war. Consider that, about a decade after the tribe's 1873 removal from central
Kansas to present-day Kay County, Oklahoma, the ethnographer Reverend James
Owen Dorsey (1883) collected some two dozen Kanza-language texts from his Kaw
consultants. About half of these texts offer either explanations of the tribe's warfare
customs or detailed depictions of specific battles. The latter are the fierce, visceral
accounts of a people living on the very brink of total societal collapse, with few
souls to spare for battle and little ground to give to enemies. Nevertheless these
are also the stories from an era of war honors, in which individuals who could

255

prove themselves in combat might be seen as courageous and resourceful leaders at a time of near hopelessness for the Kaw people.

Most of the battles described in these late nineteenth-century Kanza-language warfare texts take place in western Kansas, where many of the local tribes traveled to hunt the rapidly dwindling numbers of American bison. All tribes that engaged in this enterprise at the time were most certainly aware that an unsuccessful hunt could well mean widespread starvation and a lack of raw materials for basic shelter and tools. As such additional competition on the hunts was never welcome, least of all from old enemies. All too often the Kaws' rivals at this time were various bands of either Pawnees or Southern Cheyennes. The Cheyennes in particular happened to range along the Great Bend of the Arkansas River, a favorite hunting spot for the Kaws.

The battle described in these accounts took place during one of the tribe's last full-scale bison hunts sometime between 1867 and 1873, near what is now Larned, Kansas. At this time the area was also home to Fort Larned, a U.S. military installation built to protect travelers on the Santa Fe Trail from Natives hostile to their passage through tribal hunting territories. This area was in other words a tense confluence of both Native and non-Native activity on the Great Plains of the American West during the post–Civil War era.

Significance of the Narratives

Dorsey collected these two oral narratives in 1882 or 1883, presumably not far from what is today Kaw City, Oklahoma, the main headquarters of the modern Kaw Nation. His informants were Zhóhi^n Má^{n}yi^n and Pahá^{n}le Gáxli ("Strikes First").[1] Beyond the Kaws' decisive, if gruesome, victory during the battle in question, these stories are of importance for several reasons. First of all they offer the only known accounts of the deaths of two Kaws, Níakizhà and Cízhi^n Há^{n}ga (also Cízhi^n Hó^{n}ga). Bear in mind that there were fewer than 540 Kaws at the time (Parks 2014, 224), so the deaths of these two men on the same day amounted to a sudden and substantial reduction of the total tribal population by more than one-third of 1 percent. This may seem like a tiny fraction, but it amounts to a reduction greater than the percentage of the U.S. population that died as a direct result of World War II, military or civilian. To put it another way a proportionate one-day loss in the United States today would claim the lives of more than 1.18 million Americans— roughly equal to the combined populations of Wyoming and Vermont at the time of the 2010 census. Exact details of these Kaw deaths are, nevertheless, sketchy: Níakizhà died presumably of blood loss resulting from a serious wound to his leg. Cízhiⁿ Háⁿga is merely reported to have been killed by Cheyennes.

Second, Zhóhiⁿ Máⁿyiⁿ's account of the battle provides the historical context for the honor names of two of his comrades, Xuyólaⁿge ("Eagle Headdress") and Wádashtaye ("Burns Bare"). The use of honor names was a frequent practice among the Kaws at the time to commemorate important events in the lives of tribal members; it was not uncommon for particularly brave Kaws to have multiple names of this sort. Xuyólaⁿge is of special interest because he is one of only a few Kaws of that era to have been photographed on multiple occasions, including with the eagle headdress he obtained in the battle. Xuyólaⁿge was also the maternal uncle of Paháⁿle Gáxli, the author of one of these two accounts and the creator of the only known illustration of the battle. Zhóhiⁿ Máⁿyiⁿ's story also describes the actions of Wázhaⁿgiye ("Waits for Them to Sleep"), also known as Washungah, who would shortly go on to become the long-time chief of the Kaws from 1885 to 1908 (Unrau 1975, 70–79).

Third, the titular battle may well have been the last one fought by the Kaws as a tribe. While individual Kaws were known to have served in the U.S. armed forces for all of the major wars of the twentieth century, there are no known accounts of large-scale Kaw tribal warfare after their removal to Indian Territory in 1873. Dorsey was uncertain of when this battle took place, but speculated that it may have occurred as late as 1873. If so, this event occurred immediately prior to the tribe's removal from Kansas. It is interesting to note that the U.S. soldiers in Paháⁿle Gáxli's account appear to have the Kaws' best interests at heart. This is perhaps unsurprising given the army's violent history with the Southern Cheyenne; the Sand Creek Massacre occurred no more than a dozen years earlier, about two hundred miles to the west. Kaw soldiers, on the other hand, could conceivably have fought alongside some of the local American soldiers as part of the Union army during the Civil War.[2]

Fourth, the two texts offer some of the only extant examples of individual Kanza-language stylistic differences in narratives of the same event. Kanza ceased to be spoken in the 1980s, and very few additional monologic narratives were recorded after Dorsey's collection of texts one hundred years earlier. This means that the vast majority of the available narratives deal with very different topics from one another. These two, however, are complementary first-hand accounts of one particular Cheyenne battle. Thus they offer a rare glimpse at how the two individual speakers perceived the sequence of events (notice, for instance, that there is no mention of the fort in Zhóhiⁿ Máⁿyiⁿ's account nor of the burning of Cheyenne survivors in Paháⁿle Gáxli's account), how they treated their respective involvement in those events (note that Zhóhiⁿ Máⁿyiⁿ does not describe any of his actions during the battle, and Paháⁿle Gáxli switches to an unexpected third-person depiction of his own rather dramatic actions), and how they evoked different elements of the complex network of given and new discoursal information (both, for example, presume knowledge of the location of the bison haunts and the waterways, as well as the Cheyenne's use of shields, but whereas Paháⁿle Gáxli seems to take the presence of eagle headdresses as a given in his account Zhóhiⁿ Máⁿyiⁿ focuses on one headdress as particularly noteworthy).

Finally there are simply not many recorded examples of Kanza oral literature available. The total number is only around thirty, including the twenty-four Dorsey collected during his time with the Kaws in the 1880s. These narratives comprise therefore a not insignificant portion of the entire known Kanza corpus. While the Kaw Nation has previously published two volumes of Kanza-language texts (both of which are available on the tribal website, www.kawnation.com), including a compilation of all the oral literature in the language (McBride and Cumberland 2009) and a graded reader based on a subset of historical texts (McBride and Cumberland 2010), these two accounts of the Cheyenne battle have never before been singled out for fuller discussion and comparison.

Collection, Retranscription, and Retranslation

During his former life as a missionary to the Poncas, Dorsey had developed enough knowledge of Ponca and Omaha to assist him greatly in his work with the three other, very closely related Dhegiha Siouan languages, namely Quapaw, Osage, and Kanza. It is quite likely then that he hand-recorded directly onto scratch paper any Kaw oral texts that his consultants dictated to him in Kanza. However, if this is the case, the scratch paper has not survived. Rather, he later typed up these notes in an early phonetic alphabet that he and other Bureau of American Ethnology field-workers used. He also included a short paragraph of notes and a close English translation. These and other Kanza-language texts and notes might well have been published as a single volume, but Dorsey died before this could happen. Instead, after his death, they would eventually become part of the National Anthropological Archives' extensive James O. Dorsey Papers.

Here I have retranscribed Dorsey's collected texts using the Kaw Nation's official practical spelling system, the Kanza Alphabet (see below). I have also retranslated them directly from Kanza to spare modern readers from Dorsey's perfectly suitable but occasionally "antique"-sounding nineteenth-century English prose. These new translations may still sound awkward at times, but this is a result of including or excluding concepts as dictated by the original Kanza wording, not because of the modernity of the English used for translation.

Orthography and Pronunciation Notes

The oral texts presented here appear in the Kanza Alphabet, which has a 1:1 correspondence with the typical Americanist technical spellings used for linguistic analysis of the language. There are thirty-six letters in the Kanza Alphabet, including twenty-eight consonants and eight vowels. The characters *f*, *q*, *r*, and *v* do not appear. The consonants *b*, *ch*, *d*, *g*, *h*, *j*, *l*, *m*, *n*, *s*, *sh*, *w*, *y*, and *z* are pronounced exactly as in English. The consonants *c*, *gh*, *k*, *k'*, *kh*, *p*, *ph*, *p'*, *t*, *t'*, *ts'*, *x*, *zh*, and *'*, as well as all eight vowels *a*, *aⁿ*, *e*, *i*, *iⁿ*, *o*, *oⁿ*, and *u*, are described in relation to the International Phonetic Alphabet in the tables below.

CONSONANTS	IPA	DESCRIPTION
c	[tʃ, tʃː]	'ch' in 'ranch,' NOT 'cheese'; 't j' in 'hot jam'
gh	[ɣ]	breathy 'g,' like gargling
k	[k, kː]	'k' in 'skim,' NOT 'kale'; 'k g' in 'look good'
kh	[kʰ]	'k' in 'kale'; 'k h' in 'look happy'
k'	[k']	'k' in 'skim,' caught in throat
p	[p, pː]	'p' in 'spud,' NOT 'pancake'; 'p b' in 'top bread'
ph	[pʰ]	'p' in 'pancake'; 'p h' in 'loop hole,' NOT 'phone'
p'	[p']	'p' in 'spud,' caught in throat
t	[t, tː]	't' in 'steam,' NOT 'top'; 't d' in 'hot dog'
t'	[t']	't' in 'steam,' caught in throat
ts'	[ts']	'ts' in 'grits,' caught in throat
x	[x]	breathy 'k' or rough 'h,' like clearing throat
zh	[ʒ]	'j' in 'soup-du-jour' or 'au-jus'
'	[ʔ]	pause in 'uh-oh'

VOWELS	IPA	DESCRIPTION
a	[a]	'a' in 'pasta'
aⁿ	[ã]	'a' in 'pasta,' but nasal
e	[ɛ]	'e' in 'spaghetti'
i	[i]	'i' in 'pizza'
iⁿ	[ĩ]	'i' in 'pizza,' but nasal
o	[o]	'o' in 'taco'
oⁿ	[õ]	'o' in 'taco,' but nasal
u	[y]	cross 'ee' in 'feed' with 'oo' in 'food'; French *u*; German *ü*

The consonants *k*, *p*, and *t* are usually termed "tense," indicating that they are pronounced unaspirated when found in word-initial position and both unaspirated and geminated (that is, doubled) elsewhere. They also tend to raise the pitch of following vowels (Rankin 1989). The consonants *ch*, *kh*, and *ph* are aspirated. The consonants *k'*, *p'*, *t'*, and *ts'* are glottalized, meaning that they are accompanied by a catch in the throat.

Vowels marked with an acute accent, as in *á*, *áⁿ*, *é*, *í*, *íⁿ*, *ó*, and *ú*, receive the greatest stress, and those marked with a grave accent, as in *à*, *àⁿ*, *è*, *ì*, *ìⁿ*, *ò*, *òⁿ*, and *ù*, receive somewhat less but still more than usual. Stress patterns tend to occur regularly so that secondary stress in a word appears on every other syllable after primary stress. Some vowels may be written twice to indicate that they are pronounced about one-and-a-half times longer than normal. When this occurs, any diacritic marks—that is, for marking nasality and/or stress—appear on only the second of the two, as in *aáⁿ*. This vowel, for instance, is both nasal and stressed, and is held long. Regardless of how they are marked, stressed long vowels are pronounced with falling pitch and decreasing stress, as if marked, for instance, *óò*. Note that Dorsey did not consistently record vowel length. As such it only appears below in words, such as *Kaáⁿze*, 'Kanza,' that were known to have long vowels in modern times.

Kanza words are composed of syllables that typically take a consonant-vowel form. Other syllables are composed of either consonant-consonant-vowel combinations or just vowels. Consider for instance the word *blógaxci*, 'really all.' This divides as *bló-ga-xci*. Kanza words are rarely more than five syllables long. Primary stress usually falls on the first or second syllable.

Capitalization and punctuation in the practical Kanza orthography follow typical English rules, meaning that, for example, all proper nouns are capitalized and most declarative sentences end with a period. Graphic punctuation, however, is not strictly necessary in most cases due to the fact that Kanza typically makes use of masculine or feminine sentence- and paragraph-level evidentials, such as masculine *ao* and *hao*, respectively.

Zhóhiⁿ Máⁿyiⁿ's Account

1 Kaáⁿze akhá yegóji wakíle yushtáⁿbe-gó oyóyaha, cedóⁿga géji gaxláⁿ ayábe ao.
The Kaws, right after when the allotment payment ended, went off migrating to where the bison are scattered around.

2 Gagó cedóⁿga géji aⁿgáhibe ao.
So we arrived at where the bison are scattered around.

3 Aⁿgáhibe oyóyaha, Míhega Hí To (éji) ayábe (ao).
When we arrived there, we went to Míhega Hí To.

4 Aⁿgáhibe oyóyaha Shayáni wakáⁿyabe ao.
When we arrived there, the Cheyennes attacked us.

5 Ga Kaáⁿze Míhega Hí To ahíbe oyóyaha níka míⁿxci ts'éyabe ao Shayáni khá.
And when Kaws arrived at Míhega Hí To, one man was killed—he was a Cheyenne.

6 Gagó oyóyaha táⁿmaⁿ éji alíbe Kaáⁿze abá.
After that, the Kaws returned to the village.

7 Ga Kaáⁿze akhá wahótaⁿ blógaxci lúza-bá-daⁿ, ga wahótaⁿ blóga lúza-ba-daⁿ, ayábe ao.
And the Kaws were taking every last one of their guns and, taking all their guns, they left.

8 Ga Shayáni kítagabe ao.
And they fought with the Cheyennes.

9 Pízhixci dáge pízhi wále kukúje gashóⁿ Shayáni shóⁿge itá míⁿxci ts'éyabe ao, Gazáⁿ Naⁿge dóda ts'éyabe ao.
It was really bad fighting—very bad shooting at one another—so one of the Cheyenne horses was killed; Gazáⁿ Naⁿge killed it that way.

10 Gayó Táⁿmaⁿ Ts'éye akhá Shayáni watáⁿga khe ts'éyabe ao.
Then, Táⁿmaⁿ Ts'éye ["Kills Villages"] killed the Cheyenne leader.

11 Shayáni akhá-ji níkashiⁿga watáⁿga Wazhíⁿga Táⁿga e zhíⁿga khe ts'éyabe ao.
He killed the son of Big Bird, an important person among the Cheyenne.

12 Gá shóⁿge sábe k'áⁿsagexci míⁿ gashábe ao Pádoka Gáxli akhá.
And Pádoka Gáxli ["Strikes Comanches"] captured a very swift black horse.

13 Gayó níka akhá, Wádashtaye akhá, ka shóⁿge zhúje, Máⁿhiⁿ Táⁿga shóⁿge
itábe míⁿ gashábe ao.
Then there was a man. It was Wádashtaye, and he captured one of their
American horses, a red horse.

14 Gayó shóⁿge zhúje ijé ska míⁿ, Wazhíⁿ Waxá akhá gashábe ao.
Then Wazhíⁿ Waxá captured a red horse with a white face.

15 Gayó Tayé akhá shóⁿge míⁿ gashábe ao, óphaⁿ hiⁿ egó.
Then Táye captured a horse that had fur like an elk.

16 Gayó Wázhaⁿgiye akhá shóⁿge miⁿ gashábe ao.
Then Wázhaⁿgiye captured a horse.

17 Shayáni házabe édaⁿ shóⁿge gínashabe abá eyaó, Wázhaⁿgiye akhá.
Cheyennes were fleeing, so Wázhaⁿgiye snatched a horse.

18 Gayójidáⁿ Kaáⁿze miⁿ Níakizhà gayó tashíyaⁿmakà éji óbe ao Shayáni abá.
At that point, then the Cheyennes wounded Níakizhà, a Kaw, right on his
knee.

19 Gagóha Shayáni abá Níakizhà óbe oyóyaha Kaáⁿze akhá Shayáni gadáje
pízhi niánaⁿge ayíⁿbe ao, óxle ayé akhá eyaó.
When the Cheyennes wounded Níakizhà over there, the Kaws actually
went off to chase Cheyennes who were dealing with bad mud.

20 Gayó gódamasiⁿ ogákhaⁿ oxlóla éji Shayáni olíⁿbe ao.
Then, on the other side, there was a ravine where the Cheyennes were
camping in the hollow.

21 Ga Shayáni níka míⁿxci xuyólaⁿge ayíⁿ akhá ao.
And one Cheyenne man had an eagle headdress.

22 Shayáni akhá shóⁿge ákuyusta alíⁿ akhá eyaó.
The Cheyenne was actually riding double on a horse.

23 Ga xuyólaⁿge ayíⁿ akhá hashíta áliⁿ akhá eyaó.
And the one with the eagle bonnet was actually riding in the back.

24 Gayó Kaáⁿze míⁿxci wakáⁿya ahíbe-dáⁿ, ochíⁿ-hnaⁿbe ao, ogáxpayabe ao.
Then one Kaw arrived rushing, and he was hitting him—he knocked him off.

25 Gayó ochíⁿ-ba-dáⁿ ceháwale yiⁿkhé gínashabe che ao.
Then he was hitting him, and he apparently snatched the shield from him.

26 Ka Kaáⁿze akhá góda akhá xuyólaⁿge ayiⁿ yiⁿkhé gaxlíbe oyóyaha zházhe yuzábe che ao.
And when the Kaw who was over there killed the one who had the eagle headdress, it is said that he took that name (Xuyólaⁿge [Eagle Headdress]).[3]

27 Gagó oyóyaha Shayáni oxlábe ao.
After that, they chased the Cheyennes.

28 Shi hakháⁿzhi si-yuzábe léblaⁿ-hu noⁿbá shi ogákhaⁿ miⁿ obáyazabe che ao.
Again, not two hundred yards away—it is said that they scared them into a ravine again.

29 Ogákhaⁿ obáyazabe-gó, Shayáni ogípi olíⁿbe ao.
When they scared them into the ravine, it was full of Cheyennes.

30 Gayó Kaáⁿze akhá ánasa ógighe onázhiⁿbe ao.
Then the Kaws stood all around it, heading them off.

31 Ka yushtáⁿxci Shayáni kúdabe skaⁿ.
And apparently they shot at the Cheyennes, aiming right at them.

32 Gayó lébla yábliⁿ Shayáni Kaáⁿze akhá ts'éyabe ao.
Then the Kaws killed thirty Cheyennes.

33 Míⁿoⁿba-híye-gó, gágo-hnáⁿ dágabe ao.
When the sun set, the fighting was over.

34 Shayáni akhá xádabe ao.
Some Cheyennes had hidden.

35 Ka péje gághabe-go, osábe ao.
   So when they made a fire, they were set on fire.

36 Shayáni no[n]bá buspábe ská[n].
   Apparently, two Cheyennes had crouched down.

37 Gayó Wádashtáye akhá ówasabe ská[n].
   Then Wádashtaye ["Burns Bare"] apparently set them on fire.[4]

38 Shayáni ówasabe-gó oyóyaha, zházhe yuzábe che ao, Wádashtaye akhá.
   Right after he set the Cheyennes on fire, it is said that he took that name—
   Wádashtaye.

39 Kaá[n]ze no[n]bá ts'éyabe ao, Níakizhà, Cízhi[n] Há[n]ga éyo[n]ba.
   Two Kaws were killed, both Níakizhà and Cízhi[n] Há[n]ga.

Pahá[n]le Gáxli's Account

1 Cedó[n]ga géji a[n]gáya-bá-da[n], a[n]cíbe ao.
   We were going to where the bison are scattered around, and we had
   camped.

2 Ye Nízhuje ítata Wása Yí[n]ge Zhéga Búxo[n] Gaxá khé éji a[n]cíbe ao.
   We camped on the Wása Yí[n]ge Zhéga Búxo[n] ["Wása Yí[n]ge Breaks Leg"]
   Creek toward the head of the Arkansas River.

3 Á Yi[n]gé Gaxá oízha[n]ká ejí eyaó.
   It was actually on the fork of Á Yi[n]gé ["No Arm"] Creek [that is, the Pawnee River].

4 Ákida tá[n]ma[n]la[n] olí[n] akhá eyaó.
   There was actually a military installation there.

5 Ákida mí[n]xci achíbe ao gasí[n]xci é.
   One soldier arrived in the morning.

6 Gayó Kaá[n]ze iéwaská Ed Anderson zházhe ayí[n]be ao.
   The Kaw interpreter then had the name Ed Anderson.

7 Ákida akhá okíabe ao.
   The soldier spoke to him.

8 "Shayáni áshka-zhí^{n}ga ijé akhá eyaó.
   "Cheyennes are not too far off.

9 Níka lébla yábli^n akhá eyaó.
   There are actually thirty men.

10 Ákida watá^{n}ga akhá owíblage phú che á-da^n, owíblage achí eyaó," ábe ao.
   Hao.
   The officer said that I come here to tell you, and I am in fact here to tell
   you," he said.

11 Gagójida^n waká^{n}yabe ao Shayáni abá.
   At that time, the Cheyennes attacked us.

12 Cízhi^n Hó^{n}ga ts'éyabe ao Shayáni akhá. Hao.
   They killed Cízhi^n Hó^{n}ga.

13 Kaá^{n}ze shó^{n}ge lúza-ba-da^n, ágili^n-ba-dá^n, wahóta^n shke lúzabe ao.
   The Kaws were getting their horses and were mounting them, and they
   got their guns, too.

14 Zaní wapáhi lúzabe ao.
   They all took their weapons.

15 Ká^{n}ya yéyabe ao.
   They attacked suddenly.

16 Ká^{n}ya yéyabe Shayáni Kaá^{n}ze-baashé.
   The Kaws suddenly attacked the Cheyennes.

17 Gayójidá^n Kaá^{n}ze akhá oxlé ayábe ao.
   At that time, the Kaws went off to chase them.

18 Wékoce sáta^n hi óyaha Shayáni gahí^{n}ge watá^{n}ga khe ts'éyabe ao.
   When they reached five miles, they killed the Cheyenne principal chief.

19 Kaá^{n}ze abá é ts'éyabe ao.
   The Kaws killed him.

20 Shó^{n}ge sábe itá shke Kaá^{n}ze akhá oyí^{n}gabe ao.
   A Kaw even took his black horse.

21 Pádoka Gáxli akhá oyíⁿgabe ao.
Pádoka Gáxli ["Strikes Comanches"] took it.

22 Gayójidáⁿ oxlé ayá-ba-dáⁿ wachíⁿshka zhíⁿga Ujé Yiⁿgé Le Zhíⁿga éji obáyazabe ao, ogásta khejí.
At that time, they were going off to chase them, and they scared them
to Little Ujé Yíⁿge Le Stream [that is, Sawmill Creek] in the wide valley.

23 Gayó ejí Shayáni zaní yíⁿyabe ao.
Then they destroyed all the Cheyennes there.

24 Miⁿ-hiyé-go, yáblⁿ-hnaⁿ íyoⁿbe akhíbe ao.
When the sun set, only three made it out.

25 Gayó aⁿgéshki Shayáni akhá óbe ao.
Then the Cheyennes wounded us, too.

26 Óshe Góⁿya Shayáni wakúje-ta, wahótaⁿ íheyábe gagó ao.
Óshe Góⁿya was about to shoot at the Cheyennes and laid his gun out
like so.[5]

27 Wakúda yéyazhi shóⁿ-yiⁿkhé Shayáni akhá é paháⁿle kúdabe ao.
Having not shot yet, the Cheyennes shot at him first.

28 Á khe ópha ahú gághabe ao.
It made it come up, following the arm.

29 Máⁿzemaⁿ yiⁿkhé oyáha shóⁿ abá eyaó.
The bullet actually remained awhile.[6]

30 Shayáni míⁿxci oshtábe ao. Hao.
There was one Cheyenne left.

31 "Ats'é kóⁿbla eyaó," ábe ao.
"I really want to die," he said.

32 Paháⁿle Gáxli akhá wahótaⁿ scéje míⁿxci ayíⁿ akhá eyaó.
Paháⁿle Gáxli actually had one long gun.

33 Shayáni akhá wahótaⁿ dápa zhíⁿga, píⁿsta zhíⁿga, míⁿxci ayíⁿ akhá eyaó.
The Cheyenne had one little, short gun actually, a small pistol.

34 Kánya ayábe ao Pahánle Gáxli abá.

Pahánle Gáxli went rushing on him.

35 Gagó gashón ayábe ao, édan Shayáni akhá shápe íkudabe-zhín, níyabe ao.

So he went like this,[7] and the Cheyenne shot at him six times, but missed.

36 Pahánle Gáxli akhá áshka zhínga híbe-go óyaha wahótan mánxcan íkudabe-dán, ts'éyabe ao.

Right after Pahánle Gáxli got really close to him, he shot the gun once and killed him.

37 Xuyólange yuzábe ao, ceháwale yinkhé shke yuzábe ao, wanánp'in ska itá yinkhé shke yuzábe ao, mánze áyastale hegáxe áyastale khe zaní yuzábe ao, hegáxe shke yuzábe ao.

He took the eagle headdress, the shield, his white necklace, the metal fastened to the scalplock—all that was fastened—and the scalplock, too.

NOTES

1. The English equivalent of Kanza proper names is provided in brackets whenever possible.

2. Parks (2014, 154) writes: "By the war's end, eighty-seven Kanza warriors had served in Company L, Ninth Kansas Cavalry, and three mixed-bloods saw action with Company F, Fifteenth Kansas Volunteer Cavalry."

3. In his notes Dorsey (1883, 48) describes the events of lines 21–26 as follows:

> Of the two Cheyennes on one horse, [Xuyólange], a kinsman of [Pahánle Gáxli], killed the one in front when his horse fell, owing to a wound in the leg. The other Cheyenne fled, and at the end of the battle, being the only survivor of his party, he was killed by [Pahánle Gáxli], as told in this version.

4. Dorsey (1883, 48) clarifies the events depicted in lines 34–37 this way:

> Two Cheyennes crawled into the deep grass in the ravine. [Wádashtaye] set fire to the grass, and the south wind carried the flames to the place, where the the two were concealed. This made them stand at once, and both were killed. (Dorsey 1883)

5. The source material does not indicate the manner in which Óshe Gónya held his gun, nor the gun itself, but it was likely to have been a rifle requiring both hands to fire accurately—one on the trigger and one under the forestock.

6. There was a Kaw living around the turn of the twentieth century known as Shot Arm (he was also called Afraid of Moon or Wah-mo-o-e-ke, though the exact spelling and meaning of the latter are unknown). He was briefly chief of the Kaws following the death of

Washungah in 1908 (Unrau 1975, 79), and was photographed several times with a blanket around his arm, presumably to hide its gnarled appearance. Yet he was probably not Óshe Gónʸya. Shot Arm was listed as forty-one years old on the 1902 Kaw roll, meaning that he would have been only between six and twelve years of age at the time of this battle. He may well have fought that day, but Pahánʸle Gáxli would probably have made mention of the fact that Óshe Gónʸya was only a young boy at the time.

7. Dorsey (1883, 51) describes the manner of his running as a zig-zag, which is not the description in the Kanza-language source material. Perhaps Pahánʸle Gáxli indicated his dexterous and apparently effective maneuver through gesture while he narrated events.

REFERENCES AND RECOMMENDED READINGS

Bailey, G. A., and G. A. Young. 2001. "Kansa." In *Plains*, edited by R. J. DeMallie, 463–75. Vol. 13, Pt. 1 of *Handbook of North American Indians*, edited by W. C. Sturtevant. Washington DC: Smithsonian Institution.

Cumberland, L. A., and R. L. Rankin, eds. 2012. *Kaánʸze íe wayáje—An Annotated Dictionary of Kaw (Kanza): Kaw-English/English-Kaw*. Kaw City OK: Kaw Nation.

Dorsey, J. O. 1883. [Kansa texts. B. Historical papers]. MS 4800 James O. Dorsey Papers, circa 1870–1956, bulk 1870–1895. Smithsonian Institution, National Museum of Natural History (Oversize BAE, Folder 246, Box 33, Item 246), National Anthropological Archives, Museum Support Center, Suitland MD.

Koplowitz, B. 1996. *The Kaw Indian Census and Allotments*. Bowie MD: Heritage Books.

McBride, J. T., and L. A. Cumberland, eds. 2009. *Compiled Kanza Texts*. Kaw City OK: Kaw Nation.

——, eds. 2010. *Kaánʸze wéyaje—Kanza Reader: Learning Literacy through Historical Texts*. Kaw City OK: Kaw Nation.

Parks, R. D. 2014. *The Darkest Period: The Kanza Indians and Their Last Homeland 1846–1873*. Norman OK: University of Oklahoma Press.

Rankin, R. L. 1989. "Kansa." Translated by A. Yamamoto. In *Languages of the World*, 301–7. Vol. 1, Pt. 2 of *The Sanseido Encyclopaedia of Linguistics*, edited by T. Kamei, R. Kono, and E. Chino. Tokyo: Sanseido Press.

Unrau, W. E. 1971. *The Kansa Indians: A History of the Wind People 1673–1873*. Norman OK: University of Oklahoma Press.

——. 1975. *The Kaw People*. Phoenix AZ: Indian Tribal Series.

IOWAY

The Sister and Brother

Translated and introduced by Lance Foster, THPO Iowa Tribe of Kansas and Nebraska

Introduction

An English translation of a tale with a complicated origin was published by James Owen Dorsey in 1882 as "The Sister and Brother: An Iowa Tradition," in *The American Antiquarian and Oriental Journal*. The source of the story was Mary Gale La Flesche, half-Ioway through her mother Ni-co-ma; Mary had married Joseph La Flesche and was living up with the Omaha at the time. However, Mary had originally heard it from the father of Charles Morgan, an interpreter for the Ponca and Omaha. Although the actual tribal origin of the story may be unclear at this time, certainly it was related by an Ioway woman speaking in the Ioway language and recorded as "an Iowa tradition" by Dorsey.

HISTORICAL BACKGROUND

Glottochronology and tribal traditions indicate linguistic separation of the Ioway (Baxoje), Otoe (Jíwere), and Missouria (Ñiudači) from the Hochunk/Hocąk/Winnebago by the 1500s. The place called Red Banks or Red Earth (MaŠuje) on the shore of Lake Michigan is regarded as the traditional place of origin where the clans came together, although there is no archaeological evidence of a large settlement there. Evidence from archaeology and linguistics, as well as some tribal traditions, suggests many Siouan-speaking groups had drifted into the Midwest by the Middle-Late Woodland period, and subsequent development of some of these groups into an Upper Mississippian culture called the Oneota by archaeologists began around AD 1000. The Missouria were identifiable in the northern part of what is now the state of Missouri by the 1400s (the Utz site) and, for several hundred years (1200–1700), multiple sites indicate presence at various times for the

271

Iowa and the Otoe in western Wisconsin, southern Minnesota, the eastern parts of North and South Dakota, Nebraska, and Kansas. The center of their homelands was the land between the Missouri and Mississippi Rivers, which is now known as the state of Iowa, the source of its name being the Iowa (or Ioway) tribe.

The Ioway, Otoe, and Missouria had a reputation as traders among the tribes of the region from time immemorial; that intensive long-term interaction can be seen in even the most ancient traditions during the alliance of the clans. For example one tribal tradition states the Wolf Clan brought the bow and the arrow and spoke a different language. Indeed the bow and arrow were introduced during the Woodland period, and the words for bow and arrow are Algonquian in origin. Certainly continuing interactions and intermarriages were there among each of the three as well as with tribes like the Omaha, from precontact times onward.

Linguistically Iowa and Otoe-Missouria may be considered two dialects of the same language that began splitting in the late 1600s. This language has been termed "Chiwere" by linguists, after the Otoe's name for themselves, *Jíwere* ("Arrive Here") or *Čiwere* ("Lodges Here"); Dorsey noted an Ioway equivalent *Čikiwere*, with the meaning "the people of this place." Generally however the tribes generally prefer to term them as distinct languages, Ioway and Otoe-Missouria. Archaeologically and historically, before 1700, the Ioway and Otoe had closer association in Iowa and Nebraska, while the Missouria were further south in Missouri. One historical source indicated this was reflected in the languages, with Ioway and Otoe closer to each other than either was to Missouria. However, an attack in 1730 by Sac & Fox in Missouri soon compelled the remaining Missouria to scatter and join various tribes, with the majority joining the Otoe in Nebraska, resulting in the combined Otoe-Missouria tribal identity.

European and American explorers collected limited vocabulary lists, which are useful for archaic words and tracing phonological changes in the language.

The first substantial linguistic work, as with many indigenous languages, was that of missionaries. For the Ioway this was after they were placed on a new reservation in 1836 as a result of Indian Removal policies and Euro–American expansion. The Presbyterian missionaries William Hamilton and Samuel Irvin worked among the Iowa, and the Baptist missionary Merrill among the Otoe-Missouria, but of course the main focus of their work was conversion to Christianity, so much of it focused on translation of the Bible and other Christian texts and songs.

The publications of Irvin and Hamilton are probably the oldest and most complete source on the Ioway dialect. Hamilton was probably the one of the two who led the linguistic work with assistance of several Ioways, such as the tribe's interpreter, John Baptiste Roy.

The missionaries wrote the first grammar, a primer, and translated a number of bible verses, passages, and hymns. Although they recorded the substantive record of the Ioway language, including names of people, place names, and cultural practices, it was of course through their own worldview rather than that of the Ioways. The language materials stemmed from their purposes of proselytization. They did record some of the differences at the time between the Ioway and Otoe-Missouria dialects, both in terms of pronunciation and vocabulary.

After the split of the Iowa tribe in the 1870s, due to mounting pressures over culture, land, and allotment in Kansas and Nebraska that had been on them from the very beginning of the reservation's establishment in 1836, the larger number of traditionalists left their homes along the Nemaha country of Kansas and Nebraska to live among other Indian nations in Indian Territory, which would eventually become Oklahoma, where in 1883 they were given a reservation by executive order.

Up north, in order to survive, most of the Ioways there, diminished in land, culture, and population, turned more and more from traditional culture to become progressives and assimilated into the rural farming culture, although some individuals and families grew more inward in their culture and language. Some went to schools like Genoa, where use of Native languages was forbidden and punished. At home older people spoke their language among themselves, but were reluctant to teach it to their children, so they would not suffer as their elders had. To survive, the tribe became noted as a progressive tribe and took the path of assimilation more readily than their southern kin. Thus language use diminished much faster in the north than the south.

James Owen Dorsey collected some Chiwere texts from informants in Nebraska, where he was a missionary in the late 1800s; his focus had been on the Omaha, but he did collect some texts from Otoe-Missouria and Iowa, as well as other Siouan-language-speaking tribes.

Alanson Skinner included the Iowa among the many tribes he visited in the 1910s and 1920s as a museum collector; he published numerous articles and a few monographs on the Iowa. It is not yet clear how much linguistic work he did other than collect vocabulary for material culture, but some of his published stories also include sentences (1925).

In the early 1930s Gordon Marsh worked among the Otoe community at Red Rock, also where a small group of Iowa had gone to live and intermarry. Marsh was a student of Franz Boas and was a brilliant student of "salvage anthropology" as taught by his mentor, even developing a typewriter to record the language. Unfortunately for Marsh, he took so long working on the language that apparently Boas retired before he could graduate with his dissertation. The paradigm in anthropology had shifted again; finding faint interest among the replacement faculty, Marsh quit in disgust and became a monk. But that's another story. His notes were sent to the American Philosophical Society, which microfilmed them.

William Whitman, who had been studying the Otoe-Missouria in the later 1930s and 1940s, apparently found Marsh's notes and edited them. Marsh's work was published under Whitman's name with a nod to Marsh in 1947, as "Descriptive Grammar of Ioway-Oto."

The language continued to be used at home and in ceremonies in the southern Iowa and Otoe-Missouria communities, such as at religious services of both Christian churches and the Native American Church, and at funeral orations. By the 1960s only a few elderly people in the north had some use of the language and passed on some words and expressions in their own families.

Native speaker and Ioway tribal elder Franklin Murray and his daughter Mae Sine held a language class at Perkins; their hyphenated system of orthography (in which *Baxoje* is spelled *Bah-kho-jay*, for instance) is still used and preferred by many in the Oklahoma group.

Later in the 1970s Lila Wistrand-Robinson recorded a few stories as part of her effort with Jimm Garrett Good Tracks as part of a children's language program at Red Rock. Wistrand-Robinson was a linguist contracted for the children's project at Red Rock who worked to collect materials from elders in all three groups, including recordings of speech and songs. Jimm Garrett Good Tracks assisted her and eventually carried on the language work for many decades, with a dictionary and dedicated website.

This writer had gotten some words from my grandmother in the 1970s but really began studying the language in the early 1980s, buying a Mac and producing a lexicon from all available sources in the late 1980s.

In the late 1980s and into the 1990s a Chiwere language project based at Missouri was initiated by Louanna Furbee and her students, Lori Stanley and Jill Hopkins Greer, who continued this work, primarily among the Otoe-Missouria and Iowa who lived at Red Rock, though there was some work at Perkins as well. Several linguistic publications have resulted from this collaboration.

The last first-language elders fluent in Ioway/Baxoje are said to have died in Oklahoma by 1996, although a few semi-fluent elders still live in Oklahoma as of this writing. As Greer notes, Baxoje is a "sleeping language," and still is, as of 2017.

There have been various efforts to revive the language in both northern and southern communities, such as that by Franklin Murray (1977), enough to maintain an interest in the language, but this has been the work of individuals. Neither tribe has committed to support, staff, and fund a language program the way the Otoe-Missouria now has. There are now perhaps a dozen or two partial speakers of the Ioway language, varying in fluency from limited conversational ability to knowledge of a few words and phrases. There have been various efforts to revitalize the language among both groups of Iowa, including through language classes, but no sustained success has so far been achieved, due in part to factional disputes and lack of prioritization or support by either of the Iowa tribal governments . Individual scholars, both Ioway and non-tribal, continue to make efforts to preserve and grow Baxoje; that struggle continues despite the odds and small numbers of those actually making the effort. For example during the writing of this article, four scholars for the Ioway tribe are working at the Breath of Life language program at the Smithsonian; this writer also has a number of Ioway language videos on YouTube, as well as a Facebook page for "Chiwere."

THE TEXT: THE SISTER AND BROTHER

There are two kinds of traditional narratives among the Ioway, the *weką* and the *worage*. The weką relates sacred traditions of ancient times, and may be broken down further into several categories, from very sacred clan stories not freely shared nor spoken of to entertainment and morality tales. The worage is an account of historical events, very old or recent.

The translation into English of the weką story "The Sister and Brother: An Iowa Tradition" was published by James Owen Dorsey in 1882 in *The American Antiquarian and Oriental Journal* (Dorsey 1882). For the hunting songs musical notation and the Chiwere words were given. Comparison with the actual linguistic text and notes by Dorsey show some differences, notably the omission of the mother's affair with the bear, due to sensitivities at the time about sexual matters in the mainstream culture, but that omission also removed the incident that initiated the father's actions and his abandonment of the children.

Dorsey identified the story as an "Iowa tradition" in his published title. He had collected some texts from the Otoes as well as the La Flesche family at Omaha; those texts, including the source for "Sister and Brother," are in the National Anthropological Archives (NAA) Dorsey papers. The La Flesche family's history and social position is a complex one, with kinship and cultural ties to Ponca, Omaha, Otoe-Missouria, and Ioway, as seen in other essays in this volume. Dorsey's notes state: "This myth or legend was told many years ago to Mary Gale La Flesche by the father of the late Charles Morgan (formerly interpreter for the Ponkas and then for the Omahas). Though told to the writer by a woman, it will be noticed that the masculine 'ke' is used as the oral period, whenever a period is used in the body of the text."

Mary Gale had married Joseph La Flesche, who was an Omaha, and Dorsey met and worked with them there. However Mary was half-Ioway, not Omaha. She was the daughter of a white man, Dr. John Gale, a surgeon at Fort Atkinson (Nebraska), and an Indian woman, Ni-co-ma, which may be a spelling for "White Water Woman" (now spelled *Nixgami*). Mary Gale was called Hinnuaganun (One Woman); "woman" in Ioway is *hinaga*. Her father abandoned them; Mary would have grown up speaking Ioway from her mother and thus told the story in Ioway. This lack of certain provenance is probably why Dorsey categorized the story as "an Iowa tradition." However the person who related it was Ioway and related it in Ioway, within a cultural context of shared stories among closely tied tribes, so that is sufficient for our purposes here.

THEMES

Essentially "The Sister and the Brother" is a morality tale, with two interesting features standing out.

Circumlocution in hunting peoples: Interestingly, the hunting songs seem to record an earlier period of hunting taboos, expressed as circumlocution, that is, not saying the "real name" of the animal or bird being hunted. A series of songs pair the "hunting name" of the animal (for example, *dagure thewe xąnje iyą,* 'a big black something'), used by the brother, with the actual name (*mųnje,* 'black bear') used in response by the sister.

Wrongdoing and food-sharing: While the wrongdoing of the mother in having an affair, especially with a bear, her deceits, and subsequent murder by the father are all noted, the real focus seems to be on the abandonment of the children by the father and his attempt to deceive them into cannibalism. Also note the real sentence upon the offending father: he is not killed but banished, ignored, not allowed to share food, whether starved or not, food-sharing being foundational, especially parent to children and later children to parent. The sister said this was not to happen; the father was not to share the meat.

ORTHOGRAPHY

Information on the Ioway language is found in many sources. There are several spelling/orthographic systems used historically and also by contemporary communities; the communities contest which system should be used, and even the pronunciations of many words. Some are also based on whether the speaker favored an Ioway or Otoe dialect, or if the dialects were mixed in their family, as intermarriage was common, especially after the establishment of the reservations and of the Nemaha Halfbreed Tract and, later, the mixed Otoe-Iowa settlement at Red Rock. Such disputes can be seen in light of the complex linguistic environment occupied by the speakers and their families, and of the fragmentation of the communities. For this story I have chosen to use a modified Americanist system, with which most readers will be familiar.

A couple of sentences were rewritten here to improve comprehension, such as when the village hunting party departs. The section on the hunting songs also needed to be cleaned up and added to, due to errors, redundancy, and omissions. For example, *wayinxanje*, lit. "the big bird," was translated as "elk" in the text. Dorsey leaves out in the published translation the reason given in the text as to why the man killed his wife, which was because she was cheating on him with a grizzly bear. Additional information has been put in brackets to help the reader understand the cultural context. I wish also to acknowledge not only Mary Gale and J. O. Dorsey, but all those in our growing language community who have shared so much with me. *Warigroxi ke.*

The Sister and Brother

THE FAMILY IN THE FOREST

Či iyą dahe, añe ke.
Lodge | a | was there | they say | [declarative, male speaker].
There was a lodge, they say.

Hedą hinage naha išna xči igrą, areči ičičiŋe nuwewi, añe.

And then | woman | the | alone | really | her husband | therefore | children | two [dual] | they say.

And then the woman was really alone with her husband there, as well as two children, they say.

Igrą kinaŋgra re, añe.

Her husband | hunting | he went | they say.

Her husband went hunting, they say.

Ta č'ewahi na wošexčiwi añe ke.

Deer | he killed it | and | having plenty | very much | they two | they say.

He killed deer and they had abundant meat, they say.

Hedą kinaŋgra raje ške, igrą:

And then | hunting | he went | when | her husband:

And then when he went hunting, her husband [would say]:

"Rigixwe to, hakinaŋgra haje hñe ke."

Comb your hair | let us | I hunt | I go | [future] | [declarative].

"Let us comb your hair, I am going hunting."

Hedą gixwe, añe.

And then | he combed | they say.

And then he combed it, they say.

Hedą poroxreče šuje ki, añe.

And then | part in the hair | red | [he painted] her | they say.

And then he painted the part in her hair red, they say.

Hedą kikų̃ðe ki, añe.

And then| he painted her | they say.

And then he painted her, they say.

Hedą kinaŋgra re añe, waŋe naha.

And then | hunting | he went | they say | man | the.

And then he went hunting, they say, the man.

Hedą xtanaxči wak^į gri, añe.

And then | dusk | packing it | he returned | they say.

And then at dusk, packing [meat] he would return, they say.

Hedą hinage naha našu wahihaxči naŋe gri, añe.
And then | woman | the | hair | it really disordered | sitting there | he returned
  | they say.
And then when he returned, the woman would be sitting there, her hair
  really messed up.

Mašuje hedą wašuxči naŋe gri, añe.
Red-earth [paint] | [and] then | rubbed off | sitting there | he returned |
  they say.
The red paint was then rubbed off, and she was sitting there when he returned.

"Hakišruče haje ka;
Smooth I made it | I go | there;
"I smoothed it when I went away;

Dagure ˆų," k'are ire, añe.
Whatever | she do | about her | he thought | they say.
Whatever did she do?" he thought about her, they say.

Šige e hąŋgida, "Rigixwe to, gų re," añe.
Again | he said | he lies there | Comb your hair | let us | come | [imperative] |
  they say.
Again he said, lying there, "Let us comb your hair, come!" they say.

Hedą gixwa na kikųšeki, añe.
And then | comb | and | painted it | they say.
And then they combed it and painted it, they say.

Hedą kinaŋgra re, añe.
And | he hunt | he go | they say.
And then he went hunting, they say.

Šige xtanaxči wakˆį gri, añe.
Again | dusk | he packing | he returns | they say.
Again, at dusk, packing [meat], he returned, they say.

Šige hinage naha hįhaxči naŋe gri, añe.
Again | woman | the | hair messed up | she sitting | he returns | they say.
Again, the woman, her hair messed up, was sitting there when he returned,
  they say.

The Sister and Brother   279

"Dagure ˆųna šu ˆųŋkuñe?," ire, añe.

Whatever | she do and | possibly | they make that result | he thought |
   they say.

"What could she and the others possibly be doing to result in that?" he
   thought, they say.

Hedą dohą ikų nu, ašku.

And then | four times | thus | happen | it seems.

And then four times it happened the same way, it seems.

Hedą widoweda kinaŋgra raje ške da:

And then | the fourth time | he hunts | he goes | if | there:

And then when the fourth time he was going hunting:

"Ni aku ira re, añe ke.

Water | bring | you go | [imperative] they say [declarative].

"You go bring water!" [he told the wife] they say.

Hedą či xroške da, ičičiŋe nuwewi je, gehnaha waŋe, gehnaha hinųwe, añe.

And then | house | empty | there | children | two of them| this | the other |
   man | the other | girl | they say.

And then the lodge [was] empty, the two children; the man and the girl,
   they say.

Hedą, "Hįyuŋe, haje da, rihų ritogre šna ˆų je?," añe.

And then | My daughter | when I go| your mother | with you together | alone
   | she does | [interrogative] | they say.

And then, "Daughter, when I go, your mother, when you are together alone,
   what does she do?"

"Hiñega, hiŋka, šre da ikitą hįna re šna ˆų ki," e añe.

No | my father | you go | then | watching| my mother | she goes | alone | she
   does | [declarative] | she said | they say.

"No, Father, when you go, Mother watches and then she goes off alone," she
   said, they say.

"Hįyuŋe, hakinaŋgra haje hakuše ke," e añe.

My daughter | I hunt | I go | I pretend | [declarative] | he said | they say.

"Daughter, I will pretend to go hunting," he said, they say.

"Či naŋkeriki uhakinaxwe hayą hñe ke.
House | in back of | within I myself hide | I lay | [future] | [declarative].
"I will lie down and hide myself behind the lodge.

Dagure ˆų wopareha hagųnda ke," e añe.
Whatever | she does | what I understand | I want | [declarative] | he said | they say.
Whatever she is doing, I want to understand what it is," he said, they say.

Hedą itami gri añe, ñi agu.
And then | his wife | she returns home | they say | water | she carries.
And then his wife returned, they say, bringing water.

"Ji gixwe to! Gų re!
Come | comb [your] hair | [imperative] | Toward it!
"Come let us comb your hair! Come here!

Hakinaŋgra (ha)je hñe ke," e añe.
I hunt | I go | [future] | [declarative] | he said | they say.
I am going hunting," he said, they say.

Hedą gixwa na kikųše ki, añe.
And | he combs and | he paints her himself | they say.
And then he combs her hair and paints her, they say.

"Ho, hakinaŋgra haje hñe ke."
Ho | I hunt | I go | [future] | [declarative].
"Ho, I am going hunting."

Hedą re ške da, či naŋkerida ukinaxwe yą, añe ke.
And then | he goes | as if | house | in the back | he hides himself | he lies
  down | they say | [declarative].
And then he acts as if he is going, but goes behind the lodge, where he hides
  himself and lies down, they say.

Še wóxąče, itami: "Čičuñe gasų togre mina hą," e añe.
There | as soon as [he left] | his wife | Your little brother | already | together
  | sit | [imperative fem.] | she said | they say.
As soon as he was gone, his wife [said]: "Sit together with your little brother
  now," she said, they say.

Ida ikitą hinage naha re, añe ke.

Then | he watches her | woman | the | go | they say | [declarative].

Then he watches the woman go, they say.

Ida, "Čaa! Dagure ˆų kˆare ihare"; ira na uxré re, añe ke.

Then | Chaa | whatever | she does | as it is | I think | she goes | and | he follows [her] | he goes | they say | [declarative].

Then, "*Chaa!* I think I know what she is doing"; she goes and he follows, they say.

THE AFFAIR DISCOVERED

Hedą mąxeda hi añe, hinage naha.

And then | cropfield there | she arrived | they say | woman | the.

And then she arrives at a cropfield, the woman.

Ida ešwenaxči Mąhto iyą axewe hu, añe ke

Then | immediately | Grizzly Bear | a | appears | it comes | they say | [declarative].

Then immediately a grizzly bear appears, it comes, they say.

Jeˆe are ikų ˆų; kˆare ihare ga, are ikų ˆų ga, ire, añe ke.

This | it is | his wife | she does | it is there | I thought | there | it is | thus | she does | there | he thinks | they say | [declarative].

This is what his wife had been doing; "It is as I thought"; his wife was doing just as he had thought, they say.

Eda Mąhto naha, hinage naha, arukage, ji naŋe, añe ke.

And then | Grizzly Bear | the | woman | the embrace | coming into a sitting position | they say [declarative].

And then, the grizzly bear, the woman, they embrace, coming into a sitting position, they say.

Eda arukage na ruwañe, añe ke.

And then | embrace | and | they pull | they say [declarative].

And then, embracing, they pull [down to the ground], they say.

Hedą minaŋgri naŋewi na kikiškajewi, añe ke.

And then | returned to sitting upright | two sitting | and | they two played with each other | they say | [declarative].

And then, the two returned to sitting upright, playing with each other, they
   say.

Hedą šų našu broge wahiha xči, añe ke.
And then | thus | hair | all | disordered | really | they say | [declarative].
And then, thus her hair was all really messed up, they say.

Kikuše heda wašu xči, añe ke.
Paint | and then | by rubbing off | really | they say | [declarative].
And then, the paint had been really rubbed off, they say.

Hedą waŋe naha nayį̇ jire añe.
And then | man | the | he stands | he rises | they say.
And then, the man stands where he is, he rises, they say.

Hedą Mąhto ada na, nayį̇, añe ke, Mąhto.
And then | Grizzly Bear | he sees and | he stands | they say | [declarative] |
   Grizzly Bear.
And then, Grizzly Bear sees and he stands, they say, Grizzly Bear.

Hedą kuče na, čˆehi, añe ke, Mąhto.
And then | he shoots and | kills | they say | [declarative] | Grizzly Bear.
And then, he shoots and kills Grizzly Bear, they say.

Hedą čˆehi ške, hinage naha:
And then | he kills | if | woman | the:
And then, as he is about to kill her, the woman [cries out]:

"Hįį̇! Waŋe, ihaxˆą hagųnda ki!," e añe.
Ohh! | Man/husband | I alive | I want | [declarative]! | she said | they say.
"Ohh! Husband I want to live!" she said, they say.

"Hiñego, tąnda iraxˆą išrayį̇," e añe.
No | where | you alive | you think that way | he said | they say.
"No, you would like to think you are going to live," he said, they said.

Hedą inuki čˆewahi, añe ke.
And then | both | he-kills-them | they say | [declarative].
And then, he killed them both, they say.

Hedą ną iyą ašgida nayį.

And then | tree | a | nearby | stood.

And then, a tree stood nearby.

Hedą hįnage naha kruše na ną agráče itoda tˆąwe, añe.

And then | woman | the | taking | and | tree | limb/arm | he hung her there | he jump | they say.

And then, taking the woman, he jumped up and hung her there on a tree limb, they say.

Hedą či waagre, añe.

And then | lodge | he returned to it | they say.

And then, he returned to the lodge, they say.

Ida gri ske,

And | he return | when,

And when he [the father] returned to his home,

"Ną šedagi, ną hujeda, ta paše na rikipašnųwi ke.

Tree | that-there-towards | tree | trunk there | deer | breast | and | you-two to roast | [declarative].

"At a tree way off there, at the tree trunk, there is a deer breast and you two go roast it for yourselves.

Čičuñe inų ra na ruje inų ˆų re," e añe.

Your brother | with | go | and | eat | with | do-you | he said | they say.

Take your brother with you, go and eat with him!" he [the father] said, they say.

Hedą hįnųwe naha ičuñe ekrani na iware, añe.

And then | sister | the | her brother | leftovers | and | went forth | they say.

And then the sister and her brother went forth to get the food their father left, they say.

Hedą idahiwi, añe.

And then | they arrived there | they say.

And then they arrived there, they say.

284   The Sister and Brother

"Amina re, hi̱ruje to," e añe, išuñe ewaka.
Sit down | [imperative]| we eat | [hortative] | she said | they say | her brother
  | to him addressed.
"Sit down, let us eat," she said, addressing her brother, they say.

Ida išuñe he kipašwe ške.
Then | her brother | piece of | she cut off (a piece of) her own | if.
Then her brother cut off a piece.

Woxą̇ce wą̇xšike iyą̇ ičˆe naxų̇ ške ašku̱.
As soon as | human being | one | speech | she heard | if | it seems.
As soon as he did, she heard a person's voice, it seems.

Hedą̇ šige he pašwe ške.
And then | again | piece | she cut off | when.
And then, again, when she cut off a piece.

Heda šige wą̇xšike iyą̇ ičˆe naxų̇ ške ašku̱.
And then | again | human being | one | speech| she heard | if | it seems.
And then again she heard a human voice, it seems.

Ešwenaxči ma̱ŋgriki woruxiče ške,
Immediately | above herself | she looked for | when,
Immediately, she looked above herself [in the tree] for [the person speaking],
  and when she did,

ihų̇ čihaŋe ašku, egrata ašku̱.
her mother | dead lying there| it seems | she saw her own | it seems.
she saw her own mother lying dead there, it seems.

"Hi̱i̱! Hi̱ču̱čiñexčidha, hi̱ŋka hi̱na čˆehi na jeˆe haŋe are ki!
Ohh | my dear little brother | my father | my mother | he killed | and | this
  lying there | it is she | [declarative]!
"Ohh, my dear little brother, Father killed Mother, and this is her lying there!

Hi̱ŋgreda!" e añe.
We return home! | she said | they say.
We're going home!" she said, they say.

The Sister and Brother   285

Ida gre ašku, išuñe gratogre na čiwa.

Then | she returned | it seems | her brother | together with her own | and | at the lodge.

Then she returned, it seems, together with her own brother to the lodge.

Hedą ida griwi ške, či xroške griwi ašką.

And then | there | returned two | when | lodge | empty | return two | it seems.

And then when the two returned home, the lodge was empty, it seems.

"Hįį! Hįšųšiñexčidha, hiŋka, hųnje, hįreñe ki."

Well! | My dear little brother | my father | yes | let us go | [declarative].

"Well! My dear little brother, yes, Father's [gone], let us follow."

Hedą excą šigre uče ške, šigre ra dahe ašką.

And then | circling around | footprints | they search| for | footprints | he went | there | it seems.

And then, when they circled around, searching for footprints, there were his footprints going there, it seems.

"Hį! Hįšųšiñexčidha, hiñka šigre ra dahe ki," e ašką.

Well! | My dear little brother | father | footprints | he go | there | [declarative] | she said | it seems.

"Well! My dear little brother, Father's footprints are there, going away," she said, it seems.

Hedą šigre irowe rawi ašką.

And then | footprints | follow | they two go | it seems.

And then the two of them went, following the footprints, it seems.

THE FATHER ARRIVES AT A VILLAGE

Hedą ąnje čina xąjexči hi ašką.

And then | their father | village | really big | he arrived | it seems.

And then their father arrived at a really big village, it seems.

"Wąxšike iyą ji ke," añe ašką.

Human being | a | arrives | [declarative] | they say | it seems.

"A human being arrives," they said, it seems.

"Ani kuwi re!
Hither | bring him!
"Bring him hither!

Čįciñe mįtawe grañe hñe ke," waŋegihi e ašku.
Children | my | they marry | [future] | [declarative] | chief | he said | it
  seems.
My children will marry," the chief said, it seems.

Hedą ida añi ahiñe na grañe ašku.
And then | there | he had/was | they arrived | and | they married | it seems.
And then he arrived and they were married, it seems.

THE CHILDREN ARRIVE AT THE VILLAGE

Ida ičįčįñe anaha hiwi ašku.
Then | children | there | they two arrived | it seems.
Then the two children arrived there, it seems.

Hinaxsiñe iyą čina kixaridada čiˆakirušaˆiñe umina ašku.
Little old woman | a | village | apart from | little [tied together] lodge | sat
  within | it seems.
A little old woman sat within a small *chakiruthą*[1] a little outside the village,
  it seems.

"Hįį! Iyąhą wąxšige xšu iyą uŋkwe škuñi ga, rišuñe kˆu dagure raˆu rajiwi?"
Well! | Never | human being | now | a | enter | not | therein | your younger
  brother | give | whatever | you do | you two eat?
"Well! Never has a person ever entered before, what do you want me to give
  your brother and you to eat?"

"Hiŋkuñi, hiŋka hu na hograxre hįhuwi ki," e ašku.
My grandmother | my father | he came | and | catching up to him our own
  one | we two come | [declarative] | she said | it seems.
"Grandmother, my father came and we two came to catch up to him," she
  said, it seems.

1 A traditional lodge with tied-together framework, covered by cattail mats or elm bark

"Hų, hįtagwami, nąnje ji, añe ki.
Yes | my granddaughter | your father | came | they say | [fem. declarative].
"Yes, Granddaughter, your father came, they say.

Waŋegihi čįčiñe naha xrañe, añe ki, nąnje."
Chief | children | the | hungry | they say | [declarative] | your father.
The chief's children are hungry, they say, your father [will feed them]."[2]

Hinaxčiñe naha axewe re, añe ke.
Little old woman | the | appear/come out | went | they say | [declarative].
The little old woman went out of the lodge, they say.

Šige ičįdoiñe ada, ašku.
Again| little boy | she saw |it seems.
Again, she saw a little boy, it seems.

"Hiŋgrų, waŋegihi naha wądohą etawe ukirage re:
Firstborn son | chief | the | son-in-law | his | tell him:
"Firstborn son, tell the chief's son-in-law:

Ičįčiñe ukraxre jiwi ke."
Children | overtaken | they two came | [declarative].
The children have caught up, they arrived."

Ida ukirake ahiñe, ašku.
There | to tell him | he went | it seems.
He went there to tell him, it seems.

"Ičįčiñe ritawe irikraxre jiwi ke," e ke ašku.
Children | your | have overtaken you | they two come | [declarative] | he
    said | it seems.
"Your children have caught up to you, they two arrived," he said, it seems.

"Še wohašiñe na wohakinaxwe hahu ke.
There | I was angry with them | and | to hide myself from them | hither I
    came | [declarative].
"I was angry with them there, and I came here to hide myself from them.

2 To feed them is implying he had married the chief's daughter(s).

Ihų č^egrakiwi na wohakinaxwe hahu ke," e ašką.

Their mother | they two killed their own | and | to hide myself from them |
I came | [declarative] | he said | it seems.

Those two killed their own mother and I came here to hide myself from
them," he said, it seems.

"Ho, hįtuga, hįwakihajeda ho!"

Ho | grandfather [term of respect for chief] | let us flee here!

"Ho, Grandfather, let us flee from here!"

Ñi xąnje ške, baje ^ųñe, ašką.

Water | big | by | boats | they make |it seems.

By the big water, they made boats, it seems.

Baje ^ųñe na ruštąñe, ašką.

Boat | they made | and | they finished |it seems.

They made a boat and finished it, it seems.

"Hąhegi hįwe wawakixriwi re," e ke ašką.

Tonight | let us | close their eyes with glue | [imperative] | he said to them
| it seems.

"Tonight, let us glue their eyes shut," he said to them, it seems.

"Hąwe, harigųnda, ñi hįruče da ho."

Day | far toward there | water | let us cross | there | [optative].

"Tomorrow, let us go far away across the water."

Hedą kixrą bereñe, čina x^oje xči ašką.

And then | hunting party | they departed | village | empty | really | it seems.[3]

And then, the hunting party departed, and the village was really empty, it
seems.

"Hįyuno, išta hačupra hačus^ake ke!"

My older sister | eye | I open | I am unable | [declarative].

"Sister! I am unable to open my eyes!"

_____

3 In the original: Hedą kixrą thi, x^oje xči ašką. "And then, hunting party foot, empty really
it seems." The sentence was rewritten in order to make more sense in current usage.

"Hįšųsiñexčitha, ike išta hačupra hačušˆake ki!"
My dear little brother | likewise | eye | I open | I am unable | [declarative].
"Dear little brother, I also am unable to open my eyes!"

Hedą hįčuňe iyą wanaŋe hire ašku.
And then | mouse | a | running on her | it came | it seems.
And then a mouse came and ran over her, it seems.

"Hįį! Ušˆįdą xąnje maxéra re!
Well! | Hateful | big one | begone | [imperative].
"Well! Hateful big thing! Begone!

Dagure ųˆ na wawaranaŋewi?"
Whatever | doing and | you run on us two?
Whatever are you doing, running on us two?"

"Hinaa! Dagure ųˆ na, išta rigitaxroče dana haji.
Well! | Whatever | to do | and | eye | open them with tongue | really | I have
  come.
"Well! Whatever am I doing, I have really come to lick your eyes open.

Dagure ųˆna ųrašiñe?"
Whatever [why] | to do | are you angry?
What are you angry for?"

"Hįį! Hiŋkuñi, ihapuñe škuñe na šehe ki.
Well | my grandmother | I know | not and | so it was | [declarative].
"Ohh! Grandmother, I didn't know and so I was that way.

Hįšuñe itų kiraxroče re!"
My brother | first | open them with tongue | [imperative].
Lick open my brother's eyes first!"

"Hų," e ašku.
Yes | she said | it seems.
"Yes," she [the mouse] said, it seems.

Ida kiraxroče ašku.
Then | she licked them open| it seems.
Then she licked them open, it seems.

290   The Sister and Brother

"Hịyuno, išta hačupra ke," e ašku.
My older sister | eye | I open | [declarative] | he said | it seems.
"Sister, I opened my eyes," he said, it seems.

Hedą, "Hịyuno, ñijejedą waata ji hñe ke; kixrą waata ji hñe ke."
And then | My sister | very large lake | I see it | I arrive | [future] | [declarative] | hunting party | I see it | I arrive | [future] | [declarative].
And then, "Sister, I will go to the very large lake I see; I will go see the hunting party."

Hedą ñijejedą hi ašku, ičịndoiñe naha.
And then | large body of water | he arrive | it seems | boy | the.
And then he arrived at the large body of water, it seems, the boy.

Hedą hinaxšiñe naha pušagida naŋe ašku.
And then | little old woman | the | there on sand | she sits | it seems.
And then, the little old woman was sitting there on the sand, it seems.

"Hịị! Hịtagwayiñexčitha, uhamina kųhąnda atawi re," e ašku.
Well | my dear little grandchildren | I am sitting on | underneath | you look | [imperative] | she said | it seems.
"Well! My dear little grandson, underneath where I am sitting, you two look there," she said, it seems.

Hedą hinųwe naha xami umiye ruxe ske:
And then | girl | the | grass | covering | open by pulling up/peeling | when:
And then, when the girl pulled back the mat covering:

"Hịị! Hịšuñšiñexčitha, rikų ˆųˆewa wakipere dahe ki," e ke, ašką, išuñe.
Provisions | there | [fem. declarative] | likewise | it seems | [said to] her brother.
"Well! My dear little brother, your grandmother left those provisions there for us," she said, it seems.

GOING HUNTING

Eda, "Hịyuno, mąhdu iyaŋki ˆų re!
Then | My sister | bow | one | to make!
Then, "Sister, make one bow!

The Sister and Brother 291

Išagrehu, maša dowe rakˆų hñe, añi gų re."

Bow-ash tree[4] | arrow-reed[5] [for arrow shaft]| four | you give | [future] | have | toward | [imperative].

Go and get white ash for a bow and four river canes for arrow shafts and give them to me."

Ida išge añi gri, ašgų.

Then | likewise | she have | to return home | it seems.

Then the same way, she returned home with them, it seems.

"Či uri rexrigeda mašų iyą uje ra re.

Lodge | you go to | old site there | feather | a | you search | you go | [imperative].

"Go to the old site where the lodges were and search for feathers there.

Eda udá añi gri ašgų, mašų."

Then | some | to have | to come back | it seems | feathers.

Then, having some feathers, come back home."

Eda išge kiˆų ašgų.

Then | thus | carried | it seems.

Then, thus she retrieved them, it seems.

Hedą mąhdu ma ˆų, ašgų.

And then | bow | arrows | she made | it seems.

And then, she made the bow and arrows, it seems.

Hedą ičįndoiñe kinaŋgra re, añe.

And then | boy | hunting | he went | they say.

And then the boy went hunting they say.

HUNTING SONGS

Eda kirušdą ške, "Hįyuno, wayįxšiñe hakuče hačˆe hñe ke."

---

4 White ash (*Fraxinus americana*) is the preferred ash for bows, though Osage orange (nąpi) (*Maclura pomifera*) was the wood more preferred for bows generally.

5 Arrow shafts were made of many things, but in this case it is a "reed," that is, river cane (*Arundinaria gigantea*).

Then | finished for | when| My sister | little bird | I shoot | I kill | [future] |
  [declarative].
Then, when she had finished it for him, "Sister, I will shoot and kill a little
  bird."

Wayi̧xšiñe iya̧ čˆehi ašgu̧, togregreδiñe.
Little bird | a | he killed | it seems | blue spotted little.
He killed a little bird, it seems, a little spotted blue thing [a woodpecker].

Ida gu̧ ašgu̧.
There | [he went] toward | it seems.
He went toward there, it seems.

SONG: THE WOODPECKER

"Hi̧yuno! Hi̧yuno!
My sister! | My sister!
"My sister! My sister!

"Dagure gregreδiñe iya̧,
Whatever | little-spotted-thing | one,
"A spotted little thing,

"Čˆeharo, hi̧yuno, čˆeharo!"
I have killed | my sister | I have killed!
"I have killed, my sister, I have killed!"

"Hi̧i̧! hi̧šu̧šiñexčitha, togregreδe warajeñe ki."
Well | my little brother | woodpecker | you killed | [fem. declarative].
"Well! My dear little brother, they call that the blue spotted one, a woodpecker."

Šige heroda xči, "Hi̧yuno, šige hačˆe hñe ke."
Again | morning | really | My sister | again | I kill | [future] | [declarative].
Again, early in the morning, "Sister, again I will kill."

Šige ida gu̧ ašgu̧.
Again | there | toward | it seems.
Again, there he went, it seems.

"Hįyuno! Hįyuno!
My sister! | My sister!
"Sister! Sister!

Dagure xąnje iyą,
Something | big | a,
Something big,

Čˆeharo, hįyuno, čˆeharo!"
I killed | my sister | I killed!
I have killed, Sister, I have killed!"

Eda, "Hįį! Hįšųšiñexčitha, wayįxąñe warajeñe ki."
Then | Well! | My little brother | big bird [turkey] | what they call it | [declarative].
Then, "Well! My little brother, they call that the big bird, the turkey."

"Hįyuno, šige hačˆe hñe ke," e aškų.
My sister | again | I kill | [future] | he said | it seems.
"Sister, again I will kill," he said, it seems.

Eda šige gų aškų.
Then | again | toward | it seems.
Then, again he went there, it seems.

"Hįyuno! Hįyuno!
My sister! | My sister!
"My sister! My sister!

Dagure thįnje thka yiñe iyą,"
Something | tail | white | little | a,
Something with a little white tail,

Čˆeharo, hįyuno, čˆeharo!"
I killed | my sister | I killed!
I have killed, Sister, I have killed!"

"Hįį! Hįšųšiñexčitha, taxči warajeñe ki."
Well | my dear little brother | deer-real | what they call it | [declarative].
"Well! My dear little brother, they call that the real-deer, the whitetail deer."

"Hįyuno, šige haje hñe ke," e aškų.
My sister | again | I go | [future] | [declarative] | he said | it seems.
"Sister, again I will go," he said, it seems.

Eda šige gų aškų.
Then | again | toward | it seems.
Then, again he went there, it seems.

SONG: BLACK BEAR

"Hįyuno! Hįyuno!
My sister! | My sister!
"My sister! My sister!

Dagure thewe xąnje iyą
Something | black | big | one
Something big and black

Čˆeharo, hįyuno, čˆeharo!"
I killed | my sister | I killed!
I have killed, Sister, I have killed!"

"Hįį! Hįšųšiñe xči tha, mųnje warajeñe ki," e aškų.
Well! | My dear little brother | black bear | they call it | [declarative] | she
  said | it seems.
"Well! My dear little brother, they call that the black bear," she said, it seems.

Šige, "Hįyuno, haje hñe ke," e aškų.
Again | My sister | I go | [future] | [declarative] | he said | it seems.
Again, "Sister, I will go," he said, it seems.

Hedą gų ašku.
And then | he went toward it | it seems.
And then, he went there, it seems.

The Sister and Brother 295

"Hįyuno! Hįyuno!
My sister! | My sister!
"My sister! My sister!

Dagure thįnje ñiŋe iyą,
Whatever | tail | none | a,
Something with no tail,

Čˆeha ro, hįyuno, čˆeharo!"
I killed | my sister | I killed!
I killed, Sister, I killed!"

Eda, "Hįį! Hįšųšiñexčitha, huma warajeñe ki," e ašką.
Then | Well! | My dear little brother | elk | what they call it | [declarative] | she said | it seems.
Then, "Well! My dear little brother, they call that the elk," she said, it seems.

"Hįyuno! Hįyuno!
My sister! | My sister!
"My sister! My sister!

Dagure he thewe xąñe iyą,
Something | horn | black | large | a,
Something with big black horns,

Čˆeharo, hįyuno, čˆeharo!"
I killed | my sister | I killed!
I killed it, Sister! I killed it!"

Eda, "Hįį! Hįšųšiñexčitha, če warajeñe ki," e ašką.
Then | Well! | My dear little brother | buffalo | what they call | [declarative] | she said | it seems.
Then, "Well! My dear little brother, they call that the buffalo," she said, it seems.

Hedą išuñe axewe re, ašku.
And then | her brother | appears | he goes | it seems.
And then, her brother went and appeared, it seems.

"Hiyuno, wą^šige iyą mihį adare k^į ną amąhą dahe ke."
Sister | human being | a | robe with the hair on | at this time | wear | tree |
    leaning | there | [declarative].
"Sister, a person wearing a robe with the hair on is outside leaning against
    a tree there."

"Hįį! Hįšųšiñexčitha ritąhą are ki.
Well! | My little brother | your brother-in-law | it is | [declarative].
"Well! My dear little brother, that is your brother-in-law.

Agwira re!"
Go after him | [imperative].
Go get him!"

"Hįtąho, hiyuna hiŋgreje ke."
My brother-in-law | my sister | we go to her | [declarative].
"Brother-in-law, we go to my sister."

"Hų, hįtąhą, riyuna kagrañe hagųda na haje ke," e ašku.
Yes | my brother-in-law | your sister | marry her | I want | he said | it seems.
"Yes, brother-in-law, I want to marry your sister and [so will] I go," he said,
    it seems.

Ida togre gri ašku.
There | together | go back | it seems.
They went back there together, it seems.

Ida grañe ašku.
There | they married | it seems.
There they were married, it seems.

Heda čina are nahada wąxšige nuwe griwi ašku.
And then | village | it is | the one there | people | two | go back [dual] | it seems.
And then, the two went back there to the village, it seems.

Čina xrañi tąnrañe ke; rohą hį̂t^awi ke.

Village | hungry | great they | [declarative] many | died | [declarative].

The village had great hunger [was in famine]; many of them had died.

Wokihąwi na warujewi, ašką.

Cooked for themselves two | and | they two eat | it seems.

They two cooked for themselves and ate, it seems.

WHAT THE SISTER TELLS THE PEOPLE

"Čina woragisrageda ^o.

Village | to listen to a telling of events | [optative].

"I wish the village to listen to this news.

Agųñeda ho.

Carry it back here | [optative].

I wish you to carry [the meat] back.

Hį̂ka sna xči gų skuñe da ho!

My father | alone | really | toward | not | there | [optative].

My wish is that my father alone cannot go.

Čeroxuha če hį̂kuñi ^ų̂rakik^ų̂da ho!"

Side of buffalo [buffalo-flesh-husk] | buffalo | my grandmother | you do |
  my own to give | [optative].

I wish a side of buffalo meat be given to my grandmother!"

Hedą kixrą agriñe, ašką.

And then | the hunting party | they return | it seems.

And then, the hunting party returned, it seems.

Hedą čina broge wikigra^e, ašką.

And then | village | all | shared | it seems.

And then, they shared with the entire village, it seems.

Ida ąje snaxči he ograk^ų̂ škuñe ašką.

Then | his father | really alone | piece | his own gives | not | it seems.

Then, to their own father, alone, not a piece was not given, it seems.

298   The Sister and Brother

Gahedą.[6]
Finally/the end/then at last I started back.
Then I came home.

SELECTED SOURCES ON THE IOWAY LANGUAGE

Dorsey, James Owen. 1882. "The Sister and Brother: An Iowa Tradition." *American Antiquarian and Oriental Journal* 4: 286–88.

———. 1885. "On the Comparative Phonology of Four Siouan Languages." *Annual Reports of the Board of Regents for the Year 1883*, 919–29. Washington DC: Smithsonian Institution, U.S. Government Printing Office.

———. 1891. "The Social Organization of the Siouan Tribes." *American Folklore Journal* 9.

———. 1907. "Iowa." In *Handbook of American Indians North of Mexico*, edited by Frederick Webb Hodge, Vol. 1, 612–14. Washington DC: Government Printing Office.

Foster, Lance. 2015–2016. *Introduction to Ioway-Otoe-Missouria Language*. YouTube playlist. https://www.youtube.com/playlist?list=plyf8efKeRqFxSf1ma2lugOr0dul3k-XvJ

Furbee, N. Louanna, and Lori A. Stanley. 2002. "A Collaborative Model for Creating Heritage Language Curators." *International Journal of the Sociology of Language* 154: 113–28.

Good Tracks, Jimm. "Dictionary of Iowa-Otoe and Other Resources." Ioway Otoe-Missouria Language. Accessed June 9, 2017. http://iowayotoelang.nativeweb.org.

Good Tracks, Jimm, Bryan James Gordon, and Saul Schwartz. 2016. "Perspectives on Chiwere Revitalization." In *Advances in the Study of Siouan Languages and Linguistics*, edited by Catherine Rudin and Bryan James Gordon, 133–64. Berlin: Language Science Press.

Greer, Jill D. 2016. "Baxoje-Jiwere Grammar Sketch." In *Advances in the Study of Siouan Languages and Linguistics*, edited by Catherine Rudin and Bryan James Gordon, 183–229. Berlin: Language Science Press.

Hamilton, Rev. William, and Rev. Samuel Irvin. 1843. *Wv-wv-kvhae e-ya e-tu u-na-ha Pa-hu-cae e-cae ae-ta-wae, mv-he-hvn-yae e-cae.* . . : An Elementary Book of the Ioway Language with English Translations. Under the direction of the B.F. Miss. of the Presbyterian Church. John Battiste Roy, Interpreter. Ioway & Sac Mission Press, Indian Territory.

———. 1843. *Ya-wae pa-hu-cae e-cae ae-ta-waee-tu-hce wa-u-na-ha, Pa-hu-cae fa-kae-ku.* . . : Original Hymns, in the Ioway Language", By the Missionaries to the Ioway & Sac Indians, Under the direction of the B.F. Miss. of the Presbyterian Church. John Battiste Roy, Interpreter. Ioway & Sac Mission Press, Indian Territory.

---

6 This is the traditional idiomatic story ending for Ioway stories, like "The end," or "They lived happily ever after," often translated as "Then, I came home."

——. 1848. "An Ioway Grammar", Language used by the Ioway, Otoe and Missouri Indians. Prepared & printed by B.F. Miss. Presbyterian Church. Ioway & Sac Mission Press, Indian Territory.

——. 1849 and 1850. "The Ioway Primer". Composed of the most common words, in alphabetic order. Compiled &printed for the Ioway School by W.H. & S.M.I. Presbyterian B.F. Miss. Ioway & Sac Mission Press. 2nd edition, 1850.

——. 1850. *Ce-sus wo-ra-kae-pe ae-ta-wae, Mat-fu ae-wv-kv-hae-na-ha, a-rae kae: Six chapters of the gospel of St. Matthew in the Ioway Language.* By the Missionaries to the Ioway & Sac Indians.

——. 1850. *Wv-ro-hae: Prayers in the Ioway Language.*

——. 1850. *We-wv-hae-kju: Some Questions.*

——. 1854. "Remarks on the Iowa Language." In *Information Respecting the History, Conditions & Prospects of Indian Tribes of the U.S.,* edited by H. R. Schoolcraft. Vol. 4, 397–406. Philadelphia: J. B. Lippincott.

Marsh, Gordon. n.d. Linguistic fieldwork on the Iowa and Otoe-Missouria, American Philosophical Society collections.

Merrill, Moses. 1835. *Plkand Ioa Wdwdklhatva: First Ioway Reading Book.* Shawanoe Baptist Mission, Indian Territory: J. Meeker, printer.

——. 1837. *Wdkuntl Eeifa Cesus Kryst Wdwdklha Atva*: The History of Our Lord Jesus Christ." Translated into the language of the Otoe, Ioway and Missouri tribes of Indians by M. Merrill, Missionary of the Baptist Board of Foreign Missions, assisted by Louis Dorion, interpreter. Shawanoe Baptist Mission: J. Meeker, printer.

Murray, Franklin. 1977. "Iowa Tribe of Oklahoma Language." Accessed June 9, 2017. http://bahkhoje.com/government/library/.

Skinner, Alanson. 1925. "Traditions of the Iowa Indians." *The Journal of American Folklore* 38 (150): 425–506.

Wedel, Mildred Mott. 2001. "Iowa." In *Plains,* 432–446. Vol. 13 of *Handbook of North American Indians,* edited by Raymond J. DeMallie. Washington DC: Smithsonian Institution, U.S. Government Printing Office.

Whitman, William. 1947. "Descriptive Grammar of Ioway-Oto." *International Journal of American Linguistics* 13 (4): 233–48.

Wistrand-Robinson, Lila, et al. 1977, 1978. *Jiwele-Baxoje Wan'shige Ukenye Ich'e Otoe-Iowa Indian Language,* Books I & II. Jiwele Baxoje Language Project. Red Rock OK: Christian Children's Fund.

QUAPAW

Introduction to Quapaw

Billy Proctor

The Quapaw are a division of a larger group of Dhegiha Siouan speakers. This group consists of the Kaw, Omaha, Osage, Ponca, and Quapaw tribes. The term *Dhegiha* was introduced by James Owen Dorsey (1848–95) as a way of classifying this group based on their language and cultural similarities. James Owen Dorsey was an ethnologist and linguist working for the Bureau of American Ethnology of the Smithsonian Institution when he visited the Quapaw reservation in the late 1890s; during this time he worked with Alphonsus Valliere, Buffalo Calf, George Redeagle, and Mary Stafford in compiling a word list, stories, personal names, and ethnological information of the Quapaw people.

Today there are no longer any first-language speakers of the Quapaw language. It is through the diligent work of individuals like James Owen Dorsey that the Quapaw people hope to revive their language.

James Owen Dorsey's Quapaw work recorded stories from Alphonsus Valliere, Buffalo Calf, and Mary Stafford. These stories are quite graphic in nature by today's standards. Killing, death, dismemberment, sex, and defecation were generally part of each story. While the rabbit is the main character in a few of the traditional stories, the characters also included various animals, people, spirits, and monsters. In some of the stories there is an underlying moral, but in others it is simply a story. There is a general Dhegiha belief that these stories should only be told in the wintertime.

FURTHER READING

Baird, David. 1975. *The Quapaw People*. Phoenix AZ: Indian Tribal Series.

Ethridge, Robbie. 2008. *The Transformation of the Southeastern Indians, 1540–1760*. Oxford MS: University of Mississippi Press.

Rollins, Willard. 1995. *The Osage: An Ethnohistorical Study of Hegemony on the Prairie Plains.* Columbia: University of Missouri Press.

LANGUAGE RESOURCES

Quapaw Tribe of Oklahoma. n.d. "Quapaw Language." Quapaw Tribal website, http://www .quapaw.com/.

Rankin, Robert L. 1973–1974. Audio recordings from fieldwork and tapes acquired from various Quapaw families living in and around Quapaw, Oklahoma. Robert Rankin Quapaw language materials, Quapaw Tribal Office, Quapaw, Oklahoma.

——. 1973–74. Twenty-seven papers from field studies. Kansas Working Papers in Linguistics. Department of Linguistics. University of Kansas, Lawrence KS. Quapaw Tribal Website, www.quapawtribe.com.

——. 1978. "The Unmarking of Quapaw Phonology: A Study of Language Death."*Kansas Working Papers in Linguistics* 3: 4–52. University of Kansas, Lawrence KS.

——. 1982. "A Quapaw Vocabulary." *Kansas Working Papers in Linguistics* 7: 125 –52. University of Kansas, Lawrence KS.

——. 2005. "Quapaw." In *Native Languages of the Southeastern United States*, edited by Janine Scancarelli and Heather Kay Hardy, 454–98. Lincoln: University of Nebraska Press in cooperation with the American Indian Studies Research Institute.

The Rabbit and the Black Bears

A DHEGIHA MYTH

Narrated by Alphonsus Valliere
Recorded by James Owen Dorsey
Transcribed by Billy C. Proctor

ma-shti^n-ke e-ka^n na^n-pa ti-kde ni-k^{h}a na^n i-ya
Rabbit and his grandmother, the both of them lived together, they say.

"wa-sa ke ni-ka-shi-ka i-xa-xa ta^n-da he-we di-si-si-ke hi-ni^n-ha 'o^n-we
"The black bears make fun of humankind, they are extremely cruel to humankind,

e-ti te na-ha! i-di-si-si-ke hi ta-i e-de
you do not go there! They will sure enough abuse you,

wa-sa ka-hi-ke ni^n-k^{h}e a-ni koi-hi-de-ni^n-k^{h}e ti ti-kde ni^n-k^{h}e
the black bear chief dwells in a lodge beyond yonder distant bluff,

e-ti te na-ha!" i-yi i-ya e-ka^n-ki-dai
you do not go there!" said his grandmother, they say.

ho^n-t^{h}a^n-hi ma^n-te kdi-ze na^n e-ti de i-ya ma-shti^n-ke
But the rabbit took his bow and went there.

wa-sa ka-hi-ke ni^n-k^{h}e ti e-ti hi na^n i-ya ma-shti^n-ke
When the rabbit arrived there, to where the black bear chief resides, they say.

ti-zhe ti hi na-zhi^n a-ta^n xa-ke ko^n-ze t^{h}a^n na^n i-ya ma-shti^n-ke
The rabbit arrived to the entrance of the lodge and stood there, pretending to
  cry, they say.

"ma-shti^n-ke ho^n-ni^n-ta^n da-xa-ke e" i-yi i-ya wa-sa ni^n-k^he
"Rabbit, why are you crying?" said the black bear, they say.

"ho^n wi-te-ke
"Yes, my uncle [my mother's brother].

i^n-ka^n di-te-ke wa-sa ni^n-k^he ta e-ti da i-ye na^n a^n-na^n-ho-sa na^n
My grandmother scolded me and said, go to the black bear, your uncle,

p^hi a-ni-he" i-yi i-ya ma-shti^n-ke
so I have been coming here," replied the rabbit, they say.

"ho^n-t^ha^n-hi i-ka-xa-ta koi-ta kni^n" i-yi i-ya wa-sa ni^n-k^he
Then the black bear said, "Sit over there on the other side of the lodge,"
  they say.

ho^n-t^ha^n-hi ma-shti^n-ke e-ti kni^n ni^n-k^he i-ya
Then the rabbit sat there, they say.

ho^n te-ti ma-shti^n-ke a-shi-ti hi i-ya
When it was night, the rabbit went outside, they say.

a-shi-ti hi te-ti ti-zhe o-ka-ki-xe-xti zhe i-ya ma-shti^n-ke ni^n
When the rabbit went outside, he defecated all around the entrance of the
  lodge, they say.

*"hau i^n-kde wi-ta ha^n-ba o-ta^n-ka hi ta^n o-da-kda-x'a-x'a ta-i" i-we-ke i-ya ma-
  shti^n-ke*
"Well, my own feces, as soon as day arrives, you all will give the scalp yell,"
  Rabbit said to them, they say.

ha^n-ba o-ta^n-ka hi ta^n ho^n-t^ha^n-hi ni-ka-shi-ka zho-hi hi o-kda-x'a-x'a-we i-ya
As soon as it was day, at that time, a great many people gave the scalp yell,
  they say.

"wi-te-ke ni-ka-shi-ka zho-hi hi shko^n-wa-da-we" i-yi i-ya ma-shti^n-ke ni^nk^he
"My uncle, many people are here and will dislodge us!" said the rabbit, they
  say.

"de-do ti-a^n-hi ka^n mi^n-k^he mo^n
"I have been dwelling here a very long time.

ho^n-ni^n-ta^n shko^n-a^n-de ni-ho^n?" i-yi i-ya wa-sa ni^n-k^he

How would it be possible for anyone to make me move?" said the black bear,
  they say.

e-de ni-ka-shi-ka zho-hi hi o-kda-x'a-x'a-we i-ya bdo-ka hi

But there were a great many people, the entire group gave the scalp yell,
  they say.

koi-sho^n-ta^n a-shi-ti hi i-ya wa-sa ni^n

Thus, the black bear went outside, they say.

ni-ka-shi-ka-we i-we-ni^n-a^n ta^n-ha i-ya

Because he thought that people were making the noise, they say.

a-shi-ti hi o-ta^n-ka hi ta^n ma-shti^n-ke t'e-de i-ya wa-sa

Just as soon as the black bear went outside, the rabbit shot the black bear,
  giving him a fatal wound, they say.

"wi-te-ke t'e-di-de ta e-de" i-yi i-ya ma-shti^n-ke ni^n

"My uncle, you have surely been killed," said the rabbit, they say.

t'e-da-ta^n kde na^n i-ya ma-shti^n-ke ni^n

As the rabbit had killed him [the black bear], he started back home.

e-sho^n ti t^he-ta k^hi na^n i-ya

Then, when he returned to his home, they say.

"i^n-ka^n-e wa-sa ka-hi-ke t'e-a-de" i-yi i-ya ma-shti^n-ke t^ha^n

"My grandmother, I have killed the black bear chief," said the rabbit, they say.

"ho^n-ni^n-ta^n t'e-da-de ni-ho^n t'e-de o-te-xi" i-yi i-ya

"How would it be possible for you to kill him? It would be difficult for anyone
  to kill him," she said.

"i^n-ka^n-e t'e-a-de e-de! a^n-ka-de te" i-yi i-ya ma-shti^n-ke t^ha^n

"O Grandmother, I have really killed him! Let's go," said the rabbit, they say.

wa-x'o zhi-ka ni^n zho-kde e-ti hi na^n i-ya

The old woman accompanied him as he went there, they say.

"i^n-ka^n-e she i^n" i-yi i-ya ma-shti^n-ke t^ha^n

"There he is, Grandmother," said the rabbit.

"ho^n wi-to-shpa sho^n i^n" i-yi i-ya wa-x'o zhi-ka t^ha^n
"Yes, my grandchild, that will do," the old woman replied.

pa-te ta^n k'i^n kde i-ya
She butchered the carcass, packed it on her back, and carried it home,
   they say.

k^hi ta^n ma-shti^n-ke ni^n wa-sa sho^n-te a-ni^n a-ta^n de i-ya
Upon returning home, the rabbit took the black bear's scrotum and left,
   they say.

wa-sa ti-kde ke-ti hi na^n
When he arrived to the black bear village,

"ma-shti^n-ke t^hi e-de ma-shti^n-ke t^hi e-de" i-ke-ya-we ni^n i-ya
"The rabbit has come! The rabbit has come!" they [black bears] said to one
   another, they say.

x'a-na^n e-hi-we i-ya
There was a great uproar, they say.

"ho^n a-t^hi o-wi-ki-bda-ke a-t^hi" i-we-ke i-ya ma-shti^n-ke
"Yes, I have come, I have come to tell you something," the rabbit said to
   them, they say.

"hau ma-shti^n-ke o-da-ke t^hi i-ye" i-ke-ya-we ni^n i-ya
"Ho, the rabbit says that he has come to tell us something," they [black bears]
   said to one another, they say.

wa-sa be-ni-zhi e-ti hi-we i-ya
Everyone of the black bears went there [to the lodge where the rabbit was],
   they say.

a-k^hi-kni^n-xti ti t^he-ta hi-we i-ya
They went to the lodge, crowding together, sitting upon one another, packing
   themselves in, they say.

"hi-we o-da" i-ya-we i-ya
"Come, tell it!" they [black bears] said, they say.

"ho^n o-wi-ki-bda-ke tai mi^n-k^{h}e" i-we-ke i-ya ma-shti^n-ke
The rabbit said, "Yes, I will tell you all," they say.

"wa-sa ka-hi-ke ta^n-ka ni^n-k^{h}e ni-ka-shi-ka zho-hi hi e-ti hi-wi na^n t'e-da-we i-ya"
i-we-ke i-ya ma-shti^n-ke ni^n-k^{h}e
"They say that a great many people went there and they killed the black bear
principal chief," the rabbit said to them, they say.

"ka-hi-ke o^n-ko-ta-we t'e-wa-ki-da-we i-ya" i-ya-we i-ya wa-sa ke
"Our chief, they have killed our relation, he [Rabbit] said," the black bears
said, they say.

wa-sa be-ni-zhi xa-ka-we i-ya
Every one of the black bears cried, they say.

"ka-hi-ke ta^n-ka t'e-di-ki-de ni-k^{h}a-she sho^n-te ni^n-k^{h}e she i^n"
"You all whose principal chief has been killed, here are the testicles,"

i-we-ki ta^n we-kda-sa i-ya
he [Rabbit] said to them [black bears], when he [Rabbit] whipped them with
it [their chief's testicles], they say.

"hau ma-shti^n-ke e-wa^n ni^n di-xa a-ta^n t'e-da-we" i-we-ke i-ya
"Ho, the rabbit is the guilty one! Chase him and kill him!" said the black
bears to one another, they say.

ko-zhi hi ta^n o-xde na^n t'e-da-we i-ya
They went a long distance; when they overtook him, they killed him, they say.

zho-i-ka bdo-ka di-shpa-shpa ta^n o^n-da-we i-ya
Tearing his entire body to pieces and scattering the pieces all around, they say.

e-ka^n ni^n-k^{h}e-ti ti-a^n-hi k^{h}i-zhi i-ya ma-shti^n-ke
The rabbit had not returned to his grandmother for a long time, they say.

e-sho^n e-ka^n ni^n-k^{h}e o-ki-te de ko^n-da i-ya
Then his grandmother wanted to go look for him, they say.

wa-x'o zhi-ka ni^n-k^{h}e wa-ba-t^{h}e o-zhi-ha ni^n-k^{h}e kdi-ze na^n ma-shti^n-ke o-ki-te
de i-ya
The old woman took her sewing bag and went to look for Rabbit, they say.

"ho-wa-t^{h}e-ti t'e-dai t^{h}e i-te i-da-ki-de te" i-ye ni^n i-ya wa-x'o zhi-ka ni^n
The old woman said, "Wherever they may have killed him, I will seek him," they say.

e-ti hi na^n di-shpa-shpa ke
When she arrived there, the torn pieces were scattered about.

ki-ba-hi a-ta^n wa-ba-t^{h}e o-zhi-ha ni^n-k^{h}e o-ki-zhi ma^n-ni^n ni^n i-ya
She walked around picking up the pieces, filling her sewing bag, they say.

"ho^n ma-shti^n-ke ni-xi-te di-ni-ke
"Yes, Rabbit, you have been disobedient.

ti koi-ke ni-xi-te ni-ka-we e-ti te na-ha i-he na^n
Those lodges over there, those people are disobedient, you do not go there, I've been saying,

e-sho^n shi e-ko^n t'e-di-da-we" i-ye ni^n i-ya
then, you went and thus, like that, they killed you," she was saying, they say.

wa-x'o zhi-ka ni^n wa-ba-t^{h}e o-zhi-ha ni^n-k^{h}e ki-k'i^n kde i-ya
The old woman carried her sewing bag upon her back and went homeward, they say.

k^{h}i ta^n o-zhi-ha ni^n-k^{h}e ba-po a-kda^n ni^n na^n ma-shti^n-ke ki-ti-ta i-ya
When she reached there, she emptied the bag, and, lo! The rabbit came to life again, they say.

i-na^n-pa^n "te na-ha ti ke ni-xi-te ni-ka-we" i-yi iya
A second time, she said, "Do not go to those lodges, they are disobedient," they say.

ma-shti^n-ke ni^n-k^{h}e "bde ta mi^n-k^{h}e" i-ni^n-a^n i-ya
The rabbit thought, "I will go," they say.

ma^n-te kdi-ze ta^n de i-ya
He took his bow and went, they say.

wa-sa ti-kde ke-ti hi ta^n wa-sa mi^n ho^n-bde i-ya
When he arrived to the black bear lodges, one of the bears had a dream, they say.

wa-sa tʰaⁿ xa-ke naⁿ-hi tʰaⁿ i-ya
He alone was crying, they say.

e-shoⁿ "hoⁿ da-tʰaⁿ-she" i-ke-ya-we i-ya
Then, the others said to him, "What is the matter with you?" they say.

"hoⁿ-a-bde a-tʰaⁿ-he shi-ke-xti i-da-hoⁿ-bde
"I've had a dream, I dreamed a very bad dream,

za-ni-xti t'e-a-wa-da-we i-da-hoⁿ-bde
every single one, they killed us all, I dreamed that,"

wi-e-hoⁿ t'e-aⁿ-da-we i-da-hoⁿ-bde" i-ye tʰaⁿ i-ya
he said, "Me too, they killed me, I dreamed that," they say.

"o-x'aⁿ ni-ke da-hoⁿ-bde"
"There was no reason for your having such a dream,"

"hoⁿ-niⁿ-taⁿ za-ni t'e-a-wa-dai ni-hoⁿ" i-ya-we i-ya wa-sa ke
the black bears said, "How could anyone kill all of us?" they say.

wa-sa ke ni-ka-shi-ka e-naⁿ-xti wa-da-tʰe-we i-ya
The black bears only ate people, they ate no other kind of food, they say.

e-toⁿ ma-shtiⁿ-ke ni-ka-shi-ka o-do-wa-ki e-kaⁿ za-ni-xti t'e-wa-de koⁿ-da naⁿ i-ya
Therefore the rabbit, who sided with the people [Indians] wanted to kill all
  of the black bears, they say.

wa-sa ti-kde ke-ti hi naⁿ hoⁿ tʰe-ti ti-kde ke o-ka-ki-xe-xti zhe i-ya
When he arrived at the black bear lodges, that very night he defecated all
  around the lodges.

"hau iⁿ-kde wi-ta haⁿ-ba saⁿ-haⁿ ti-he taⁿ o-da-kda-x'a-x'a ta-i
"Ho, my feces, when it is daybreak, you all will give the scalp yell.

wa-sa ke za-ni hi t'e-aⁿ-wa-de ta-i
Let's kill all the black bears.

*wi-taⁿ-niⁿ hi wa-te-paⁿ ta miⁿ-kʰe e-ti-tʰaⁿ o-kda-x'a-x'a-we ka" i-we-ke i-ya ma-
  shtiⁿ-ke tʰaⁿ*

I will give the attack cry first, immediately afterward you must give the scalp
  yell," the rabbit said to them, they say.

*ha*ⁿ*-ba o-ta*ⁿ*-ka hi ta*ⁿ *wa-te-ba*ⁿ *i-ya ma-shti*ⁿ*-ke t*ʰ*a*ⁿ
As soon as day arrived, the rabbit gave the attack signal, they say.

za-ni hi o-kda-x'a-x'a-we i-ya ni-ka-shi-ka ke
All of the people gave the scalp yell, they say.

wa-sa za-ni hi a-shi-ti hi-we i-ya
All of the black bears came outside [of their lodges], they say.

wa-sa-pa za-ni hi t'e-wa-de i-ya
All of the black bears were killed, they say.

*ni-ka mi*ⁿ*-xti wa-x'o mi*ⁿ*-xti na*ⁿ*-pa o-ka-shte i-ya*
One male and one female, two remained after the striking down of the others, they say.

*ma-shti*ⁿ*-ke wa-sa na*ⁿ*-pa ni-k*ʰ*a o-wa-na*ⁿ *i-ya*
The rabbit took hold of the two black bears, they say.

*ma-shti*ⁿ*-ke wa-sa na*ⁿ*-pa ni-k*ʰ*a o-wa-ki-e i-ya*
The rabbit spoke to the two black bears, they say.

"*di-shi-ka-we ta*ⁿ*-ha wa-kdi-shka e-na*ⁿ*-xti da-t*ʰ*e ta-i-t*ʰ*e*
"Because you all have been bad, you all shall eat nothing but insects and
  reptiles in the future.

*wa-na-xe di-ni-ke ta-i-t*ʰ*e*
You all shall be without a soul, spirit, and mind.

*i*ⁿ*-da wi-te-ke e-ta-we di-da-t*ʰ*e ta-i-t*ʰ*e*
My mothers, my uncles, their [offspring], they will eat you.

da-we-ka"
You all begone!"

*sho*ⁿ
The end.

PART SEVEN

Uto-Aztecan Language Family

COMANCHE

Blind Fox and Two Girls

Narrated by Mow-wat
Translated by Juanita Pahdopony
Introduced by Brian Daffron

Mow-wat tells the story of Blind Fox trying to live with two sisters who ran away from home. Wearing a cloth around his head to conceal his inability to see, he deceives the sisters into staying with him. When he builds a shelter with large openings, he lies by saying it is for an easy escape route. By luck, he accidentally shoots a buffalo, thereby causing the sisters to think he is a good provider.

While Blind Fox sleeps, the sisters discover that he is blind and then decide to get revenge. Placing an ant-infested log underneath him, they wait for the ants to bite.

When Blind Fox awakens from the ant bites, he threatens to kill them with his bow. The sisters run to the edge of the cliff. One of the sisters, known for wearing a bell, throws it over the cliff. Blind Fox then follows the sound of the bell over the cliff, with Blind Fox breaking a leg as a result. This is where Mow-wat's version of the story, told in June 1940, ends.

According to Cruikshank and Sidney, the Trickster "is a figure of chaos, the principle of disorder. He embodies two distinct and conflicting roles: creator of the world and bringer of culture on the one hand; glutton and instigator of trouble on the other" (1994, 139–40).

In this instance, Blind Fox is neither a "creator" nor a "bringer of culture." Instead he is "a blunderer who is often the victim of his own tricks and follies" (Ricketts 1966, 327).

Juanita Pahdopony, a Comanche artist and storyteller who is a retired dean of academic affairs and interim president for Comanche Nation College, was not familiar with Fox being a Trickster figure in the stories of her childhood. For her,

317

Coyote is a more common Comanche Trickster. However, for her, "Fox is considered a Little Brother to Coyote" (personal interview, April 8, 2015).

St. Clair and Lowie identify a Comanche story that is similar in content to the story of Fox and his two wives. In this story the Trickster is not Fox but Coyote. However, this version gives a prelude as to why Coyote is blind—two yellow birds tricked him into pulling out his own eyes (1909, 278–79).

This story continues to follow a parallel of the Fox story with three key components: 1) meeting the two girls 2) the girls having no knowledge of Coyote's blindness 3) the killing of buffalo 4) building a house with large holes for escape purposes and 5) the girls luring Coyote off the cliff. However instead of breaking his legs as Fox does, Coyote "was crushed to pieces" (St. Clair and Lowie 1909, 279).

Although many Comanche storytellers use Coyote as their protagonist, Mowwat was not the only one who uses Coyote's "Little Brother" as his medium. One of these storytellers, Niyah, tells of Fox killing his wife in order to trade her for food. From what Fox is told by humans, it is acceptable because the wife will come back to life in seven days. However the humans trick Fox, and he "turn[s] toward home very much broken up over the death of his wife" (Kavanagh 2008, 113). Thus, Fox kills his wife out of greed.

On the other hand, Fox is the protagonist in another story told by Niyah in which he successfully tricks a group of white men in a horse trade (Kavanagh 2008, 113).

Another Comanche storyteller, Atauvich, shares a story in which Fox lies in wait for a ball of fat and a ball of meat. When they roll toward him, he begs for small bites of each one. By the fourth time Fox tricks them into giving him pieces of themselves, and the balls of fat and meat both roll away to safety (Kavanagh 2008, 369).

Pahdopony told another version of this story on April 13, 2015, to an American Indian oral literature class at Comanche Nation College in Lawton, Oklahoma. This version differs in that "Fatball" and "Meatball" are the protagonists, and Coyote fulfills the role of the Trickster.

Atauvich is also recorded telling a story of Fox duping a group of prairie dogs into dancing with their eyes closed so that he can kill them with a club and eat them. The story actually shares a high degree of similarity with the Kiowa story of "Sende [Saynday] and the Prairie Dogs." Near the end of Atauvich's story, while Fox is finishing his meal of *turukuu* (Comanche for "prairie dog"), a younger—and hungrier—Fox enters his camp. In order for Younger Fox to get a meal, he not only has to race Fox, but also wear a rock tied to one of his feet. Younger Fox agrees to this, only to find at the end of his race that the prairie dogs have all been consumed (Kavanagh 2008, 368).

For Pahdopony, a key element that a specifically Comanche audience would recognize is plural marriage. For Blind Fox to take two young ladies as companions—especially sisters—was not unusual in older times. For example if a wife "had a little sister that someone couldn't take care of or something happened to the family, then [a husband] could take them into the marriage and be part of the family too" (personal interview, April 8, 2015). Another key element is a sense of community, with Blind Fox and the sisters seeing to each other's needs for survival.

On the other hand an element that is potentially missing from Mow-wat's story is a formulaic opening that would be recognized by a Comanche audience. For example many Kiowa stories begin with *Cáuigú á cí:dê*—"The Kiowa were camping" or—in the case of a Sende Trickster story—*Sende ahel*—"Sende was reportedly coming along." When either Pahdopony or her husband, Harry Mithlo, tell stories, they open with "A long time ago, when the animals could talk . . ." Although Pahdopony acknowledged that many of these types of story conventions could be band-specific, the absence of this opening in this version could potentially have been lost in translation or in the editing of the written text.

Ricketts acknowledges that the role of the Trickster is to make people laugh at themselves despite all of their failures:

The myths of the trickster enabled the Indians to laugh off their failures in hunting, in fighting, in romance, and in combatting the limitations imposed upon them by their environment, since they saw in the trickster how foolish man is, and how useless it is to take life too seriously. (1966, 347)

Yet this may be a more shallow interpretation of the Trickster's role, especially in a Numunuu (Comanche) context. For Pahdopony, the "cliff-hanger" ending of this story is indicative of the abrupt endings that many Comanche stories had. Pahdopony sees this as an inherent way to teach Comanche children problem-solving and critical-thinking skills:

One of the things I've noticed about our stories is that they have an unresolved conclusion. They will leave you hanging. When I was a girl, that used to be really upsetting to me, because I would hear "and they lived happily ever after" at school. I would cry, "What happened?" My dad would say, "That's all we know. That's what we were told." I would be so upset. . . . As I became an adult, I realized they were probably problem solving. They caused the kids—the listeners—to think about solutions. "What would I do?" It was a way for us—a very superior way—to problem solve and learn to make decisions. (personal interview, April 8, 2015)

Whether it's Fox or Coyote, when serving in the role of Trickster, he is in many instances giving an example of how not to behave. Yet for the Comanche audience, the thematic elements are not pulled out artificially from the story so that the morals are clear. There is no denouement, and there is definitely no "happily ever after" for Blind Fox. Instead the Comanche audience is part of the story. They are the ones who draw the conclusions and determine what exactly they should learn from them.

Blind Fox and Two Girls

BY MOW-WAT

JUNE 1940

Blind Fox one day was wandering along the creek. He was lonesome for companions. Since he had become blind, no one cared for him. He tied a cloth around his head so that people couldn't see that he was blind. When he heard the sound of a bell across the creek, he called, "Who are you?"

"We are of the Indian tribe," came the answer from two girls. One of them was wearing a bell.

"So am I," said the fox. "Why are you out here alone?"

"We had a quarrel with our mother. She whipped us," they said.

"What are you doing?" asked the fox.

"Just fooling around," said one.

"So am I," the fox replied, "Let's live together."

"All right," said the girls, and they went across the river.

Fox was very soon busy building a house with poles and brush while the girls gathered firewood. As the girls returned, they noticed the queer house that Fox had built. On all sides were large openings. Fox couldn't see to build it properly.

"This is no house," they complained. "It has too many openings."

"W-well," the fox stammered reassuringly. "I purposely built it that way. When the enemy approaches, we can escape from the house in any direction."

After a while the girls saw a herd of buffalo in the distance. "Get your bow and arrow and shoot one of those buffalo," they yelled. "Hurry!"

"Why, yes," said the fox, "I'll do that. You circle them from the other side, while I get my bow and quiver, and don't let them run away." Fox accidentally killed a buffalo, and the girls were very much pleased. The girls prepared some of the meat and hung the rest on a pole to dry.

"We'll have food for many days to come," they said. "You are a good provider."

"Oh, yes," said Fox, "I usually hit my mark." He leaned up against the house and began singing. He prided himself with being a real warrior. He was also proud of his two wives.

He ate so much that after dinner he had to rest. In keeping with his dignity, Fox rested with his feet on the lap of one girl and his head on the lap of the other. "Delouse me, now, while I rest," he said. He was soon sound asleep.

"I wonder why he keeps that cloth on his head," remarked the girl at the foot.

"Let's take a peep at his face while he is asleep," said the other, looking up from her delousing. Immediately after lifting the cloth, she drew back. "O-o-oh," she said, "he's blind; his eyes are full of sores, and worms are crawling out of them."

"The nasty man!! Let's play a trick on him," said the girl at the foot disgustedly.

Without waking the old fox, they went out to find two stumps. One of the logs had wood ants all over it. This one they placed beneath his head for a pillow, the other they placed under his legs. They then stood by to see what would happen.

Half-asleep, as he stretched, he felt something tickling him. He thought it was the girls and smiled. The tickling continued and soon the ants were biting him. In kicking and moving about he struck wood, and the girls laughed to see him in his misery. Now fully awake he heard them.

"I'll kill you for this," he yelled as he stumbled after them with his bow and arrows.

The girls ran to the edge of a steep red rock cliff. "He can't see us," one said. "He is just following the sound of my bell. I'll throw the bell down the cliff, and he'll follow after it. That will serve him right, and we shall be rid of him."

Fox followed the sound of the bell and fell down the cliff and broke his leg.

REFERENCES

Cruikshank, Julie and Angela Sidney. 1994. "How the World Began." In *Coming to Light: Contemporary Translations of the Native Literatures of North America*, edited by Brian Swann, 139–40. New York: Vintage.

Kavanagh, Thomas W., ed. 2008. *Comanche Ethnography: Field Notes E. Adamson Hoebel, Waldo R. Wedel, Gustav G. Carlson, and Robert H. Lowie.* Lincoln: University of Nebraska Press.

Ricketts, Mac Linscott. 1966. "The North American Trickster." *History of Religions* 5 (2): 327–50.

Pahdopony, Juanita. Storytelling presentation to the American Indian oral literature class at Comanche Nation College, Lawton, Oklahoma. April 13.

St. Clair, H. H., and R. H. Lowie. 1909. "Shoshone and Comanche Tales." *The Journal of American Folklore* 22 (85): 265–82.

The Boy Who Turned Into a Snake

Narrated by Dorothy Martinez
Translated by Juanita Pahdopony
Introduced by Brian Daffron

Introduction

Kwasinaboo—the Comanche word for "snake." This reptile invokes a lot of emotion and is highly symbolic for Comanche people. When driving on I-44 near Lawton, Oklahoma, the Comanche Nation Complex is visible. Signs and flags bearing the Comanche tribal seal are boldly evident. In the middle of the red, yellow, and blue seal is a wavy line that represents the snake.

Yet the snake isn't how the Comanche view themselves necessarily. Instead it is a perception of how other tribes viewed the Comanche. In intertribal Plains sign language, the sign for "Comanche" is a sinuous movement of the hand going backwards, an S-like motion (Pahdopony 2015, 2). Other interpretations are that the Comanche's home country was originally in the Snake River region before they split off from the Shoshone people. Juanita Pahdopony, a Comanche storyteller and retired dean of academic affairs for Comanche Nation College, also interprets the Kwasinaboo symbolism as suggesting that the Comanche were as "mean as snakes" (personal interview, April 8, 2015).

In the story told by Dorothy Martinez one of the central motifs that drive this story is a taboo against eating a snake. Two young men—around twenty-one years of age—set out on a hunt. Their mother packed them plenty of non-perishable foods that were supposed to last at least two weeks. Before they left, their mother warned them not to eat a snake.

By the fourth day of searching for game, all of their food was gone. By the third night, large eyes studied them in the darkness. Although one of the brothers heeded their mother's words, the other did not. When the snake came toward them, they both killed it, but the hungry brother threw the snake in the fire and proceeded to cook it for dinner. After consuming the food the boy eventually turned into a creature that was half-snake and half-human.

The Boy-Snake instructed his brother that he would retreat into the mountains to live, and that he needed to return home and tell their mother. Out of grief the mother went to the mountains to see her son and kill food for him. Eventually the weary mother shot the Boy-Snake and then "shot herself."

This story is significant in many ways. First, it addresses the Comanche taboo against eating snakes. Second, there is a primary indicator that the story was told in at least the twentieth century. When Martinez said the boys saw something "shiny" in the woods, she makes the statement that "two big eyes looked like car lights." Furthermore the story ends with a mother killing her son and inflicting a gunshot wound on herself. For Pahdopony, Comanche stories end almost abruptly because it is an almost Socratic way "to problem solve and make decisions" (personal interview, April 8, 2015). Yet when asked specifically about this ending, Pahdopony said that it was the first reference she had ever read or heard in a Comanche story in which suicide was used as part of the subject matter.

For Pahdopony, Kwasinaboo is particularly significant. In the essay "Kwasinaboo Puha (Snake Medicine)," she not only writes of snake imagery and herbal medicines such as snakeroot, but also of her inheriting a snake medicine through listening to the stories of her late paternal grandfather, Oliver Pahdopony. The story she heard was that, as a baby, Oliver Pahdopony rode with his elders to the present-day site of Lake Lawtonka, which is now the water source for Lawton, Oklahoma. A snake appeared to the Comanche present and warned them that that portion of land would eventually be covered by water (2015, 3–4). Another story with an environmental theme was that when the Comanche first discovered the sacred site of Medicine Bluff at present-day Fort Sill, Oklahoma, a serpent that resided there said to them, "'Take a good look at me because you will never see me again!'" (Pahdopony 2015, 3).

Pahdopony knows at least two other versions of this story told by Martinez. First, there is a story about a boy who turns into an alligator instead of a snake. However the version that most closely parallels the Martinez version is one she credits to Comanche tribal member Thomas Niedo. In Niedo's version, the boys hunt for days, with no game in sight, not even pecans. They have been warned by their mother not to eat game at night. After one of the boys eats a snake during the night, the boy who does not eat at night awakens to see nothing but a pile of clothes where his brother had been. Looking for him, the boy sees evidence of something being dragged, which eventually leads him to a cave. When the boy calls his brother's name, a snake comes out. The snake says to apologize to their mother on his behalf for not listening about the consumption of game at night. "Now I can't go home ever," the snake says at the end of the story. "Tell her she can come see me here. I can't ever go home again" (Pahdopony, personal interview, April 8, 2015).

The significance of this version isn't merely that there are variations in detail from the Martinez story. Where lies the significance as a story is the context in which it was told. According to Pahdopony this version was told at a Comanche sacred site—Enchanted Rock, the area of which is now in a state park near Fredricksburg, Texas. Niedo was part of a group of Comanche touring the area. For Niedo it is important to tell this story because this is *exactly* where the story took place:

> The location of an event is an integral aspect of the event itself, and identifying the event's location is therefore essential to properly depicting—and effectively picturing—the event's occurrence. (Basso 1996, 86–87)

The power that lies in telling the story and tying the story to a physical, tangible place cannot be underestimated. Although stories can certainly be told without knowing what a setting looks like, the ability to tie words to a place that can be known through the physical senses gives power and dimension to the story.

A variation of the Martinez and Niedo stories is found among the Comanche's distant relatives to the north—the Shoshone. In a story published by St. Clair and Lowie, a Shoshone story of two weasels is similar in plot in that one of them is warned by the other not to eat at night. But the other weasel does not heed the warning and is captured by an owl. One difference, however, is that the weasel escapes (1909, 272).

It is no surprise that a Shoshone story would parallel a Comanche story, because they are, in fact, the same people. Although the Comanche split from the Shoshone before c.1700, they still recognize each other as relatives, being speakers of the Numic branch of the Uto-Aztecan language family. For the past fifteen years, the Comanche and the Shoshone tribal divisions throughout the Plains take turns hosting an annual Shoshone Reunion.

On the surface, the Martinez story may be simply a tale about the need to follow a distinct Comanche dietary code. However when seen within the context of other Comanche stories and beliefs, the snake is a valued spiritual entity that can both tell the future and teach ecological standards. Moreover when the story is tied to a sacred site, the Boy-Snake has even greater significance, especially for a Comanche audience. In essence the snake encircles Comancheria—the traditional Comanche domain—and bonds the Comanche people to their land and heritage.

The Boy Who Turned Into a Snake

BY DOROTHY MARTINEZ

They were going hunting. They'd go hunting every year. Everyone in the family, when they'd get to be twenty or twenty-one, would go. They'd have to become a man.

So these two boys went and their mother told them while they were starting off, "Boys, I want to tell you something before you leave. You are going to meet a lot of things. A lot of things are going to be before you. If you ever get hungry, you can eat everything else, but never eat a snake, because it's not good for you."

They wanted to go so the mother packed up a lunch for them of dried meat, grease bread, and some other food that would last them a whole two weeks without spoiling. She fixed it so they could eat it when they got hungry. She told them to eat just so much a day so that it would last the full two weeks. They said they would.

So they started out one morning, and it took four days before they got to where they were going. When they got up on a hill and they looked around, they said, "This is a good place to stay. We better make our beds up there, and sleep there."

So they had blankets, all rolled up so that when they were going to sleep they could just roll them out.

They went up there on the hill and they slept up there that night and the next night.

But on the third night when they were down in the woods they saw something and it looked shiny. Its two big eyes looked like car lights. They didn't know what it was, but they just got prepared for it, whatever it was, and they waited and waited.

They had already eaten all their meat and other food, and they were hungry. One of them thought, no matter what, [I] wouldn't eat a snake. His brother said, "I would if I was real hungry."

When that animal came close they saw it rolling around. It was a big snake. It was coming to them. So they killed it. And then the boy who said he would eat it went and cut it up in the middle, and they had a fire already, so he just threw it in the fire. After it browned up, it looked good enough to eat. But the other boy wouldn't give in. He said, "No, mother told us not to eat it. So I'm not going to eat it."

But this other one said he was going to eat it because he was hungry. So he ate it. That night they went back up there and while they were asleep, toward morning, the brother who didn't eat the snake turned over and felt something cold. When he looked at his brother, there was a half-snake, half-human. He knew then what had happened.

He just slept with him until morning and then he said, "Now see what you have done. I have to go back home and tell the folks what happened."

So this boy, the one who turned half-snake, said, "Well, you tell my mother just where I'm going. I'm going way up there in the mountains. There's a big hole up there. I'm going to be in there. If she wants to see me she can come up there."

So that [other] boy went back home and, of course, they asked where his brother was. He had to tell them. The mother just cried, but she said she was going to go see him. She got ready and got her some meat and everything and got on a horse and went.

She stayed up there with him as long as she could, but she had to go and kill rabbits and deer or whatever she could find for him. He didn't like that because he couldn't go and kill anything. She had to keep on feeding him that way and she got tired, so one day she said to the boy, "Son, I'm tired. I can't stay here any longer. I can't live this way." But she didn't tell him what she was going to do.

She had a gun with her and so when he came out of his hole to talk to her, she said, "I can't stand it any longer." Then she took her gun and she shot him. Then she turned around and shot herself.

WORKS CITED

Basso, Keith H. 1996. *Wisdom Sits in Places: Landscape and Language among the Western Apache*. Albuquerque: University of New Mexico Press, 86–87.

Pahdopony, Juanita. 2015. "Kwasinaboo Puha (Snake Medicine)." *IK: Other Ways of Knowing* 1 (1): 1–8.

St. Clair, H. H., and R. H. Lowie. 1909. "Shoshone and Comanche Tales." *The Journal of American Folklore* 22 (85): 265–82.

PART EIGHT
Language Isolate

Introduction to Language Isolates

Gus Palmer Jr.

In Oklahoma, there are two language isolates: Yuchi and Tonkawa. According to David Crystal, a language isolate or isolate language is a language with "little or no structural or historical relationship to any other language. . . . Many such cases have been noted. They include languages which remain undeciphered, languages where there is insufficient material available to establish a family relationship, and languages where, despite a great deal of data, the relationship is undetermined" (2008, 256). Tonkawa is included in this book along with the other tribes of the southern Plains, with Yuchi featured in the language groups of Southeast United States region. Harry Hoijer, the primary linguist who investigated the Tonkawa language and published the first description of Tonkawa in 1933, writes:

> The Tonkawa appear to have been an important and warlike tribe living in central Texas during most of the 18th and 19th centuries. From the scanty accounts of their culture which have come down to us through mission and governmental reports, they were a nomadic people living on the buffalo. Their myths and stories, of which I have collected about thirty, give indications of their dependence upon buffalo and deer, and, insofar as this sort of evidence is reliable, indicate a Plains type of culture. A more complete account of their culture—or, rather, of what little is known of their ethnological relations—may be found in the Handbook of the American Indian. (Hoijer 1933–38, ix)

This introduction to Hoijer's work on Tonkawa, shown only in part here, is important in demonstrating how, early on, Tonkawa was a subject of intense interest in the work of many of the outstanding linguists working on American Indian languages in this country.

TONKAWA

The Young Man Who Became a Shaman

A TONKAWA MYTH STORY

Transcribed, translated, and introduced by Don Patterson
Text prepared by Miranda Allen Myers

The Tonkawas belong to the Tonkawan linguistic family, which was once composed of a number of small subtribes that lived in a region that extended west of south-central Texas and western Oklahoma to eastern New Mexico. The Tonkawas had a distinct language, and their name, as that of the leading tribe, was applied to their linguistic family. They were one of the most warlike tribes during nearly two centuries of conflict with enemy tribes on the western Plains and with the Spanish and, later, American settlers in the Southwest. Their men were famous warriors, and their chiefs bore many scars of battle. The Tonkawa women were also reputedly physically strong and vindictive in disposition.

The people of this tribe were nomadic in their habits in the early historical period, moving their tipi villages according to the wishes of the chiefs of the different bands. They planted few crops, but were well known as great hunters of buffalo and deer, using bows and arrows and spears for weapons, as well as some firearms secured from early Spanish traders. They became skilled riders and owned many good horses in the eighteenth century. From about 1800 the Tonkawas were allied with the Lipan Apache and were friendly to the Texans and other southern divisions. By 1837 they had for the most part drifted toward the southwestern frontier of Texas and were among the tribes identified in Mexican territory.

The Tonkawas were removed from Fort Griffin, Texas, in October 1884. They were transported by railroad from a station in Cisco, Texas (a child born on the way was named "Railroad Cisco") to a temporary stop at the Sac-Fox Agency near Stroud, Oklahoma. The entire tribe wintered at the Sac-Fox Agency until spring, then traveled the last hundred miles by wagon, fording many rain-swollen rivers and axle-deep mud caused by severe spring rains. They reached the Ponca Agency on June 29, and then finally arrived at "Oakland" on June 30, 1885. This was the Tonkawa "Trail of Tears." The Tonkawa tribe currently lives on an approximately 1,500-acre reservation called Fort Oakland near the town of Tonkawa, Oklahoma.

TONKAWA STORIES

The Tonkawas divided their tales into two broad categories: night stories and old stories are accounts of happenings that took place at a time when no humans existed and when animals and birds roamed the earth and spoke like humans. As among many of the western Indians, Coyote is portrayed, for the most part, as a gullible and easily deceived character. He is also, however, pictured as a cultural hero; he brought both fire and the buffalo to the Tonkawas. In one tale Coyote is given an exceptionally evil character.

In general, however, Coyote was a kind of divinity. His name, Ha'cokonay, means, literally, "the owner of the earth," a divinity who owns in particular all the animals on which the Tonkawas depended for food. In this capacity hunters always requested Coyote's permission to hunt and always left a portion of the game killed for Coyote. Failure to observe this rule resulted in failure both to find and to kill food animals.

Night stories are so called because of the ritual associated with their telling. They were told only at night and during the winter. Each man around the campfire told four stories and, when all had finished, the group went to the nearest river to bathe. Failure to observe this procedure led to being "bothered by snakes." If too many Coyote stories were told, Coyote might well appear and warn the group to desist.

Old stories recount adventures that took place in the distant past. One recounts the fate of a Tonkawa who married a bear; another is a tale in which a young man is transformed into a fish. Only one concerns hostilities between the Tonkawa and their hereditary enemies.

All the stories, whether night or old, recount events known only from cultural tradition, not because anyone now living participated in the events or was told of them by a participant. As a result most of the verbs in these tales, excepting only those occurring in direct discourse, contain the narrative enclitic *k-lakno'o*, roughly translated by the phrase "it is said."

Don Patterson is an elder of the Tonkawa tribe and former tribal chairman, having served seven terms as chairman and one term as vice chairman over the years. Don is a veteran of the United States Air Force; has a masters degree in education; and is a former chairman of Native American Studies at San Francisco State University in San Francisco, California. Also an adjunct professor of Native American Cultural Studies at Oklahoma State University, Don has dedicated his life to protecting, preserving, and perpetuating Tonkawa native culture as well as all Native cultures for the benefit of future generations. It is from this rich background that Don has submitted this brief presentation of Tonkawa traditional oral literature.

PRONUNCIATION GUIDE

Short Vowels

a as in 'about,' 'above'
e as in 'bed,' 'met'
i as in 'it,' 'hid'
o as in 'onward,' 'ongoing'
u as in 'put,' 'push'

Long Vowels

a· as in 'saw,' 'call'
e· as in 'hey,' 'they'
i· as in 'field,' 'wield'
o· as in 'own,' 'bone'
u· as in 'Yule,' 'rule'

Consonants

c as in 'church,' 'chair'
h as in Standard English
k as in Standard English
l as in Standard English
m as in Standard English
n as in Standard English
p as in Standard English
s fluctuates between 'ship' and 'sip'
t as in Standard English

w as in Standard English
x as in German 'Ba**ch**,' 'i**ch**'
y as in Standard English
' glottal stop

Vowels

Tonkawa vowels are pronounced with both long and short duration. Short vowels are indicated by the English equivalent. Long vowels are indicated by a dot (·) following the vowel, that is, *a·*, *e·*, and so on. No two vowels ever occur next to each other in Tonkawa: vowels are always separated from one another by one or two consonants.

Consonants

The Tonkawa consonants referenced above are: *h, k, l, m, n, p, s, t, w,* and *y*; all are pronounced as in Standard English. The consonant *c* is pronounced like the initial sound of '**ch**urch' or '**ch**air.' The consonant *x* is pronounced like the German 'ch' as in 'Ba**ch**' with a strong 'kh' sound. The raised ('), also a consonant, is called a glottal stop and is pronounced by momentarily closing and opening the air flow in the throat as in the English utterance 'uh-oh.'

The English consonants *b, d, f, g, j, r, v,* and *z* do not appear in Tonkawa.

Syllables

Each syllable of a Tonkawa word must begin with a consonant and, if possible, be composed of consonant plus vowel plus consonant (CVC). Where there is a series of sounds like CVCVC, the first syllable will be CV and the second, CVC.

If only one consonant (C) comes between vowels (V), the first consonant (C) will go with the preceding syllable, and the remaining consonants (C) will go with the following syllable.

Stress or Accent

Stress is evenly distributed in Tonkawa. Each syllable receives substantially the same accentuation. Words of two syllables tend to be pronounced with a slightly greater stress on the latter syllable. Words of two syllables or more usually have a slightly greater stress on the next to last syllable.

Intonation appears to have little or no impact upon meaning.

The Young Man Who Became a Shaman: A Tonkawa Night Story

1 yacox'ana·'as'ita / tickanwa·cka / yacox'o·noklakno'o.
In many tipis / Tonkawas / they were encamped, he said, it is said.

2 'e·noklak / ha·'ako·nosaskosamkapayla / "hecu·'axeykak / hecocxo·peno'o," / nonoklakno'o.
This being so / a reckless young man / "Of anything / I have never been afraid," / he was saying, he said, it is said.

3 'e·kla / we·'is / ha·'ako·nkwa·lowla / "wa·xes?" / nonoklakno'o.
Then / one / an important man / "Truly?" / he was saying, he said, it is said.

4 'e·kla / "hey'," / noklakno'o.
Then / "Yes," / he said, it is said.

5 'e·kla / "'o·'o·l'ok / cakawkwa·lowe'e·k / ta·taklana·s'ok / naxcankwa·low / 'e·ta / naxcana·cin'a·y'ik / heylapan'an /
Then / "When night comes / to that big river yonder / when I take you / a big fire / making / close to the fire / standing /

hetew'an'ax / nesexwe·l'ok / na·xwa / nesexwew," / noklakno'o / ha·'a-ko·nkwa·lo·'a·la.
from any direction / if someone shouts / you also / shout," / he said, it is said / the important man.

6 'e·kla / "hey'," / noklakno'o.
Then / "All right," / he said, it is said.

7 'e·ta / cakaw'a·y'ik / ta·taklanaklakno'o.
And then / to the river / he took him down, he said, it is said.

8 'e·kla / ha·ako·nosaswa·'a·la / kwa·lo·tak / naxceta / ha·cin'a·y'ik / hay-lapaklakno'o.
Then / that young man aforementioned / very big / making a fire / in its vicinity / he stood, he said, it is said.

9 'e·kwa / cakawaklana'a·w'an / nesexweklakno'o.
When he did so / from down river / someone shouted, he said, it is said.

10 'e·kla / ha·'ako·nosaswa·'a·la / 'a·xwa / nesexweklakno'o.
Then / that young man aforementioned / he also / he shouted, he said,
it is said.

11 'e·t / papasan'e / 'e·kwa / naxcan'a·y'ik / we·l'at / hatxiltaklakno'o.
And / a little while / when it had passed / to the fire / that one yonder /
he came out, he said, it is said.

12 'e·l'ok / xal'o·n'a·lak / ketay / nokota / 'a·'a / xal'o·nwa·'a·lak / x'el'enokla-
kno'o.
When he did so / knives / two / having / and / that knife aforementioned /
he was sharpening, he said, it is said.

13 'e·ta / ha·'ako·nosaswa·'a·lak / ta'anceklakno'o / 'e·t / totopoklakno'o.
And then / that young man aforementioned / he grasped him, he said, it
is said / and / he cut him to bits, he said, it is said.

14 'e·kla / ha·'ako·nkwa·lo·wa·'a·la / ya·ceta / ha·naklakno'o / yacox'an'a·y'ik.
Then / that important man aforementioned / having seen it / he went
away, he said, it is said / to the camp.

15 taxso·kwa / ha·'ako·nosaswa·'a·la / xa·xaklakno'o / 'e·t / x'ax'ay'anoklakno'o.
When daylight came / that young man aforementioned / he arrived, he
said, it is said /and / he was laughing, he said, it is said.

16 'e·kla / ha·'ako·nkwa·lo·'a·la / "wa·xes / cocxo·penonekawe," / noklakno'o.
Then / the important man / "Truly / you are not afraid," / he said, it is said.

17 'e·klak we·tic / he·saxewlak / coxnanweklakno'o / ha·'ako·nosaswa·'a·la.
He so treated / in that manner / [by] a giant / he had become a shaman,
he said, it is said / that young man aforementioned.

18 na'a / he·pano·no'o.
So / it has customarily been told.

REFERENCES

Crystal, David. 2008. *A Dictionary of Linguistics and Phonetics*. 6th edition. Malden MA:
Blackwell Publishing.
Hoijer Harry. 1933–38. *Tonkawa: An Indian Language of Texas*. Pt. 3 of *Handbook of American
Indian Languages*, edited by Franz Boas. New York: Columbia University Press.

Himmel, Kelly F. 1999. *The Conquest of the Karankawas and the Tonkawas 1821–1859*. College Station: Texas A&M University Press.

Hodge, Frederick W., ed. 1910. *Handbook of American Indians North of Mexico*. Washington DC: Government Printing Office.

Powell, J. W. 1888. "Work of Mr. A. S. Gatschet." In *Sixth Annual Report of the Bureau of Ethnology to the Secretary of the Smithsonian Institution 1884–85*, xxxiii–xxxvi. Washington DC: U.S. Government Printing Office.

Schilz, Thomas Frank. 1983. *People of the Cross Timbers: A History of the Tonkawa Indians*. Fort Worth: Texas Christian University Press.

CONTRIBUTORS

MOSIAH BLUECLOUD is the director of the Kickapoo Language Development Program out of McLoud, Oklahoma. He graduated from the University of Oklahoma with his bachelors in linguistics. Mosiah Bluecloud started his language journey in high school while attending Shawnee-language community classes and private Kickapoo lessons from his grandmothers. When he graduated in 2007 from Norman High he started advocating for the revitalization of his heritage languages; later that fall Mosiah began studying linguistics at the University of Oklahoma. Mosiah simultaneously began working with the Sauk Language Department, where he developed the skills necessary to navigate language-teaching and -learning through the modified master apprentice technique, and the teaching of languages at the collegiate and secondary level.

SKY CAMPBELL is the director for the Otoe-Missouria Language Department and has worked for the Otoe-Missouria Tribe for over six years. He has degrees in Native American Studies and computer programming. He has appeared in documentaries and co-authored or contributed to academic papers and magazine articles.

WALLACE CHAFE received a PhD in linguistics from Yale in 1958 with a dissertation on the Seneca language of New York. He was then employed by the Smithsonian Institution in Washington as a specialist in Native American languages before moving in 1962 to the Berkeley campus of the University of California, where he was chair of the Linguistics Department for six years. During the 1960s he spent considerable time working with the Caddo language in and around Anadarko, Oklahoma. In 1986 he moved to the Santa Barbara campus of the University of

California, where he is now research professor emeritus. He has continued to enjoy a productive relationship with the Seneca Nation for more than fifty years.

DAVID J. COSTA is the program director for the Language Research Office at the Myaamia Center at Miami University of Ohio. He earned his PhD in linguistics at UC Berkeley in 1994 with his dissertation on the Miami-Illinois language. He has been studying the Miami-Illinois language since 1988, and has worked extensively with the Miami Tribe of Oklahoma on language revitalization for twenty years. In 2010 he published *Myaamia neehi peewaalia aacimoona neehi aalhsoohkaana: Myaamia and Peoria Narratives and Winter Stories*, a collection of traditional Myaamia, Wea, and Peoria narratives. He is continuing to work on a fully annotated collection of interlinearized Miami-Illinois texts. In addition to his work on Miami-Illinois, he has also done extensive research on the Shawnee language, the Algonquian languages of southern New England, and comparative Algonquian. Dr. Costa is a third-generation northern Californian and presently lives in El Cerrito, California, with his wife and daughter.

BRIAN DAFFRON is a former dean and faculty member at Comanche Nation College, where he taught composition, Native American literature, and beginning Kiowa language. His publications have appeared in *Indian Country Today Media Network*, *American Indian Art*, *Mid-America Folklore*, and *Tribal College Journal*. He is married to Maya Torralba, an enrolled member of the Kiowa Tribe, and they have four children. A member of the O-Ho-Mah Lodge, Kiowa Tia-Piah Society, and Caddo County Election Board, he currently serves as interim director of the Anadarko Chamber of Commerce.

DURBIN FEELING holds an associate of arts degree from Bacone College in Muskogee, Oklahoma. After studying at Bacone he served in the U.S. Army for two years in Vietnam. After returning from the service he continued with his education and studied journalism at Northeastern Oklahoma State University in Tahlequah, receiving a bachelor of arts in journalism. He also studied descriptive linguistics at the University of California, Irvine, and received a master of arts in linguistics. In 2004 Ohio State University in Columbus conferred upon him a doctor of letters honorary degree. Feeling has taught Cherokee literacy all of his adult life. He is full Cherokee, and speaks, reads, and writes his native language. He has co-authored the Cherokee–English dictionary along with a number of monographs and refereed research papers regarding Cherokee verbs.

LANCE M. FOSTER (b. 1960) is an enrolled member of the Iowa Tribe of Kansas and Nebraska, and serves as the Tribal Historic Preservation Officer (THPO), tasked primarily with the protection and preservation of tribal sites and burials (NAG-PRA). He learned only a few words from his grandmother, and began his study of Ioway as an undergraduate student in anthropology and Native American studies at the University of Montana, in 1981. He has an MA in anthropology and an MLA in landscape architecture (cultural landscapes) from Iowa State University. His graduate theses focused on Ioway tribal bundles linguistic taxonomy (MA), and cultural landscapes and the Ioway (Chiwere) language (MLA). He also started the tribal museum and is the language point of contact for the tribe. He is the author of *Indians of Iowa* (University of Iowa Press, 2009), created a language coloring book for preschool children on the reservation, and has appeared in several videos about his tribe, including *Lost Nation* (Third Wall Films, 2007). He continues to engage tribal members in use of the tribal language, and is sending a team of younger scholars to the Breath of Life Workshop in Washington DC the summer of 2017. All his language efforts are voluntary, as the tribe does not have a language program. He has made a number of language videos and uploaded them to You-Tube, as well as creating a Chiwere language group on Facebook.

BRYAN JAMES GORDON works with the Joint PhD Program in linguistics and anthropology at the University of Arizona, Tucson. He is also affiliated and works with the Omaha-Siouxan Language and Culture Center of the *Unón hon* Nation Public School in Nebraska.

JULIA A. JORDAN holds a master's degree in anthropology from the University of Oklahoma. As a research anthropologist she conducted extensive fieldwork among Indians of western Oklahoma as a part of the Doris Duke Indian Oral History Project of the University of Oklahoma. In later work at the Sam Noble Oklahoma Museum of Natural History she served as consultant and co-principal investigator for several anthropological projects. Her book, *Plains Apache Ethnobotany*, was published by the University of Oklahoma Press in 2008. She is retired and lives in Norman, Oklahoma.

JUSTIN T. MCBRIDE has been actively involved in Kanza-language revitalization efforts since 2001 and has overseen the Kaw Nation's Kanza Language Project for nearly a decade. His work in this area has involved extensive Kanza-language research, teaching, and materials development. He has also consulted with various tribal language documentation and maintenance projects throughout the central United States. In addition, he recently completed an ethnographic and sociolinguistic survey of Native American English varieties in Oklahoma. McBride is currently employed with Northeastern State University's Department of Languages and Literature as an assistant professor of linguistics. He is a citizen of the Cherokee Nation.

JUSTIN NEELY was born July 1, 1977, in Kansas City, Missouri. Justin did not grow up speaking Potawatomi but acquired the language as a second-language learner, starting first with tapes and then attending classes. In 2002 he received an Endangered Language Fund grant from Yale University and spent several months shadowing a fluent first-language speaker, Don Perrot, in Escanaba, Michigan. Justin graduated in 2003 from Missouri State University in Springfield, Missouri with a bachelors in education. After graduation he was hired by the Hannahville Potawatomi community to teach in their K-12 school. Justin spent two school years teaching in the Nah Tah Wash school for the Hannahville Potawatomi people in Wilson, Michigan. Justin has been a yearly presenter at the annual Potawatomi Language Conference from 2003 to the present. In 2005 Justin was hired to be the director of language for the Citizen Potawatomi Nation in Shawnee, Oklahoma. He has been director of language for the last ten years.

SEAN O'NEILL is a linguistic anthropologist who specializes in the expression of oral literature in multilingual and multicultural settings, especially the languages of California and Oklahoma. Early in his career he contributed to the *Collected Works of Edward Sapir*, and more recently he edited William Bright's posthumous book, *A Traveler's Guide to Native American Placenames of the Southwest*. In his capacity as an associate professor of anthropology at the University of Oklahoma, he has worked extensively with the Plains Apache Tribe of Oklahoma and the Ponca Tribe of Oklahoma, which represent the Athabaskan and Siouan language families respectively, as illustrated in his contributions to this volume. He is the author of *Cultural Contact and Linguistic Relativity among the Indians of Northwestern California* (University of Oklahoma Press, 2008).

JUANITA PAHDOPONY was an adjunct professor of American Indian art at the University of Science and Arts of Oklahoma (USAO) in Chickasha, Oklahoma (2000–Summer 2002). Pahdopony also served as project director of Chickasaw and Kiowa language courses funded by Sarkeys/USAO Foundation/Oklahoma Arts Council (2001–02); and tribal administrator for the Comanche Nation (1997–2000). She writes, "The disappearance of tribal language represents one of our greatest losses. Recently, I was asked to offer a prayer for the city of Lawton's Arts for All festival opening. My Comanche prayer offered a blessing for everyone and many non-Natives thanked me after the ceremony. It's been my goal to use at least one Comanche word a day in speaking, writing, speaking, and thinking. Our tribal languages are worth preserving!"

GUS PÀNTHA̱I:DÊ PALMER JR., a professor emeritus of anthropology and Native American studies at the University of Oklahoma, is a Kiowa speaker, doing work in Kiowa language and Kiowa oral literatures. A published poet, Palmer has published many articles and book chapters on Native languages and literatures.

DOUGLAS R. PARKS is professor of anthropology and co-director of the American Indian Studies Research Institute at Indiana University, Bloomington. Over the course of his career he has focused his research on the Pawnee and Arikara people, beginning work with tribal members in 1965 and continuing until 2001, when the last two speakers passed away. Among his publications are *A Grammar of Pawnee* (1976), *Ceremonies of the Pawnee* by James Murie (as editor; 1981), *Traditional Narratives of the Arikara Indians*, 4 vols. (1991), and *A Dictionary of Skiri Pawnee* (2008). He is currently finishing reference dictionaries of both dialects of Pawnee and Arikara. He is also editor of the journal *Anthropological Linguistics*.

DON PATTERSON is an elder of the Tonkawa Tribe and former tribal chairman. Patterson has a master's degree in education, is a road chief in the Native American Church, and a former chairman of Native American Studies at San Francisco State University. He is an adjunct professor of Native American Studies at Oklahoma State University.

BILLY PROCTOR is a member of the Osage, Quapaw, and Cherokee tribes of Oklahoma. He currently works for the Quapaw language program, compiling audio recordings of first-language speakers from the 1950s and 60s as well as historical written works on the Quapaw language dating back to 1827. Prior to working for the Quapaw Tribe, he worked for the Osage language program as a teacher in the public schools and of adult classes.

JIM REMENTER, project director, grew up in southeastern Pennsylvania, the original home of the Lenape. He began his study of the Lenape or Delaware language in the summer of 1961, returning the following summer and resuming his study with James H. Thompson, one of the oldest tribal members. After Mr. Thompson's death in 1964, Jim continued his study primarily with Nora Thompson Dean, daughter of James Thompson. Jim continued his studies with other speakers, and in 1997 the Delaware Tribe appointed him director of the Lenape Language Project. He recently discovered that his fifth great uncle, Nicholas Ramstein, was a captive of the Delaware Indians for fifteen months beginning in January 1756.

JOSH RICHARDS holds an MA in linguistic anthropology from Indiana University, where he is a research associate at the American Indian Studies Research Institute. Much of his work has focused on the oral literatures of the Arikara, Pawnee, and Kitsai, with an emphasis on analyzing the complex word structure of these polysynthetic languages.

DAVID S. ROOD, currently professor of linguistics at the University of Colorado, has been studying Wichita since 1965. When he started, there were several hundred speakers, but today (2016) there is only one who is truly fluent, Ms. Doris Lamar. Ms. Bertha Provost, the narrator of the story reported here, was Rood's main teacher and consultant from the beginning until her death in the early 1980s. Rood has published, a book-length grammar of the language (*Wichita Grammar*, 1976) and several papers about Wichita language and culture and about Wichita in relation to theoretical linguistic issues, and has deposited annotated videotapes of Wichitas speaking Wichita for the archive "Documentation of Endangered Languages (DoBeS)" at the Max Planck Institute for Psycholinguistics in Nijmegen, the Netherlands. He also worked with the tribe to create language lessons for anyone who would like to learn to speak a little Wichita.

JADE ROUBEDEAUX is a language assistant with the Otoe-Missouria Tribe of Red Rock, Oklahoma. His focus is researching, transcribing, and translating the

Otoe-Missouria language. He is an accomplished singer, a member of the Native American Church, and has been culturally active all his life. He has composed many songs for his tribe that are heard all over Indian Country today.

ADRIAN SPOTTEDHORSECHIEF is a member of the Pawnee Nation of Oklahoma. A traditional Pawnee chief, Adrian has spent many years working with the Pawnee Language Program. He has also worked as a member of the Pawnee Nation Council.

VIDA WOODHULL STABLER directs the Indian Education program at Umóⁿhoⁿ Nation Public School. Her belief that Umóⁿhoⁿ culture is taught best by the community has led her to document and develop authentic materials for use within schools and the community. She has created a place for the Umóⁿhoⁿ community to contribute their knowledge and to teach our children as well as a place to learn from one another.

JOYCE TWINS is a member of the Cheyenne Tribe of Oklahoma. She has spent many years working for Cheyenne tribal education, language, and cultural programs. She has taught Cheyenne for the Native Language Program at the University of Oklahoma.

ALAN R. VELIE is David Ross Boyd Professor of English at the University of Oklahoma. Velie is the author of many articles and several significant books on American Indian literature. His special interests are Shakespeare, American Indian literature, poetry and poetics, and the Bible as literature.

PAULINE WHITE WAHPEPAH was born near Tecumseh, Oklahoma. Her first language was Absentee Shawnee, her second language was Kickapoo, and her third language was English. She would interpret for her grandmother in Shawnee and then her grandfather in Kickapoo. She attended the boarding schools of Pawnee Indian School in Pawnee, Oklahoma, and Riverside Indian School in Anadarko, Oklahoma. She also attended Haskell Institute (now Haskell Indian Nations University), Lawrence, Kansas. She began her higher education pursuits at St. Gregory's University, Shawnee, Oklahoma, and received her graduate education from the University of Central Oklahoma, where she obtained a master's degree in bilingual education in 1995. She has worked for the Kickapoo Tribe of Oklahoma and

Absentee Shawnee Tribe of Oklahoma on various language programs from 1986 to present. She helped to develop the Kickapoo Language Pictionary and has taught Shawnee throughout the years. She has composed poetry in both the Shawnee and Kickapoo languages.

GORDON YELLOWMAN is an enrolled member of the Cheyenne and Arapaho Tribes. He has extensive knowledge of Cheyenne history, customs, traditions, and religious beliefs. Gordon's Cheyenne grandparents, father, and elders provided him with teachings on the Cheyenne way of life. Gordon served as an adjunct professor for the Cheyenne and Arapaho Tribal College for some years. He studied architectural technology and has over thirty years of experience working for the Cheyenne and Arapaho Tribal Government. In addition, Yellowman has taught Cheyenne and Arapaho history to educate and empower the tribal youth.

INDEX

236–37, 238–41; Ponca works by, 213; recordings by, 305–12; text collections by, 273; other text information by, 275–77; transcriptions by, 241; translation and a tale by, 271; translations by, 275–76

Dougherty, John, 237

Dúba-Mo^{n}thi^n, 235, 249n6, 249–50n7

Dunn, Jacob, 42, 45, 47n4

Dust Bowl, 60

Edmunds, David, 51

Enchanted Rock, 325

Erdrich, Louise, xxiii, 196; *LaRose*, xxii; *Love Medicine*, xxi

ethnopoetics, xviii

ethnopoets, xviii, xix

Euro-Americans, xix

Eurocentrism, xxi

European ethnology, xxi

evidentiality, xlin1

Finley, George, 45

Fletcher, Alice Cunningham, 195, 242

formulaic openings in storytelling, xxxiii, 319

Fort Berthold Reservation (North Dakota), 123

Fort Griffin TX, 335

Fort Sill OK, 324

Fox, xxiii, 45–47, 319, 320

Fredericksburg TX, 325

Furbee, Louanna, 274

Gale, John, 276

Gatschet, Albert, xli, 42; work of, 43–44

General Allotment Act of 1887, xxxv, xlin4

Godfroy, Gabriel, 45

Goodin, Barbara, xxxix

Good Tracks, Jimm Garrett, 274

Gordon, Bryan James, 236

gourd dance tradition, Kiowa, xxxv

Great Lakes, 41, 51, 214

Great Southern Plains, xxvii

The Green Book of Language Revitalization (Hinton and Hale), xlin2

Greenwood, Kennetha, 226

Grist Mills, 177

Haddon, Tom, 145

Hale, Kenneth, xxx, xxxi

Hamilton, William, 272–73

Harrington, John P., xli, 195, 207n1

Hastings, Dennis, 237

Hawaii, xl

Heap of Birds, Edgar, xxii

heritage languages, xxix, xxxiv–xxxv, xxxix–xl

High Backed Wolf, 11

Hitchcock County, Nebraska, 119

Ho-Chunk (Winnebago), xix, 237

Hoijer, Harry, 59–60, 64, 65, 331

Hollywood, xvii

Homer NE, 238

Hopkins Greer, Jill, 274

Huh-dawh 'long ago', 5

Hupa, 60

Hymes, Dell, xviii, xxx

Illinois River, 41

Indiana, University of, xxxix

Indian Country, xxxv, xlin3; language revitalization in, xxxi, xxxix

Indian Removal Act of 1833, 19

Indian Territory, 29, 83, 85, 211, 213, 214–15, 217, 218, 220, 273

indigenous verbal arts, xli

interlinearized translations, xxix

International Phonetic Alphabet (IPA), 64

Ioway (Baxoje), 271, 274; as "sleeping language," 275

Irvin, Samuel, 272–73

Já:mátàunhè̩:jègà (Star Girls Story): as magical realism, 196; versions of, 195
James O. Dorsey Papers, 259
Jicarilla tribe, 59
Jordan, Julia A., 8, 9, 11, 13

Kai Kai (Kitsai), 145
Kanza Alphabet, 259–60
Kanza language and oral literature, 257–58
Kaskaskia (kaahkaahkiaki 'katydids'), 41
Kaw City OK, 256
Kaws (Kanza or Kansa), 255–56; in warfare and military service, 257
Káxe-Thoⁿba, 236, 245, 247–48
Kickapoo language, 25, 51
Kickapoos, 41
Kiišikohkwa 'Sky Woman' (Elizabeth Valley), 42–43; Story of Wiihsakacaakwa, 47n1
King, Thomas, 196
Kiowa-Apaches (Plains Apaches), 59
Kiowa Five, xxi
Kiowa language, xix, xxxi–xxxii, 195; pronominal system of, xxxii; speakers of, xl; nineteenth-century translator-documenters of, xli; writing system of, 197–200. See also Já:mátàunhè̩:jègà (Star Girls Story); Kiowa storytelling
Kiowa storytelling, xxxii–xxxiii, xli; formulaic opening in, xxxiii; texts of, xxxvi
Kiowa Voices I & II, xxxvi
Kitsai language and people, 145
Kodaseet, Dorothy, xl
Kroeber, Karl, xx–xxii
Kwasinaboo (snake), 323, 324
"Kwasinaboo Puha (Snake Medicine)" (Pahdopony), 324

La Flesche, Frank (Francis), 195, 213, 215–16, 240
La Flesche, Joseph, 213, 215, 229, 271, 276
La Flesche, Mary Gale (Hinnuaganun 'One Woman'), 271, 276
La Flesche, Susette (Bright Eyes), 215
La Flesche family, 215–16
Lake Mohonk Conference of Friends of the Indian, 240
Lakota language, 213
Landes, Ruth, 51
Land Run, 214
language endangerment and loss, xl
language isolates, 331
language preservation, xxxiv
language revitalization, xxxix; in Indian Country, xxxix
Larned KS, 256
Lenape language and people (Delaware), 29
Lenape Talking Dictionary, 29–30
Lesser, Alexander, 145
Lipan Apache, 335
literature, American, xli
Littlecrow, Shawna, 226
"Little Red Riding Hood," 75
Longbone, Willie, 29
Louisiana Purchase, 213
Lowie, R. H., 318, 325
Lykins, Johnston, 237

Macy Standard, 240–41
Mad Bear, Harry (Tiʔaakaciksuukuʔ 'He Has Good Thoughts for People') (Skiri Pawnee), 106
Manabozho, xxiii
Marquez, Gabriel G., 196
Marriott, Alice, xvii, xli
Marsh, Gordon, 273–74
Martinez, Dorothy, 323–25

Ónpʰonₜ-tonga, 236, 245–46
oral texts, documentation of, xxix, 145
oral tradition(s), xxxvi, xxviii
origin stories, xxxv, 123
Osage language, 213, 258, 291, 303
Óshe Gónₜya, 266, 267–68nn5–6
Otoe-Missouria language (Otoe), 213, 225; community revitalization of, xxxix; Gordon Marsh work in, at Red Rock, 273
Otoe-Missouria Language Department, 225–26
Ottawa County, Oklahoma, 41, 177, 180, 182

Pahánₜle Gáxli (Strikes First), 256–58, 267n3, 268n6; account of, 264–67
Pahdopony, Juanita, 317–19, 323–25
Pahdopony, Oliver, 324
Pahé-thonₜ Átonₜwonₜgthonₜ ("The Village on a Hill"), 238
Palmer, Alice, xl
Palmer, Gus, xl
Palmer, Gus, Jr. (Gus pàntha̠i:dê Palmer), xviii–xix, xxiv, 19, 195, 331
Papillion Creek, 238
Parks, Douglas R., xxxix, 85, 106, 123
Parsons, Elsie Clews, xli
Páthinₜ-Nonₜpazhi, 236, 247
Patterson, Don, 337
Pawnees, xxxix, 85; culture of, 119; Skiri band of, 106
Peoria Tribe of Oklahoma, 42
phonotactics, xxxii
Piankashaws (peeyankihšiaki 'torn ears people'), 41
Pidgin English, xvii
Plains Apache language, orthography and pronunciation of, 63–65
Plains Apache Tribe of Oklahoma, 59–61; oral tradition of, 61–63
Plains Apache Trickster, 61–63, 146
Pleiades, 196, 207n2

plural marriage, 319
poetic devices, xxix
Polelonema, Otis, xxi
polysynthetic languages, xix, xxix
Ponca language, 213, 215, 242; pronunciation guide, 216–18
Ponca oral literature, 213, 216, 242
Poncas, 213–16, 236, 242, 303; agency of, 336
Potawatomi Tribe, 51–52
Powell, John Wesley, 195
Prairie Flower, 214
Provost, Bertha, 161, 164
Pulitzer Prize, xxii

Quapaw Agency, 41–42, 189
Quapaw language, 63, 213, 303
Quapaws, 189, 303
Quapaw stories, features of, 303

Rabbit, xxiii, 227–28, 229–32, 305–12
Raven (Crow), xxiii
Red Banks (Red Earth, MaŠuje), 271
Redeagle, George, 303
Red Rock, Oklahoma, xxxix, 272, 274, 277
Rementer, Jim, xxxix, 29
Ricketts, Mac Linscott, 319
Rock Monster, 62, 63, 65–68
Rocky Mountains, xxvii
Rood, David S., 164
Roosevelt, Theodore, 195
Rothenberg, Jerome, xviii, xxx
Roubedeaux, Jade, xxxix, 226
Roy, John Baptiste, 273

Sac & Fox language, 51
Sac-Fox Agency, 335
salvage anthropology, 274
Sand Creek Massacre, 257
Sapir, Edward, 60
Saynday (Séndé), xxiii, 319

IN THE NATIVE LITERATURES OF THE AMERICAS
AND INDIGENOUS WORLD LITERATURES SERIES

*A Listening Wind: Native
Literature from the Southeast*
Edited and with an introduction
by Marcia Haag

*Inside Dazzling Mountains:
Southwest Native Verbal Arts*
Edited by David L. Kozak

*Pitch Woman and Other Stories:
The Oral Traditions of Coquelle
Thompson, Upper Coquille
Athabaskan Indian*
Edited and with an introduction
by William R. Seaburg
Collected by Elizabeth D. Jacobs

*When Dream Bear Sings: Native
Literatures of the Southern Plains*
Edited by Gus Palmer Jr.
Foreword by Alan R. Velie

*Algonquian Spirit: Contemporary
Translations of the Algonquian
Literatures of North America*
Edited by Brian Swann

*Born in the Blood: On Native
American Translation*
Edited and with an introduction
by Brian Swann

*Sky Loom: Native American
Myth, Story, and Song*
Edited and with an introduction
by Brian Swann

*Voices from Four Directions:
Contemporary Translations of the
Native Literatures of North America*
Edited by Brian Swann

*Salish Myths and Legends:
One People's Stories*
Edited by M. Terry Thompson
and Steven M. Egesdal

To order or obtain more information on these or other University of Nebraska Press
titles, visit nebraskapress.unl.edu.

CPSIA information can be obtained
at www.ICGtesting.com
Printed in the USA
LVHW101810260220
648293LV00015B/403